A History of
JUDAISM *and*
CHRISTIANITY

BOTH JEWISH AND GENTILE
BELIEVERS BEING GRAFTED INTO THE
RICH OLIVE TREE: TOWARDS HEALING OF
THE ORIGINAL WOUND OF DIVISION

Second Edition

DONALD SWENSON

WESTBOW
PRESS®
A DIVISION OF THOMAS NELSON
& ZONDERVAN

WestBow Press books may be ordered through booksellers or by contacting:

WestBow Press
A Division of Thomas Nelson & Zondervan
1663 Liberty Drive
Bloomington, IN 47403
www.westbowpress.com
844-714-3454

ISBN: 979-8-3850-3463-5 (sc)
ISBN: 979-8-3850-3464-2 (e)

Library of Congress Control Number: 2024920732

Print information available on the last page.

WestBow Press rev. date: 10/23/2024

A REVIEW OF

A HISTORY OF JUDAISM AND CHRISTIANITY.

TOWARDS HEALING OF THE ORIGINAL WOUND.

SECOND EDITION

BY

MR BOB GARRETT

ELDER & OVERALL COORDINATOR OF
THE ALLELUIA COMMUNITY
AUGUSTA, GEORGIA.

In the first edition of this work, Don Swenson laid the foundation of the division between Judaism and Christianity that commenced in the first two centuries of Christianity. The division happened and was well documented through the Patristic Fathers and has extended through to the periods of Medieval, Early Modern, Modern and Post-Modern Eras of Western societies.

Using a sociological, historical method, he was able to paint a history of Jewish antisemitism that has been ongoing for 1700 years. However, this history can, and should, end in a new hope for a new heaven and earth populated by Gentile believers in Jesus and Jewish believers in the same Yeshua.

The second edition includes a study of Tertullian, (c. 200) a prolific early Christian author, who shaped much Roman Catholic theology & practice through to current times. Within his writings, there exists blatant antisemitism that formed the fabric of the various families of Christianity, including Roman Catholic, Protestant and Orthodox traditions.

Tertullian promoted this antisemitism in a way that ultimately manifested in persecutions, discrimination, exiles and pogroms that led to inquisitions, and, worst of all, massacres and finally the Holocaust.

Swenson has proposed that this genocide is the ultimate expression of human depravity unlike anything else in human history. But this does not end the story, he argues. There are now many signs of redemption and healing finding their way to the surface, including a signifiant move towards réconciliation and restoration. There are such groups of Christians for Jews, Catholic-Jewish dialogues, prayer gatherings and monies being raised for suffering Jews in the Middle East.

The book ends with an in-depth study of eschatology. Yeshua, the Messiah is the source and foundation for the ultimate reconciliation and healing that will live into eternity. The text can be seen as a framework for healing of the relationship between Jews and Christians from many different traditions.

Swenson is convinced that the Body of Christ, can and will ultimately be restored to perfect unity for which Jesus prayed in John 17:21 . . . "that they may all be one, just as you, Father, are in me, and I in you, that they also may be in us, so that the world may believe that you have sent me." It is thought by many that this unity of Christians and Jews will pave the way for the greatest evangelistic event in history and will precede the return of Yeshua for his glorious and perfected bride.

CONTENTS

CONTENTS

INTRODUCTION

REMEMBERING, REPENTING
AND RECONCILING

ORIENTATION

Many articles and books have been written on the relationship between Judaism and Christianity. The unique feature of this writing is its pastoral emphasis. By this I mean it is a document that calls for response as the history is told. It is told not only to inform the reader of the contents of this history but also to seriously remember the past and to anticipate the future. Much of the history between the two religions is fraught with pain and suffering as Christianity has dominated Judaism for nearly two thousand years. This is to be remembered that, in turn, is to be repented of. In this way, reconciliation will happen. Reconciliation will happen primary in the future when Israel is restored and the one true humanity (Jewish and Gentile believers in *Yeshua*[1]) are united in an eternal, supernatural eschaton when *Yeshua,* and *Adonai*[2], is king of the whole earth and the cosmos as written in Zechariah "Then *Adonai* will be king over the whole world. On that day *Adonai* will be the only one, and his name will be the only name" (14:9).

Two primary themes capture this document: the mysteries of the kingdom and the many branches of Christianity being grafted into Israel as branches are on an olive tree (see Romans 11:17). Relying on the scholarship of Rabbi Mark Kinzer (2018), it is argued that an aspect of the mystery of the kingdom is the link between *Yeshua* being crucified and raised from the dead and Jerusalem (an acronym for the Jewish people) being crucified and raised from the dead as well). Except for the first 150 years of Christianity, Jerusalem has been "crucified" or has suffered much, both at the hands of Christians and secular governments. Much of this history of suffering will be documented in this text. The theme of resurrection is the theme of hope, healing, and restoration so well evidenced by *Yehsua's* resurrection and Israel being "born in a day" in 1948. Subsequent

---

[1] Throughout this text, the name of *Yeshua* will be used for it is the Hebrew name for the Greek name, Jesus.

[2] *Adonai* literally means "my Lord", a word the Hebrew Bible uses to refer to God as *Yud-Heh-Vav-Heh* or *YHWH*.

to that date, there has been many "resurrections" consisting of reconciliation among Jews, Christians and Messianic Jews.

Mysteries of the Kingdom

Paul visited the disciples (both Jewish and Gentile believers) in Ephesus for his last time and gave encouragement to them. He reiterated to them the Good News of *Yeshua* in many ways of which three stand out as central to his proclamation: (1), that all are to turn from sin to God and to trust in *Yeshua* the Messiah; (2), to declare in depth the Good News of God's love and kindness; and, (3), the Kingdom of God consisting of the whole plan of God (Acts 20:17-27[3]).

This document is an attempt to address what could be part of the mystery of the whole plan that God has for His original people, Israel, the believers in *Yeshua* (known primarily as Christians), the whole of humanity and, indeed the vastness of *Adonai's* creation. The primary source, besides the *Tanakh*[4] and the New Testament, is the work of Mark Kinzer (2018) in his text: *Jerusalem crucified, Jerusalem risen.*

In this introduction, I will outline the primary thesis that Kinzer offers along with the many sub-theses in his work that serve as a structure of this chapter. These themes will form the base of the following chapters. This will be followed by the inclusion of Gentile believers in the divine plan for all of humanity and as "being grafted into Israel" and then, the methodology of the text.

Jerusalem Crucified, Jerusalem Risen.

The title of the text by Kinzer (2018) carries within itself the fundamental thesis of his work. Kinzer, an Emeritus Rabbi in the

---

[3] The Biblical translation used throughout this work is from Stern (2016).

[4] This is an acronym for the first letters of the Hebrew Bible: **To**rah, **Ne**vi'im (Prophets) and **K**'tuvim (Writings). It is God's authoritative word to humanity (Stern, 2016:1850).

Messianic Jewish movement, compares the crucifixion of *Yeshua* to the suffering of Jerusalem from the exile in 70 CE of the Jewish people to the termination of the *Shoah* in 1945. As *Yeshua* did suffer in his passion and death, so did the people of Israel suffer over these long centuries. One may describe His passion compared to the passion of the Jewish people from their exile in 70 CE to the beginning of World War II in 1939. His crucifixion can be compared to the *Shoah* with the death of six million European Jews. As did the Jewish people suffer, so did *Yeshua* weep along with the millions of cries of *Adonai's* people in the death camps of the Nazi's. As we journey through the historical eras, we will find that Christians have not joined themselves with *Yeshua* in this regard but have, sadly, rejoiced in the suffering of the Jewish people. The *Tanakh* clearly says that those who rejoice or celebrate the tragedies of Israel or Jerusalem will be punished. A text that confirms this is from Ezekiel who, in speaking to the nation of Amon, is:

> *Adonai Elohim* says, "Because you gloated when my sanctuary was profaned, when the land of Israel was laid waste, and when the House of Judah went into exile and because you clapped your hands and stamped your feet, full of malicious joy over the land of Israel; I'm going to stretch out my hand over you and deliver you as plunder to the nations; I will cut you off from being a people and cause you to cease from being a nation; I will destroy you. Then you will know that I am *Adonai* (Ezekiel 25:3 and 6-7).

A second confirming text is: "Anyone who injures you injures the very pupil of my eye. But I will shake my hand over them, and they will be plundered by those who were formerly slaves" (Zechariah 2:12-13).

Rather than rejoicing, Christians are called to lament and cry with *Adonai's* original people who lived in exile and suffering. In this way, there may be an acknowledgement of sin against *Adonai's* chosen people followed by repentance.

But this is only part of the story. *Yeshua* did not stay in the grave as proclaimed by the psalmist "For you will not abandon me to *Sheol* or allow your holy one to rot in the grave" (Psalm 16:10). Fundamental to the Christian faith, *Yeshua* was raised from the dead. So also did Israel rise from the dead as recorded in the Book of Ezekiel (37:1–14). The genesis of this rising corresponded to the establishment of the nation of Israel in 1948[5]. Since that time, millions of Jews have come back to the land of Israel. They made what is known as *Aliyah*. It is now the resurrected *Yeshua* who is with the beginning of the resurrected Jerusalem or Israel that is culminated in his return in glory when he will set his feet on the Mount of Olives, just east of Jerusalem (see Zechariah 14:4).

Kinzer expands the meaning of the Gospel, the *euangelion*, beyond its basic meaning of salvation through belief in *Yeshua* as Messiah and the Son of God. He offers two more interpretations. First, *euangelion* also includes the restoration of Jerusalem, the land and all of Israel where *Yeshua* will be king or sovereign. The wider vision is cosmic-the restoration of the earth with a new heaven and a new earth[6] with Jerusalem as the epicenter.

Emerging from this foundational interpretation is that Jerusalem, the Holy City and "City of Great King" (Psalm 48:3), is under the lordship of *Yeshua* as king. The city is the locus of God's action in human history for she is both *axis mundi* and *axis temporis*[7].

From 63 BCE, when the Romans conquered Israel under Pompey (106–48 BCE), until 1948, this land, and Jerusalem, has been under the aegis of the Gentiles. This long period is known by *Yeshua* (Luke 21:24) and others "The Age of the Gentiles." In 1948 and 1967, the

---

[5] This is the understanding of Stern (2016:769) that is shared by many Messianic Jewish believers.

[6] There are four references to the new heaven and the new earth that are created by *Adonai*: Isaiah 65:17, Isaiah 66:22, II Peter 3:13 and Revelation 21:1.

[7] *Axis mundi* is a term relatively common in anthropology that means "the axis of the world" or that the whole world revolves about a specific place. Here it is used as "the city of the Great King" (Psalm 48:3). *Axis temporis* refers to time revolving about the temporality and eternity of Jerusalem.

Age of the Gentiles ceased. It is after these two momentous years that the ultimate restoration of Jerusalem begins. It appears that the prayer of Isaiah has partially been fulfilled: "You who call on *Adonai,* give yourself no rest; and give Him no rest until He restores Jerusalem and makes it the praise on earth" (Isaiah 62:6-7). But the restoration of the land of Israel and Jerusalem has much wider implications. It is through Israel and Jerusalem that the whole of creation is renewed for "That Day will bring on the destruction of the heavens by fire, and the elements will melt from the heat; but we, following along with his promise, wait for the new heavens and a new earth (II Peter 3:12-13).

An implicit interpretation of replacement theology is that the rejection of *Yeshua* as Messiah has meant the rejection of Israel as *Adonai's* people. Some second and third century Gentile believers believed that the destruction of Jerusalem and the exile of the people was an indication of this rejection. Paul disagrees. He wrote:

> Isn't it that they have stumbled with the result that
> they have permanently fallen away? Heaven forbids!
> Quite the contrary, it is by means of their stumbling
> that deliverance has come to the Gentiles, to provoke
> them to jealousy (Romans 11:11).

The apostle continues to argue that if Israel's stumbling has meant so many riches to the Gentiles then how much greater riches will there be to the Gentiles when Israel receives *Yeshua* as Messiah? Kinzer expands on this theme with another sub-thesis that their rejection does not imply a nullification of Israel's covenantal status nor the surrendering of the hope for an eschatological reversal of her rejection. If her rejection is not this, then what is its effect? It is a punishment or discipline. Punishment for the purpose of purification. Purification for what? For rejecting *Yeshua* as Messiah. The good news, however, as taught by Paul is "that all of Israel will be saved" (Romans 11:26).

Another issue Kinzer addresses is what is the role of the role of the

Jewish people since the Roman exile and even though they rejected *Yeshua* as Messiah? He offers two roles: the continued presence of the Temple along with the *Torah*.

The primary function of the temple is to remind Jews, Messianic Jews and Gentile believers in the divine presence (*Shekinah*) among his people. His presence, in human history, has been manifested in a variety of ways. Before the prideful disobedience of Adam and Eve, he was present in his creation for he made it. This presence takes on various forms in Israel with the construction of the Tabernacle as recorded in Exodus 25-31. It is written that "They are to make me a sanctuary, so that I may live among them" (Exodus 25:8).

The key elements of this presence were the ark, the altar, the bread of presence, and the tabernacle. The ark served as the earthly throne of Israel's God (I Samuel 4:4). In the first book of Samuel, it is recorded: "the ark for the covenant of *Adonai* of Hosts, who is present above the cherubim." This ark, within the wider sanctuary, was held in Shiloh. It was later that King David brought the ark to his newly established city, Jerusalem termed the city of David or of the Great King (see Psalm 48:3). But where in Jerusalem? According to the tradition that stretched back to Abraham, the place was Mount Moriah. Upon this mount, was built the first temple that, sadly, was destroyed by the Babylonians in 586 BCE. The second temple was built in 516/515 BCE but also was destroyed by the Romans in 70 CE. So, what role did the temple play from 70 CE to the present?

According to Kinzer, the physical temple is a symbol pointing to realities beyond itself. These realities consist of the temple as of heaven, cosmic, eschatological, and human. The heavenly temple is the holy of holies in heaven. It was the Essenes[8] who accented this that consists of *Adonai*, sitting on a high and lofty throne. The

---

[8] One of the three religious expressions of Judaism from about 150 BCE to 70 CE. In the Qumran, they lived as celibate monks and sought to live as authentic *Torah* believers practising immersions for purification, studying and praying the *Tanakh*, writing scrolls of the sacred texts and in composing original literature. Also, some of them lived married lives with families in rural Israel . (Karesh and Hurvitz 2008:145 and Swenson, 2018:17-24).

physical temple housed his robe while *Serafim* stood over him. His presence was awesome, and the angels shouted praises such as: "More holy than the holiest holiness is *Adonai*-T'zva'ot" (Isaiah 6:3). Other images come from the Book of Revelation: "The one sitting there gleamed like diamonds and rubies, and a rainbow shining like emerald encircled the throne" (Revelation 4:3). An extended attempt to envision this divine presence is outlined in the prophet Ezekiel, Chapter One[9].

The second reality is the cosmic temple. This temple begins to be present in the creation narrative of Genesis 1-2. *Adonai* created the earth, the heavens, the cosmos to share his presence to the epitome of his creation: humans, male and female, made in his image (Genesis 2:27). In the mind of Isaiah, the creation is the effect of an infinite artist: "For thus *Adonai,* who created the heavens, God, who shaped and made the earth, who established and created it not to be chaos, but formed it to be lived in" (45:18). There remains a promise of restoration and redemption for the whole of this cosmos for, Paul writes: "creation waits eagerly for the sons of God to be revealed" (Romans 8:19) and …"We know that until now, the whole creation has been groaning as with the pains of childbirth" (Romans 8:22).

The third temple is eschatological. Ezekiel (40-48) envisions it reflecting a house of various gates, doors and rooms with a special accent on the "especially Holy Place" (41:4 and 41:23). The height of the vision is the coming of *Adonai* "who filled the house" (43:5). A special feature of this temple is water flowing eastward from under its structure. It starts as a small stream but expands to become a mighty river. On both sides of the river all kinds of trees grow. In the river itself will dwell many varieties of fish. Part of the river will flow to the west of the Temple and the other to the east that will make the salty sea (The Dead Sea) like fresh water. The core of the temple is the same as the heavenly and cosmic kinds: the continued divine presence. Ezekiel concludes his prophetic message with this

---

[9] There are many other images in the Scriptures describing the heavenly temple. Some of them are Daniel 7:9-10, 13-14, Psalm 98:4-9 and Psalm 104:1-4.

statement: "And from that day on the name of the city will be *Adonai Shamah* or *'Adonai* is there'" (Ezekiel 48: 35).

The last temple is the human one. Very early in the history of Israel, while the people were still in the desert, the author of Numbers indicated "the camp where I (*Adonai*) live among you" (5:3). Israel is this temple for *Adonai* did not forsake his people even after they did not accept *Yeshua* as Messiah. Paul teaches that God has not repudiated his people (Romans 11:1) and that they have not permanently fallen away (11:11). The gifts given to them have not been taken away. "They were made God's children, the *Shekinah* has been with them, the covenants are theirs, likewise the giving of the *Torah,* the Temple service and the promises; and the Patriarchs are theirs" (Romans 9:4-5).

But how does this temple continue after its physical manifestation was destroyed in 70 CE? Rabbinic Judaism[10] has a response. The synagogue becomes a concrete and physical structure. It is here, and in Jewish homes, that believers can study the *Torah,* pray towards Jerusalem, observe the festivals of the Jewish calendar and celebrate life cycles. Kinzer writes: "Israel as the human temple was thus linked not merely to the pre-70 CE institution, but even more to the transcendent realities to which it had pointed. As a result, the people of Israel obtained an extraordinary place in the universe and in the divine plan" (2018:78).

As indicated above, the second role that Israel plays in the post 70 CE history is the continued presence of the *Torah.* This term is referred to many times in this document. What does it mean? The authors of the *Encyclopedia of Judaism* offer us its meaning:

---

[10] Rabbinic Judaism, the normative form of Judaism that developed after the fall of the Temple of Jerusalem originating in the work of the Pharisaic rabbis, it was based on the legal and commentative literature in the *Talmud* it set up a mode of worship and a life discipline that were to be practiced by Jews worldwide down to modern times (The Editors of Encyclopaedia Britannica, https://www. Britannica. com/topic/ Rabbinic Judaism)

The *Torah* (Hebrew for teaching) refers to: sacred scripture, the five books of Moses (Genesis, Exodus, Leviticus, Numbers and Deuteronomy), oral law which includes the *Talmud* and all Jewish law (Karesh and Hurvitz, 2008:521-522).

As was the presence if the temple an important feature of post-Roman exilic Israel so also was the presence of the *Torah*. Kinzer argues that many Gentile Christian theologians deny the need for *Torah* observance based on Acts 10 to 11 (Peter's dream-vision) and Acts 15 (no need to observe the *Torah*). He offers a different perspective.

By interpreting the infancy narratives, *Yeshua's* life and teachings, the lives of the first disciples, and the life of Paul, Kinzer makes a strong point that all were *Torah* observant women and men. He especially accents *Yesuha* who said: "But it is easier for heaven and earth to pass away than for one stroke of a letter in the *Torah* to become void" (Luke 16:17) and:

> Don't think that I have come to abolish the *Torah* or the prophets, I have come not to abolish but to complete. Yes, indeed! I tell you that until heaven and earth pass away, not so much as a *yud* or a stroke will pass from the Torah—not until everything must happen has happened (Matthew 5:17-18).

Stern (2016) explains the verb "to complete." *Yeshua* came to teach *Torah* correctly and to affirm its fulness and its truth and to establish *Torah's* full and intended meaning so that the followers would know how to follow God.

As it was with *Yeshua*, so it was with Miriam, the mother of *Yeshua*, Joseph, her spouse, Zechariah, Elizabeth, Simeon, Anna, Stephen and Paul. Kinzer accents both Miriam and Paul.

...His (*Yeshua's*) mother should be seen and honored as 'blessed,' but wishes to focus less on the bodily life he derived from her and more on her faithful hearing of the divine word that made her worthy to bestow that life. Here Miriam becomes the paradigmatic disciple, hearing and performing the living word of the *Torah* (Kinzer, 2018:196).

Paul was also a serious observer of the *Torah*. He was committed to attend all the feasts of Israel, took a Nazirite vow and saw that his disciple, Timothy was circumcised. He was frequently accused of denying the *Torah* and in all cases, he defended himself as a model *Torah* observer.

What is the second role of the Jew who does not accept the Messiahship of *Yeshua*? It is what the whole of the *Tanakh* has taught: to be a righteous *Torah* observer who lives blamelessly according to all the commandments and regulations of *Adonai*. This forms a basis and for each Jew to continue to look to Jerusalem. In this way, the observant Jew contributes to the coming of the reign of *Adonai* and the Messianic Age.

To add to this important role, it is to the credit of Rabbinic Judaism, that the *Torah* has been preserved in its originality, the earth is seen to be the place of redemption, the teaching of the geographical centrality and the Messianic significance of the land of Israel, Jerusalem, and the Temple Mount. Jews have always and to the present long for the Messiah that could very well coincide with the return of *Yeshua* to be discussed in Chapter Eight. Believers of Rabbinic Judaism and *Yeshua* both believe the one day the kingdom of Israel will be restored (Acts 1:6).

As many of these Jewish believers-maintained hope and practiced *Torah* observance for two-thousand years, two major processes happened within the Gentile church: acceptance of the gift of the Jews and her rejection. Kinzer expands. The Gentile Church, to its credit, kept the *Tanakh* as canonical, adhered to the fundamentals of the Apostle's Creed, called more and more Gentiles to repent and believe in the message of the Messiah and practiced Baptism. She also created a way of life founded on apostolic teaching, communal sharing and relationships, celebrating the Eucharist, liturgy and private prayer. Of all Christian traditions, Roman Catholicism is one which has maintained many of the Jewish traditions. Some of these are: the construction of a hierarchy of priests, an established regular liturgical prayer similar to the *Siddur*[11], the celebration of feast days that always have a vigil the evening before, the presence of sacred bread, and the centralization of a tabernacle. Kinzer acknowledges: "The ecclesia (church) guarded this rich treasure and kept it safe for generations through fierce storms, and we should be grateful for her faithful stewardship" (2018:235).

However, many of the treasures of the Jewish faith have not been received. Some of these treasures consist of: the denial of an earthly Jerusalem, a disregard of the land of Israel as belonging to the Jews, the down-playing of the covenantal status of Israel, the suppression of Jewish rituals especially the Sabbath, a rejection of the church being composed both of Jewish and Gentile believers in *Yeshua,* not accenting the role of Israel in the eschaton and the major role that Israel will have in the unification of the Gentile faith in Jesus and the restoration of the earth.

However, as to be argued in Chapter Seven, the Catholic Church has repented of much of her part in the many collective sins against Jews. This has come from the highest authority in the church in the documents of Nostra *aetate* of the Vatican Council, *The Catechism of the Catholic Church* and *A reflection on theological questions pertaining to the Catholic-Jewish relations on the occasion of the 50th Anniversary of Nostra Aetate.*

---

[11] "The Siddur is the Jewish prayer book. It presents all the prayers to be recited at the various daily and Sabbath worship services, in their proper order according to the tradition of the community that printed it." Since it was written the first time in the ninth century, it has evolved and changed a lot but still maintaining the heart of Judaism. It consists of collections of the Tanakh, material drawn from the *Talmud,* a special prayers and humns composed by individual writers and poets over the centuries (Karesh and Hurvitz 2008: 478-479).

To summarize this section, I would accent a vision of not only salvation in *Yeshua* and the promise of eternal life with him but also of *Adonai's* intent is to establish on earth the reign of his Son with Jerusalem as the epicenter (the *axis mundi*) in the land of Israel that combined both Jewish and Gentile believers in him as "one new humanity" (Ephesians 2:15). Further, the role of Jewish believers during Israel's long exile with their hope of the restored temple and their *Torah* observance is important in God's plan for both Jewish and Gentile believers, all of humanity and the whole cosmos. It was also during this long exile that *Yeshua's* suffering was joined with the suffering of the people of Israel. Also, as he rose from the dead, so is also Israel rising from the dead to complete the amazing and awesome plan of God.

BEING GRAFTED IN

The phrase "being grafted in" needs some explanation. All peoples of the earth who are not of Jewish heritage are called "Gentiles or of the Nations." Those who are disciples of Jesus, are then Gentile believers in Jesus and if Jewish, the term to be used is "Jewish believers in Yeshua." All the people in the New Testament (*Br'it Hadashah* or Books of the New Covenant) are Jewish and, especially, *Yeshua* as the Messiah of Israel, who completes Israel but does not replace it. Israel is still intact after the first coming of Messiah.

Consider two olive trees, one a cultivated olive tree and another an uncultivated olive tree. The text reads of a wild olive tree which was uncultivated (Romans 11:17). Those of Gentile origin are rooted in pagan gods and goddesses or, in modern times, under the yoke of secularism. The Apostle wrote that they were: "without a Messiah, estranged from the national life of Israel. We were foreigners to the covenants (from Israel) with the promises. They were in the world without hope and without God" (Ephesians 2:12). Further, "You used to be dead because of your sins and acts of disobedience. You walked in the ways of this world (*'olam hazel*) and obeyed the Ruler of the Powers of the Air (Satan or the Adversary) who is still at work among the disobedient" (Ephesians 2:1-2). They were "spiritually dead" (II Corinthians 5:14). This is what an uncultivated olive tree looks like.

The cultivated olive tree is opposite: "They were made God's children, the *Sh'kinah Glory* (the Divine Presence) has been with them, the covenants are theirs, likewise the giving of the *Torah* (the teaching), the Temple service and the promises; the Patriarchs are theirs; and from them, as far as his physical descent is concerned, came the Messiah, who is over-all" (Romans 9:4-5). The true olive tree, called beautiful in Hosea 14:7 and "Beautiful. Full of leaves and good fruit" (Jeremiah 11:16) was cultivated by 1800 years of Jewish tradition (from Abraham to *Yeshua*), is a mature tree with rich roots. Part of this tradition is that the Jews are chosen and loved for the Patriarchs' (Abraham, Isaac and Jacob) sake. *Adonai's* free gifts are never revoked. The great promise is that at the end of the ages, when all the Gentiles destined to salvation enter the kingdom, all of Israel will be saved (Romans 11:25).

Gentile believers in Jesus (called Christians) are like a branch, broken off from a wild olive tree and are grafted into this true, cultivated olive tree with Messiah *Yeshua* at its core. They who are Gentile believers in Jesus become equal sharers in the rich root of the olive tree. They immensely enjoy the root and the rich sap of Israel.

This carries major responsibilities. Never think that the grafted in branch is the root but, rather, the root is Israel that supports the Gentile believers. Paul warns the newly grafted branch not to be arrogant but stand in awe and show mercy to the Jews just as you have been shown God's mercy.

Yet so much is mystery for he is humble enough to know he knows little. Standing before the whole wonder of *Adonai's* plan for world-wide redemption, he sings: "O the depths of the riches and the wisdom and knowledge of God! How inscrutable are his judgments! How unsearchable are his ways!" (Romans 11:33) [12].

Archdeacon Fichtenbauer (2019) and Swenson (2021) demonstrate the life-giving connection of Gentile believers with Israel with the imagery of the true olive tree. The roots and trunk of the olive tree represent the Patriarchs, the covenants, the *Torah*, the Prophets and the Writings (such as the Psalms, Proverbs, Job, Song of Songs, Ruth, Lamentations, Ecclesiastes, Esther, Daniel, Ezra–Nehemiah, and Chronicles) and the Messiah, *Yeshua*. Gentile believers are like a branch taken from a wild olive tree and grafted into the true olive tree (Romans 11:13-14). The mature and full life in God depends on the Gentile branches being connected to this true olive tree-with its roots. The blood of Messiah has made us adopted sons and daughters. Gentile believers are very much part of the Jewish people in a spiritual sense. This means a deep unity with Israel without Gentile believers becoming Jews.

- According to Paul, many of the Jews in his time were dead parts of the tree, broken off branches that could be grafted in again later (Romans 11:17- 23).
- The Gentiles have a place in salvation history because they are part of God's people and are linked to Israel through the Jewish part of the church (Romans 11:18). The full measure of the Gentiles participation in God's plan for salvation depends on their connection to their Jewish roots.
- The realization obvious link between Gentile believers and Israel only functions well when the Messianic Jewish Movement[13] acts as the bridge between the gentile church and the Jewish people (Fichtenbauer, 2019:24-25)

---

[12] Some of this richness is that Israel is God's child, has the *Sh'khinah*, received the covenants, the *Torah,* the Temple service, the promises and the Patriarchs (Romans 9:4-5).

[13] To be discussed in detail in Chapter Seven.

However, Paul warns us Gentile believers not to boast as if we were better than the other branches. "Remember, you do not support the root, but the root supports you" (Romans 11:18). Further, we are not to be arrogant but should stand in awe of God. We are to maintain ourselves in divine kindness for if we do not, we can be torn off from the Olive tree!! We are called to show mercy to Israel who have not yet received *Yeshua* as Messiah may come to faith in him.

To what have we been grafted in? We turn to the election and choice of Israel in ancient times. We read:

> You are a people set apart as holy for *Adonai* your God. *Adonai* your God has chosen you out of all the people on the face of the earth to be his own unique treasure. *Adonai* didn't set his heart on you or choose you because you numbered more than any other people—on the contrary, you were the fewest of all peoples. Rather, it was because *Adonai* loved you, and because he wanted to keep the oath which he had sworn to your ancestors, that *Adonai* brought you out with a strong hand and redeemed you from a life of slavery under the hand of Pharaoh, king of Egypt. From this you can know that *Adonai* your God is indeed God, the faithful God, who keeps his covenant and extends grace to those who love him and observe his commandments, to a thousand generations. But he repays those who hate him to his face (Deuteronomy 7:6-10).

Indeed, Israel is the apple (or pupil) of God's eye (Deuteronomy 32:10 and Zechariah 2:12) and "He is like a shepherd feeding his flock, gathering his lambs in his arm, carrying them against his chest, gently leading like the mother sheep" (Isaiah 40:11). We, Gentiles, are invited to partake in the rich olive tree!

THE METHODOLOGY OF THE TEXT.

Several academic disciples are used in gaining more understanding of the relationship between Judaism and Christianity. They consist of sociology and Jewish, Christian and Messianic Jewish theologies. All four are vital in our interpretation of the intricate relationship between the two Abrahamic traditions. One of the accents is how indebted is Christianity is to its predecessor, Judaism. This indebtedness has been compromised by century old conflicts between the two faiths with Christianity more likely the initiator of the conflicts.

Sociological Ideal Types

In the tradition of Max Weber (1864-1920) and H. Richard Niebuhr (1894-1962), I posit *ideal types* (Weber) and *types* (Niebuhr) to structure much of this work. The term *type* comes from the Greek word *typos* and can be translated as a pattern or a model. Weber (1894/1978) uses to term ideal type as an analytical construct that serves as a measuring rod to determine similarities and differences in concrete cases. It usually does not exist in its pure form, but it is of heuristic value for discussing the real world. The use of ideal types permits comparisons between different types of relations between Christianity and Judaism.

In a similar way does Niebuhr (1951) use the analytical construct, type, to describe the relationship between the sacred culture of Christianity with the secular culture of Western society from the time of The Late Classical Era (from the time of Jesus to 395 CE) to the modern era (1775-1970). Bearing in mind a wide variety of ways these two cultures intersect, he wrote:

> Yet it is possible to discern some order in this multiplicity, to stop the dialogue, as it were, at certain points; and to define typical partial answers that recur so often in different eras and societies that they seem to be less the product of historical conditioning

than that of the nature of the problem itself and the meanings of its terms (1951:40).

He noted what Weber says, no person or group ever conforms completely to a type. The advantage of this typology is to call attention to the continuity and significance of the great motifs that appear and reappear in the long history of Christianity, and applied here, with Judaism.

Sociological meaning of Secularization.

A general definition of this term is provided to us by Bowker (2000):

> From the Latin, *saeculum,* 'age' or 'world', i.e., this world. The process whereby people, losing confidence in other-worldly or supernatural accounts of the cosmos and its destiny, abandon religious beliefs and practices, or whereby religion loses its influence on society. It then came more loosely to refer to the transition from the religious to the non-religious world.

This definition is best applied in the modern and post-modern eras to indicate a migration of the sacred from the center of society and mind to the peripheries of the same. However, if we use the term in its original meaning, its roots in Latin, means "of this world and of this age or time" or, in Hebrew, *'olam hazel.* In the first centuries of Christianity, it means how some of the Church Fathers (also called Patristic Fathers) adapted some of their understanding of Christianity and Judaism not from the Hebrew (sacred) tradition but from the secular tradition of the Egyptians, the Greeks and the Romans. Fichtenbauer concurs: "Theologians, not using the Hebrew worldview, used the Greek, Roman and Germanic mindsets. This trend (secularization) continues today in churches whose teaching reflects modern philosophy" (2019:44).

Documented in Chapter Three, the Egyptian, Greek, Roman cultures and societies were fundamentally Anti-Semitic. Thus, because most of the Church Fathers were educated in the Greco-Roman schools, they adapted similar Anti-Semitic perceptions that emerged from these ancient cultures.

Sociology: An interpretation of history or Historical Sociology

Another methodology from sociology is known as historical sociology. Sample scholars include Sckopol (1984) and Bloch (1961). Sckopol argues that historical sociology can be considered as a science wherein one can look at causes and effects of historical phenomena. Both she and Bloch focused on causal regularities that will be the pattern used in this text.

CONCLUSIONS

This introduction sets the ground for what will follow. According to the sub-title of this work, it is vital to remember, to repent, and to reconcile. Historical events that had negative effects on Israel and the Jewish people need to be remembered, then repented of and to be reconciled.

The whole plan of God (as recalled in Acts 20:27) must necessarily include the role of Israel in this plan. Some of this plan is presented by Kinzer (2018) in his theme of *Jerusalem crucified and Jerusalem risen*. By this he means that *Yeshua*, Messiah, walked with the people of Israel through about 1800 years, sharing their suffering and pain as he did during his passion and death. But the Christian faith knows that *Yeshua* rose from the dead. The mystery is that he has walked with them also as the risen Messiah and shared their joy, especially the joy of Jews coming home to their own land in 1948.

Another part of this mystery of *Adonai's* plan is that even though most of the people of Israel rejected *Yeshua* as Messiah, they continued to have a role in the divine plan. Their role, in part, was to preserve the meaning of the temple and to live the *Torah* as much as they could. Through this, a sense of the Shekinah, the divine glory, was maintained.

Part of the mystery has already begun that refers to the inclusion of Gentile believers into Israel that is formed in the Messiah. Paul uses the imagery of an olive tree to describe this mystery:

> But if some of the branches were broken off and you, a wild olive, we're grafted in among them have become equal sharers in the rich root of the olive tree, then don't boast as if you were better then the branches! However, if you do boast, remember that you are not supporting the root, the road is supporting you (Romans 11:17-19).

The finishing part of the introduction was to inform the reader the methodology of the work. Theology from Judaism, Christianity, and Messianic Judaism inform much of this document. In addition, specialty terms that were utilized consisted of sociological ideal types, secularisation, and historical sociology. In historical sociology, what is accented is not only defining the events of history but also out looking for causes and effects of these events. This will be very helpful as we investigate the tragedy of the *Shuah* in Chapter Six.

REFERENCES: INTRODUCTION

Abbot, W 1966. Editor. *Nostra Aetate* (Declaration on the Relationship to non-Christian religions. *The Documents of Vatican II.* New York: Guild Press.

Bloch, M. 1961. *Feudal society.* Volume I. Translated by L.A, Manyon. Chicago: The University of Chicago Press.

Bowker, J. 2000. "Secularization" *The Concise Oxford Dictionary of World Religions* Edited by J. Bowker. Oxford University Press. *Oxford Reference Online.* Oxford University Press. Mount Royal College. 13 September 2006<http://www.oxfordreference.com/views/ENTRY.html?subview=Main&entry=t101.e6503.

Commission for religious relations with the Jews, 2015. *A reflection on theological questions pertaining to the Catholic-Jewish relations on the occasion of the 50th Anniversary of Nostra Aetate.* Rome: The Vatican.

Editors of Encyclopedia Britannica, https://www. Britannica.com/topic/ Rabbinic Judaism

Fichtenbauer, J. (Archdeacon). 2019. *The Mystery of the Olive Tree: Uniting Jews and Gentiles for Christ's Return.* Luton, Bedfordshire: New Life Publishing.

Karesh, S. and M. Hurvitz 2008. *Encyclopaedia of Judaism.* New York: Checkmark Books.

Kinzer, M. 2018. *Jerusalem crucified; Jerusalem risen.* Eugene Oregon: Wipf and Stock Publishers.

Niebuhr, H. Richard. 1951. *Christ and culture.* Harper and Row: New York, New York.

Stern, D. H. 2016. *The Complete Jewish Bible.* Peabody Massachusetts: Hendrickson Publishers.

Skocpol, T. 1984. "Sociology's historical imagination." In *Vision and method in historical sociology,* edited by T. Skocpol, p. 1-22. Cambridge: Cambridge University Press.

Swenson, D. 2009. *Society, spirituality and the sacred. A social scientific introduction*. Second edition. Toronto: University of Toronto Press.

Swenson, D. 2018. *Alleluia: The return of the prototype*. Texas: New life Publishing.

Troeltsch, E.1931. *The social teachings of the Christian churches. Vols I and II*. New York: Harper and Row.

United States Catholic Conference. 1994. *The Catechism of the Catholic Church*. New York: Image Books.

CHAPTER ONE

THE PROPHETIC FAITH:
THE *TANAKH* REMEMBERING,
REPENTING, AND RECONCILING

Orientation

The title of this document is "The Prophetic Faith" which is a Jewish interpretation of the Judeo-Christian tradition. A Messianic Jewish understanding will complete an in-depth outline of the tradition. The term, *the Prophetic Faith* comes from Buber (1949), a Jewish scholar and philosopher, who addressed the meaning of Judaism by referring to it as a unique faith that posits it as being of divine origins. This tradition is rooted in God (*Elohim*) communicating, revealing, and acting in the history of a people, Israel, for her own salvation but also for the salvation of humanity. It is written in the Book of Genesis:

> Now *Adonai* said to Avram, 'Get yourself out of your country, away from your kinsmen and away from your father's house and go to the land that I will show you. I will make of you a great nation, I will bless those who bless you, but I will curse anyone who curses you; and by all the families of the earth will be blessed (12:1-3).

The text reveals that *Adonai* called a people to be a blessing to all the nations. It is this document that revealed how Israel did this (and failed to do it) from this time of a call to one man that would be as numerous as the stars of heaven and be an instrument of salvation to all peoples.

The chapter begins with Buber's historical analysis of the people of Israel known today more commonly as Judaism[14]. He begins his interpretation of the faith by starting not with Abraham but with the Song of Deborah which led him to outline the origins of Israel, the God of the Fathers, the Holy event, the great tensions, the turning to the future and the God of the sufferers. Subsequent to this is a

---

[14] The title Judaism comes after the two tribes, Judah and Benjamin, are exiled in Chaldea (or Babylon) in 587 BCE. In the land of their exile, they become known as Jews emanating from the one tribe, Judea.

Messianic Jewish interpretation of the *Tanakh* from the scholarship of Stern (2016).

TIME LINE OF DIVINE INITIATION AND HUMAN RESPONSE OR REJECTION

The following figure, Figure 1:1:

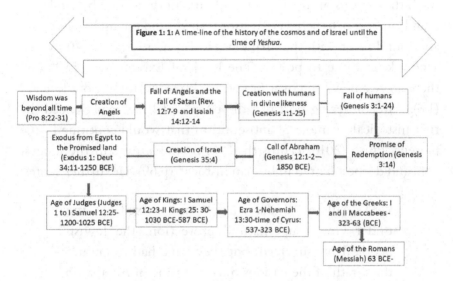

Figure 1: 1: A time-line of the history of the cosmos and of Israel until the time of *Yeshua*.

Wisdom, was before all and an attribute of *Adonai*. *Adonai's* primary action towards us as humans was His creation. The first of the divine creations were angels that was followed by the rebellion of Lucifer against God who then, falls to the earth with all of his followers (Revelation 12:7-9 and Isaiah 14: 12-14). It is after this that the cosmos is created by the hand of *Elohim* who kept saying that it was good. With the creation of humans (Genesis 1:26 and 2:7 and 21-24), *Elohim* gazed and said "it was very good" (Genesis 1:31).

The man was created to care for the earth and, together with his wife (woman or *Ishah*) to increase and multiple and fill the earth with humans. The divine plan for the increase of the image of God on earth was thwarted by Satan (in the form of a snake) who inspired Eve and Adam to disobey their creator and eat of a tree in order to have knowledge and make decisions of what is good and bad. *Adonai*, walking in the garden with them, challenged both and they experienced a judgment that barred them from the Tree of Life but with a promise of redemption.

The genesis of redemption is the call of Abram (about 1850 BCE). He became the instrument in the creation of a people called Israel (named after Jacob). Her call was immense as she was to be a blessing to all the nations of the world for all humanity is loved by God. His grandson, Jacob, fathered twelve sons who found themselves in Egypt and found favor with the Pharaoh. However, after about 400 years, a new king came to power. The book of Exodus records: "Now there arose a new king over Egypt. He knew nothing about Joseph" (1:8). After suffering horribly, the people of Israel experienced the first historical example of antisemitism that would continue to the present. Finto (2016) claims that "Antisemitism is still the longest held and deepest hatred in human history" (p.69). He further writes:

> God's call to Abraham has been a mixed blessing under God's supernatural protection, the Jewish people have survived, but they have had to endure the wrath of the nations since the time of Abraham's call. Satan has targeted this family for extinction. If he could destroy Abraham's descendants, he would thwart the purpose of God in bringing the world's deliverer through Israel's promised Son (2016:69-70).

Adonai called Moses who led the people to freedom and eventually, by the hand of Joshua, were carried to the Promised Land. After Joshua (about 1200 BCE) came the judges who led the Israelites through to the era of the kings (1030-587 BCE). During the time of the kings, two major disasters hit the people because they would not obey *Adonai* and follow His *Torah*. The ten tribes of the northern kingdom (called Israel) were attacked by the superpower of the age, the Assyrians in 722 BCE. They were then exiled. The southern part of the land, (Judea and Benjamin) suffered a similar tragedy in 587 when the new superpower, Babylon, attacked and exiled these two tribes. After about seventy years, the superpower of that age (550–330 BCE), Persia, allowed the people, now called Jews after the name Judea, to return to their land. Governors were the political authority until 323 BCE when the Greeks conquered the land. The Jews rebelled against this empire and were successful under the hand of the Maccabees. For a short period of time, the Jews enjoyed independence until the Romans conquered them and confiscated the land in 63 BCE.

THE SONG OF DEBORAH: JUDGES 5:2-5

This text is a song of an historical event of a war between Israel and the Canaanites. The background is that because Israel had done evil and had forsaken *Adonai*, He judged her and put her under the control of the Canaanites whose king was *Yavin*. In despair, the Israelites cried out to *Adonai* and he had compassion on them. The judge of Israel at that time was Deborah, a prophetess. She summoned a general of Israel, Barak, and told him that *Adonai* had given her orders to call the army and engage in battle with the King of the Canaanites, *Yavin*. She ordered him: "Go, march to Mount Tabor, and take with you 10,000 men from the people of Naftali and Z'vulun. I will cause Sisera, the general of the army of the Canaanites, to encounter you at the Kishon River with his chariots and troops; and I will hand him over to you" (Judges 4:7). Thereafter, the entire army of the Canaanites was thrown into panic and Barak defeated them.

Martin Buber[15], of whom much of these reflections are based, noted that in the full song, seven verses end with the word Israel and seven verses with *Adonai* 's name, YHVH. This is to show the intimate link between Israel as a people and *Adonai*. He presented four points:

1. *Adonai* is the God of Israel and Israel is *Adonai* 's people.

---

[15] Buber, M. 1949. *The Prophetic Faith*. New York: Harper and Row, Publishers.

2. If Israel acts and obeys *Adonai* and lives out its calling as *Adonai 's* people, *Adonai* is blessed.
3. *Adonai* is to lead, and Israel is to follow.
4. The important point is to love *Adonai*.

This deity, this God, is also master of nature (for nature fought against *Yavin*), master of the world, and master of Israel. Buber quotes the song: "Blessed are you, Israel, who is there like you, a people upheld by *Adonai*, shield of your help, and sword of your majesty." This song, hidden away in verses not referred to, is the heart and soul of the prophetic faith. God, the God of the universe, creator and Lord, is intimate with Israel and leads her in victory and success. She only needs to say "yes" but if she says no, she will never be denied her special place but she will suffer as an effect of disobedience.

ORIGINS

Buber offers to us teaching that challenges our focus of the "individualization" of our faith wherein the accent is on personal growth, being spiritual, and personal piety. This is important but it loses the meaning of Israel and Christianity as communitarian realities.

His insight is that *Adonai* relates to us as a people—a people whose "peoplehood" is fundamentally linked to our relationship to Him. There are definite personal calls in the First Testament, but it is always linked to others. In our study of eschatology in the final chapter of this book, *Yeshua* marries a bride, a people who has become pure and spotless, Let us consider the journey of Israel as a journey to become more and more a pure people who exhibit abundance love of God and love of one another. That is the focus—the creation of Israel being a people of God, a people of *Adonai*.

The new element from an assembly at Shechem (Joshua 24) is that the people, as a people, are called to make a collective or group commitment—a renewal of the covenant made at Sinai. Joshua stands erect and proclaims: "As for me and my household, we will serve *Adonai*, for he is our God" (Joshua 24:15). This must have been an encouragement to the whole assembly of Israelite who themselves claim:

> Far be it from us that we would abandon *Adonai* to serve other gods; because it is *Adonai* our God who brought us out and our fathers up out of the land of Egypt, from a life of slavery, and did those great signs before our eyes, and preserved us all along the way we traveled and among all the peoples we passed through; and it was *Adonai* who drove from ahead of us all the peoples, the *Emori*[16] living in the land. Therefore, we too will serve *Adonai,* for he is our God (Joshua 24:16-18).

A truth in this commitment, a kind of a renewal of a covenant, is that there cannot be an Israel unless she is linked to *Adonai* as her God and her Lord, sovereign in all what they do and stand for.

The assembly of Shechem was a point in time after Israel had entered the land promised to them from their father, Abraham. It was not the first assembly but a renewal of the assembly at Mount Sinai when the first covenant was made for all the people. This covenant has a sacramental dimension when an ox is sacrificed and the blood is sprinkled on the altar as well as on the people to create a bond, a "blood bond", stronger than words (see Exodus 24:1-8).

Something new happened before the Sinai event. Israel is not only known as a people but now as a son, a member of the family of God, of *Adonai*. Not only is she under His sovereignty, but now under *Adonai* as a father, of one who begets a child. The texts: "Then you are to tell Pharaoh: *Adonai* says, 'Israel is my firstborn son. I have told you to let my son go in order to worship me'.... (Exodus

---

[16] This is the Hebrew name for the Amorites.

4:22-23) and "When Israel was a child, I loved him; and out of Egypt I called my son" (Hosea 11:1).

Buber enumerates additional elements of the intimate relationship between *Adonai* and Israel. *Adonai* is one who is holy and is not present in unholy places. He who walks with them, communes with them and is the One who will be there with them. He gives direction to where the people are to go (as He did with Deborah) and is not only their God but also the God of their fathers: Abraham, Isaac and Jacob (known later as Israel that means "'God rules" [Genesis 32:29]).

THE GOD OF THE FATHERS

The God of the Patriarchs is a God of intimacy with those who He called. He is also a God of leadership and sovereignty who is for those He has summoned and called. The journey of Israel, whom He called and summoned, begins with one man, Abraham, who lived in Ur, a Sumerian city in the nation of the Babylonians. The pivotal text is:

> Now *Adonai* said to Avram[17], "Get yourself out of your
> country, away from your kinsmen and away from your
> father's house and go to the land that I will show you. I
> will make of you a great nation, I will bless you, and I
> will make your name great and you are to be a blessing.
> I will bless those who bless you, but I will curse anyone
> who curses you; and by you all the families of the earth
> will be blessed (Genesis 12:1-3).

The meaning and impact of this revelation is profound. Implied is that *Adonai* is keen on blessing all of humanity, but He selects a person whom He blesses first and then, through him, and his descendants, would bless the whole human race. It is striking, however, to note

---

[17] This was the original name of Abraham who became known as Abraham in Genesis 17:5-6 which means "father of many."

that those who bless Abraham (and Israel, his descendent) will be blessed but those who curse or are against Israel, will be cursed.

Several themes were given to the fathers that became paradigms for the future of Israel. As the fathers were called, so was Israel called. Likewise, as Abraham was summoned to leave his land to go to another, so was Israel called to a new land called, eventually, Israel. As Abraham was called to leave his homeland, so also was Israel called to leave Egypt and all the gods and goddesses in the land of Canaan. And, of utmost importance, all three patriarchs were called to decide to obey and follow *Adonai*. This is at the heart of the nation of Israel and the religion of Judaism: to say yes and obey the God who loves so dearly.

THE HOLY EVENT

The call to the fathers was primarily a call to individuals. As we journey with Israel, we come to the time of not only a call to individuals but the call to a people, an extended family, and, eventually, a nation. This is what happened at the Holy Event. One may call this a series of holy events but for Israel, it is one holy event that has five elements:

1. The Passover from Egypt into the land of Canaan.
2. The person who led the people, Moses.
3. The Passover meal.
4. The revelation at Mount Sinai.
5. The origins of the Shabbat.

All of these elements reveal a God who loves, cares, guards, protects, empowers, and initiates. This God, *Adonai,* is the God not only of the universe, earth, and humans, but the God of history who acts and shows himself to a people destined to be his kingdom here on earth.

This holy event, is the core of the creation of a people that were promised to Abraham. One may call this, as Buber does, the *supra-historical election* when *Adonai* revealed Himself not to any other people except to Israel. The first of the events in the major holy event is the Exodus of the Hebrews who were living in slavery over 400 years in Egypt. In the midst of distress, they cried: "The people of Israel still groaned under the yoke of slavery, and they cried out, and their cry for rescue from slavery came up to God. God heard their groaning, and God remembered his covenant with Abraham, Isaac and Jacob. God saw the people of Israel and God acknowledged them" (Exodus 2:23-25).

Thereafter, *Adonai* called and commissioned Moses to be the person who would do this. It all began when *Adonai* meet Moses in a burning bush which was on fire but was not burned. It is written: "Don't come any closer! Take your sandals off your feet, because the place you are standing is holy ground. I am the God of your father, he continued, the God of Abraham, the God of Isaac, and the God of Jacob (Exodus 3:5-6).

After, Moses, and his brother Aaron, confront the Pharaoh to let the Hebrews go to offer sacrifice in the desert. Pharaoh refuses and only after ten plagues (the last being the death of the first-born son in all the families of Egypt), does he grant them freedom. Yet, even after that, Pharoah races after the Hebrews, who are by now, passing on dry land through the Sea of Reeds. As the soldiers pursued them, the waters flowed down and destroyed them all. This event was immediately celebrated by Moses, his sister Miriam, and all the people in a song of thanksgiving and praise as recorded in Exodus 15. One verse sums up the exuberance: "Sing to *Adonai*, for He is highly exalted! The horse and its rider he threw in the sea" (Exodus 15:21).

So that the people and the generations that followed would remember this event, the Passover meal was created by *Adonai*. It consisted of a lamb (the blood of the lamb was painted on the doorway so that the angel of death would not destroy the first-born son of the families of the Israelites), unleavened bread, bitter herbs, and was eaten with haste as all the people would begin their journey of freedom out of the land of slavery.

The fourth element of the holy event was the covenant and

giving of the ten words. A fundamental base of the revelation is that these ten words (the Decalogue) reversed the sin of Eve and Adam as recorded in Genesis 3: 1-7. The Adversary told Eve that she would learn how to distinguish between good and evil or that she would be the one who could decide what is good and evil without any divine direction. The Decalogue reminds the people of Israel that it was not her who made decisions as to what is good and evil, but it is by *Adonai*, the creator of all that is.

At the heart of the covenant was the offering to the people, awesome gifts by *Adonai* and the decision (just as the decision was made by Abraham, Isaac and Jacob) by the people to obey. *Adonai 's* offer: "Now if you will pay careful attention to what I say and keep my covenant, then you will be my own treasure from among all the peoples, for all the earth is mine, and you will be a kingdom of priests for me, a nation set apart" (Exodus 19:5-6). The Israelites responded, "Everything *Adonai* has said, we will do" (Exodus 19: 8).

At the heart of the covenant and the ten words given is so the people be like *Adonai*. To be like him is to allow him to be involved in every part of the people's life. The Israelites are to follow after him, to know in their hearts that His way is the right way and that this relationship is taken as an all-embracing relationship that is founded on an everlasting bond. Vital to the covenant is its mutuality. The people are called to surrender to the divine power and grace. This grace and power are accented when *Adonai* reveals to Moses more of who He is: "*Yud-Heh-Vau-Heh* is God, merciful and compassionate, slow to anger, rich in grace and truth" (Exodus 34:6).

Another way that the Israelites are to be like *Adonai* is to celebrate the Shabbat. It is the fourth word given in the Decalogue or the Ten Commandments:

> Remember the day, Shabbat, to set it apart for God.
> You have six days to labor and do all your work, but
> the seventh day is a Shabbat for *Adonai* your God.
> On it, you are not to do any kind of work—not you,
> your son or your daughter, not your male or female

slave, not your livestock, and not the foreigner staying
with you inside the gates of your property. For in six
days, *Adonai* made heaven and earth, and everything
in them, the sea and everything in them; but on the
seventh day, the Shabbat, He separated it for himself
(Exodus 20:8-11).

The Shabbat observance is key to living the life of *Adonai* the rest
of the week. As indicated above, living the Israelite life is to have
Adonai at the very center of one's life so that there is no distinction
between the sacred and the secular. Even the land, which appears to
be secular or of this world, is sacred. The true Israelite is empowered
in keeping the Shabbat, to live life more fully in his or her daily
labor. Fundamental to this word the Shabbat is separated for *Adonai*
himself. A Messianic scholar, Stern, 2016: 99: "It is clearly the queen
of the holidays."[18]

This holy event, which is not one but five, stands at the heart of
Judaism and the Israelites themselves. Its core is divine love, divine
action and divine initiation. If the *Torah* is key to Judaism, then this
holy event is the core of the *Torah*. The rest of the *Torah*, the prophets,
the writings are extensions of this very holy event. There is much
that we can learn as Gentile believers in Jesus to drink deeply of the
rich sap of the Olive Tree, Israel.

THE GREAT TENSIONS

Major challenges await the newly founded people not yet a nation and
more of a nomadic tribe. The book of Joshua chronicles the initial
settlement of the people in the Promised Land. Yes, they arrived! The
story revealed the historical truth of the words of Moses in the Book
of Deuteronomy. Chapter Twenty-Eight outlined the blessings and
the curses given to the people. Blessings if they obeyed and curses if
the disobeyed and follow after the Canaanite Baal and Astarte.

---

[18] For an extended discussion on the Sabbath is Heschel, 1951.

Some of the blessings if they obeyed (Deuteronomy 28:3-6):

- Blessing on you in the city and the countryside.
- Blessings on the fruit of your body, the fruit of your land and the fruit of your livestock.
- Blessings on your grain-basket and kneading bowl.
- A blessing on you when you go out and a blessing on you when you come in.

However, "if you refuse to pay attention to what *Adonai* your God says, and do not observe and obey the commandments of which I am giving you today, then all the following curses will be yours in abundance" (Deuteronomy 28:15-43):

- Cursed in the city and the countryside.
- Curse on your grain-basket and kneading bowl.
- A cursed on you when you go out and a curse on you when you come in.
- You will be defeated before your enemies, robbed of your possessions, build a house and not live in it and plant a vineyard and not use the fruit.

During the exile in Babylon, Daniel, the prophet prayed and recalled a warning given to Moses:

> It is for *Adonai* our God to show compassion and forgiveness because we rebelled against him. We didn't listen to the voice of *Adonai* our God, so that we could live by his laws, which he presented to us through his servants the prophets…. Therefore, the curse and oath written in the *Torah* of Moses the servant of God has poured out on us, because we sinned against him (Daniel 9:10-11).

These blessings and curses are illustrated in the history of the people from the time they arrived with Joshua between 1220 and 1200 BCE all the way through to the era of the Romans in 70 CE when Israel lost her land until 1948.

The book of Joshua lays out the history of Israel from the arrival in the promised land (1220 BCE) when Joshua headed the people (as Moses's successor) to the time of the Judges (1200 to 1030 BCE) until the era of the kings.

Something tragic was written in the book of Judges after the generation of Joshua died. It is written: "When the entire generation had been gathered to their ancestors, another generation arose that knew neither *Adonai* nor the work he had done for Israel. Then the people of Israel did what was evil from *Adonai 's* perspective and served the Baals and Astarte" (Judges 2:10-13).

Tensions existed on this front for centuries. One may think of it this way that both in Judaism and Christianity, there exists a strong pull to adapt the faith to the culture of the time. Sociologists use the term "secularization" to describe religious organizations and people to adjust their faith and behavior to values of this world and this age or time. This is exactly what the Israelites did after Joshua. As outlined in the book of Judges, for a period of time, the Israelites obeyed and lived the covenant made with them and they were blessed with the blessings outlined by Moses. However, when the disobeyed and followed the ways of the local god (Baal) and goddess (Astarte) of Canaan, they experienced the curses. Then, *Adonai* raised up judges to call them back. They repented and then experienced blessings.

We meet the first judge of Israel, Deborah, a woman and a prophet. She led the Israelites to victory over the Canaanites. Several judges followed suit that included Gideon, Tola, Jair, Jephthan, Ibzan, Elan, and Sampson. The pattern repeated itself as indicated until the death of Sampson. Until the time of Samuel (1040 BCE), the leadership in Israel was vague to the extent that "At that time there was no king in Israel; a man simply did whatever he thought was right" (Judges 21:25).

As predicted by Moses, when the people were disobedient, they suffered the consequences. Eli, a priest who led Israel in Shiloh, did not discipline his sons who took advantage of their priestly position to abuse their power and to take advantage of the daughters of Israel. Great was their offense: "they were having sex with the women doing service at the door of the tent of meeting" (I Samuel 2:22). It was also a time of darkness for …"in those days *Adonai* rarely spoke, and visions were few" (Samuel 3:1).

It was then that *Adonai* called Samuel to be prophet and judge. Through the sin of Eli and his sons, the priests as leaders begin to falter. Samuel is anointed to speak as a prophet to the people to strengthen the despairing hearts and to fix them again on *Adonai*.

However, the people complained again. They claimed a judge and prophet are not sufficient to lead them. They want a king. The leaders of Israel gathered around Samuel and said: "make us a king to judge us like the other nations" (I Samuel 8:5). *Adonai* responded to Samuel: "Listen to the people, to everything they say to you; for it is not you they are rejecting; they are rejecting me: they don't want me to be a king over them" (I Samuel 8:7).

And so, it came to be. Saul became king followed by David and Solomon. For the next 400 years, kings ruled both in Judea (Juda and Benjamin) and Israel (the northern ten tribes). Yet, their history does not depict Israel as being obedient for, except for a few kings, the people fell to a deadly syncretism combing the faith of *Adonai* with the Baal and Astarte deities. Both of these deities brought defeat, drought, and tragedy to the people. Baal means 'master" as well as "owner". Thus, the people become "owned" by Baal and they became his possession (Cahn, 2016: 179).

Yet, *Adonai* continued to love His people, so he sent more prophets to them. One such person was Elijah. He was a zealous and inflexible nomad, long-haired, wrapped in a hairy garment, with a leather girdle and spoke with an authority that subdued kings. He challenged the priests of Baal on Mount Carmel. There the priests and Elijah set up altars of the sacrifice of bulls. The Baal priests cried aloud but there was no answer. Elijah prays and: "then the fire of

Adonai fell. It consumed the burnt offering, the wood, the stones, the dust and licked up the water in the trench" (I Kings 18:38).

The people exclaimed: "*Adonai* is God! *Adonai*, the God of Abraham, Isaac, and Israel, He is God and there is no other!! The people acknowledged the sovereignty of their own true Lord. "There is no Israel and there can be none except as *Adonai* 's people" (Buber: 1949:78).

This victory over Baal was a victory over who is the lord of the earth, *Adonai* or Baal? Elijah, breaking through to the very heart of the political system of Israel, shows without doubt that *Adonai* is not only the Lord of the people of Israel, He was also the Lord over the earth–its trees, its water, its valleys, and its abundant fruit. Baal and Astarte were false and they stood for lies. They also seduced, hurt and maimed people. A lesson to be learned: the struggle of Israel was a struggle over history, land, politics and family life. *Adonai* was not just a God of the altar and the temples but of the whole person and the whole body politic.

TURNING TO THE FUTURE

In this section, Buber assists us in understanding in our hearts the prophetic faith through the persons of Amos, Hosea and Isaiah. All three challenged the Israelites. Amos and Hosea addressed the sins and the redemption of the ten tribes of the north while Isaiah's prophetic message challenged the people of Judea.

For the sake of righteousness-Amos.

The heart of Amos is justice and the sins that the people committed were not only against *Adonai* but also sins against each other. *Adonai* called Israel his firstborn son, adopted by him from out of all the nations. The call to Israel: a place of brotherly love as the people of God but, in contrast, she had become a self-seeking band, ignorant of everything except egotism and greed. She sold the poor for the price of sandals (Amos 2:6) and father and son had a sexual relationship with a prostitute. Her leaders enticed the Nazirites[19] to become drunk and they silenced the prophets.

But *Adonai* did not leave them in their sin and continued to lead them as their king again. If they were willing to be led, then, "justice should roll down as the waters, and righteousness as a mighty stream" (Amos 5:24). He established equity, He betrothed Israel to Himself in righteousness, justice, in grace and in compassion (Hosea 2:21). God sought after Israel for her to follow Him, to keep "*Adonai's* way in which He walked." Buber wrote: "The unity of justice and righteousness is in Israelite thought one of the basic concepts of the divine-human relationship" (1949:102).

The call to repentance was a constant theme but the people and their leaders would not repent. The inspired text reads:

> Their deeds would not allow them to return to their God, for the spirit of whoring was in them, and they did not know *Adonai* (Hosea 5:4) and the more they (the priests) increased in numbers, the more they sinned against me…. They fed on the sin of my people; they were greedy for their crimes (Hosea 4:7-8). However, they didn't listen, but followed their old pagan practices and served their carved idols (II Kings 17:40)

In the end, a major disaster captured all the ten tribes of Israel by the Assyrians in 722 BCE. The king, Shalmaneser V (726–722 BCE), carried Israel away captive to Ashur, the capital of Assyria and they were scattered. and became known as the "lost tribes of Israel." According to the warning of Moses and the *Torah*, if Israel sinned and did not repent, disaster will follow.

But *Adonai* was so loving, so faithful that he promised to "restore the broken hut of David" (Amos 9:11-12) in the time of the restoration.

---

[19] In Numbers 6:1-21, *Adonai* created the Nazirites to be consecrated to Him and be holy. They were commanded not to drink wine or any intoxicating liquor, to approach a corpse, and to wear long hair. Sampson (Judges 13-16) was one of them.

This happened at the Council of Jerusalem when James, the head of the church in Jerusalem, quoted Amos and said that *Adonai* would rebuild the ruins of David so that the rest of humankind would seek *Adonai*.

For the sake of loving kindness-Hosea.

In Hosea, we meet a prophet whose very life is prophetic. The book begins with a command from *Adonai* to Hosea that he was to marry a prostitute and engage in a suffering love of his wife who continued to commit adultery. The symbolism is striking. Hosea represents *Adonai*. His wife is like a whore, unfaithful to him over and over again.

Love takes on several meanings in the text. It means the love a husband has for his wife; adulterous love that breaks the bond; divine love of *Adonai* for His people, Israel; and the so-called love of the Baal. The accent in the book is the third kind of love which is a demanding love for He called Israel as a son out of Egypt, drew her with "cords of love," grew to be very fond of her but, in the end, she turned away (Hosea 11:1-2).

Buber goes further to describe the kind of love *Adonai* has for his people. He uses the Hebrew word *hesed* which is translated as "loving kindness and faithfulness." The accent is on the response of Israel to imitate *Adonai* who exhibits this kind of love to Israel, she in return is to exhibit it to all people, not only her own people but all of humankind.

Hosea builds on the original covenant established at the hands of Moses. This covenant is depicted as a marital relationship. To disobey is to be unfaithful to *Adonai* as husband—the sin of Israel, and our sin, is a sin of adultery.

Another element that Buber elucidates for us is who did Israel love? It was Baal. Israel pretended that she could have both a love for *Adonai* as well as love for the Baal (and by implication Astarte). The Canaanites went to Baal and the Astarte to solicit them to create abundance for the land. So did Israel. She engaged in the "banalization" of *Adonai*, making him into an idol and only a nature god. This action of the priests and kings of Israel was a shameful action. The people engaged in sexual activity just as did the priests and priestesses of the ancient Canaanite cult.

Yet, the everlasting love of *Adonai* never ceased. He promised to be there for Israel as well as for us with these words:

> I will heal their disloyalty; I will love them freely; for my anger has turned from them. I will be like dew to Israel; he will blossom like a lily and strike roots like the L'vanon. His branches will spread out, his beauty be like an olive tree and his fragrance like the L'vanon...I am like a fresh, green cypress tree; your faithfulness comes from me (Hosea 14:5-7, 9).

For the sake of holiness-Isaiah.

Like the calls to Abraham, Moses, and the judges, there was also a call to Isaiah. It is an amazing call for Isaiah was in the Temple, praying when suddenly, *Adonai's* glory appeared:

> I saw *Adonai* sitting on a high and lofty throne! The hem of his robe filled the temple. *S'rafim* stood over him, each with six wings---they were crying out: More holy than the holiest holiness is *Adonai –Tzvabt* (Hosts)! The whole earth is filled with his glory (Isaiah 6:1-3).

Isaiah responded in humility and said he is unclean among the people who also were unclean. Isaiah identified himself with the rebellious, faithless kings for they are unclean. Through them, an unclean breath permeated the land and was even mingled with the holy smoke in the temple. Isaiah became clean with a glowing coal put on his lips by one of the angels.

Then, *Adonai* raised his voice and asked: "Whom shall I send?

Who will go for us? Isaiah did not wait for he was ready: "Here I am, send me" (Isaiah 6:5 and 8).

Isaiah would continue to be an amazing prophet who kept saying "yes" to all and everything *Adonai* had him do despite opposition. The author of the text continues the long line of prophetic utterances given to many in the history of Israel: the patriarchs, Moses, Joshua, the judges, kings and the major and minor prophets[20].

In this text, *Adonai* is the absolute master of the Judeans and the whole world. He is especially holy (Leviticus 19:1) and calls his people to be holy as well to create and re-create over and over again a holy nation.

Isaiah presents an image of *Adonai* and the people. He is a vinedresser and Israel are a vineyard. In Chapter Five, the prophet "sings" a song about *Adonai's* beloved, Israel. The vinedresser creates a vineyard on a very fertile hill, he digs up stones to clear the land, plants it with the choicest of vines, builds a watchtower and constructs a winepress. Sadly, though, the vinedresser expects good grapes but wild, sour grapes were produced.

In a subsequent chapter (seven) Ahaz, the king of Judea, trembles at the sight of the king of Israel and the king of Aram who are about to attack Jerusalem. Isaiah counsels the king to be calm and peaceful and to have firm faith in *Adonai* while the enemies put Ahaz under siege, but they could not overcome him" (II Kings 16:5). Buber comments that here appears a special kind of politics that he calls *theopolitics*. He wrote:

> What prevails is indeed a special kind of politics, *theopolitics,* which is concerned to establish as certain people, in a certain historical situation under the divine sovereignty, so that his people are brought nearer to the fulfilment of its task, to become the beginning of the kingdom of God. Men trust the Lord of this

---

[20] The Major Prophets were Isaiah, Jeremiah, and Ezekiel. Some authors include Daniel as the fourth. The Minor Prophets were: Hosea, Joel, Amos, Obadiah, Jonah, Micah, Nahum, Habakkuk, Zephaniah, Haggai, Zechariah, and Malachi.

kingdom, that He will protect the congregation attached to Him; but at the same time, they also trust in the inner strength and the influence of the congregation that ventures to realize righteousness in itself and toward its surrounding (Buber, 1949:135).

The base of all of this is trust and to keep still. Buber then links trust to holiness. Keeping still is holiness in regard to the political attitude of God and His people. Built into this vision of politics is the Messianic promise of the coming of Immanuel, or "God with us." He will set up a kingdom of God through the Branch of Jesse. For Christians, this is *Yeshua* or Jesus who has the Spirit of *Adonai* upon him to judge the impoverished justly, to decide fairly for the humble for "Justice will be the belt around his waist, faithfulness the sash around his hips (see Isaiah 11:1-5). He is to set up with human forces and human responsibility for the divine order of the human community until "…. the earth will be as full of the knowledge of *Adonai* as water covering the sea" (Isaiah 11:9).

THE GOD OF THE SUFFERERS

The image of who God is in this section of probing for the "Hebrew Truth" is a God who suffers with those who suffer. One can feel the anguish and suffering of *Adonai* when his glory rises from the Temple, hesitating to leave, for He cannot continue to abide in a temple that is filled with idolatry, adoration of false gods, and sexual promiscuity (Ezekiel 11:22-25). Another part of this suffering is that *Adonai* informs Ezekiel that the prince in Jerusalem, the house of Israel, the priests, the people, the false prophets and leaders will be deported to Babylon. They will be scattered and the land left behind will be abandoned and desolate with its cities without inhabitants (see Ezekiel 11-12).

The prophet Jeremiah and the author of the second book of Isaiah are illustrative of the suffering of the prophets, the people and *Adonai* himself. One may also fast-forward to the nearly two thousand years of the people of Israel suffering that culminated in the worst tragedy of human history, the Holocaust or the *Shoah*.

We begin this section with Jeremiah who like Isaiah before him was directly called by *Adonai* "Before you were formed in the womb, I knew you; before you were born, I separated you for myself. I have appointed you to be a prophet to the nations" (Jeremiah 1:5). Jeremiah, however, complains but turns to listen and obey the call. His task is monumental. He is to speak to the kings of Judah and the priests of the temple. He will suffer much at their hands but he will prevail in the power of the Highest.

Jeremiah was a son of a priestly family of the country. Along with his predecessors, Moses and Samuel, Jeremiah was a man of the Word of God that comes again and again as something new and fresh. For him, the word of God is: "like a fire burning in my heart, imprisoned in my bones" (Jeremiah 20:9). The prophet has to speak this out and bear much derision and suffering. "Let's denounce him! All those who were on good terms with me watched for my downfall.... But *Adonai* is at my side like a mighty hero" (Jeremiah 20:10).

Jeremiah was not only a man of the word but a man of imagery that *Adonai* used to express his prophetic ministry. He was told to take a linen waistcloth and bury it near a river. He was then to come back to find that the waistcloth was ruined. When he showed this to the people, he said that the pride of Judah was to be ruined and all the people will be good for nothing (Jeremiah 13:1-13).

Once he visited a potter who had shaped the clay that did not produce what he wanted. So, he began again to make a proper vessel. Likewise, the Israelites. Speaking to them he said that "you are like clay in the hands of *Adonai* so be malleable to let him form you. But you refused to listen and obey" (Jeremiah 18:1-12).

The prophet continued speaking against the false use of the Temple. Some of the false use consisted of worshipping *Adonai* without sincerity, adoring false gods and goddesses such as "the Queen of Heaven," living in a world of bad faith, trusting in a delusion, and abandoning *Adonai* as the fountain of clear water and drinking from a spoiled well. The Judeans were also guilty of working on the Shabbat, abandoning the covenant of *Adonai* they made earlier, shedding innocent blood, and engaging is their own private interests rather than living the life of the *Torah*.

However, Jeremiah bore the costs of speaking like this. For some of the people said "Come on, let us concoct a plot against Jeremiah, for the *Torah* will not perish for lack of priests, nor advice for lack of wise men, nor the word for lack of prophets. Come on, let us slander him and pay no attention to anything he says" (Jeremiah 18:18). *Adonai* however, supports him with these words: "They will fight against you but will not overcome you because I am with you to save you and rescue you" (Jeremiah 15: 20).

So tragically the kings, the priests and the people did no listen, did not obey and they suffered horribly by being taken into captivity and brought to Babylon in the year 587 BCE. Yet, the mercies of *Adonai* were there with many prophesies of renewal. Several are most striking:

> I love you with an everlasting love; this is why in grace I draw you to me. Once again, I will build you; you will be built, virgin of Israel (31:2-3) and for the plans I have in mind for you, plans for well-being, not for bad things; so that you can have hope and a future. When you call to me and pray to me, I will listen to you. When you seek me, you will find me and then I will reverse your exile and gather you from all the nations and places where I have driven you and bring you back to the place from which I exiled you (Jeremiah 29:11-13).

The second book of Isaiah (40-66) speaks much of the future of Israel that is full of hope and anticipation of the "New Heavens and the New Earth" (Isaiah 66:22). *Adonai*, "the Holy One of Israel" is centerfold to this text. Through Israel the nations, are destined to be holy, redeemed, liberated, and saved. The author of this book, speaks of a theology of world-history, or in Buber's term, theopolitics, that declares the Rule of God over all the world, all the nations, and the whole of creation. God was seen as one who makes history and is actively involved in the very existence of creation. Buber comments: "*Adonai* is God living in history" (1949:11). It is through Israel and the Gentile believers, who are grafted into Israel. A further channel is through the servant of *Adonai* who appears in four songs in this text. This servant will be gentle and be a light to the nations (Isaiah 42:1-9). He will bring back Jacob to *Adonai* and will be a light to all the nations (Isaiah 49:1-6). This servant will be open every morning to hear like a disciple and will not rebel (Isaiah 50: 4-9). Like the prophets who suffered, this servant will suffer much as the hands of sinners but will be instrumental in their redemption (Isaiah 52:13-53: 1-12).

The message of suffering hope is redolent with meaning:

> After this ordeal, he will see satisfaction, by knowing pain and sacrifice, my righteous servant makes many righteous, it is for their sins that he suffers. Therefore, I will assign him a share with the great, he will divide the spoil with the mighty, for having exposed himself to death and being counted among the sinners, who's actually bearing the sin of many and interceding for the offenders (Isaiah 53:12).

This is so well summed up as a prophetic word speaking of Jesus at the hands of Paul:

> On the contrary, He emptied Himself, in that He took the form of a slave by becoming like human beings are. And when He appeared as a human being, He humbled Himself still more by becoming obedient even to death—death on a cross as a criminal but God raised Him to the highest place and gave Him the name above all names. (Philippians 2: 7-9).

A MESSIANIC JEWISH INTERPRETATION OF THE *TANAKH*

Taken together, the *Tanakh* and the *B'rit Hadasha*, form a whole. According to Stern, to have the *B'rit Hadasha* without the *Tanakh* is heresy but to have the *Tanakh* without the *B'rit Hadasha* is incomplete. The goal of both together is bring repair to a broken world. The constant theme in both series of texts is to recognize that humans need to be saved and *Adonai* provides salvation. God created us in His image to have an intimate, loving, and abundant fellowship with Him (Genesis 1:20–2:25).

Stern offers a new perspective in understanding the *Tanakh*. He integrates a nearly 2000-year history of rich Jewish thought with the text. He makes abundant use of the Babylonian *Talmud*, completed in 600 CE that is composed of *Mishnah* (an interpretation of the *Tanakh*), the *Tosefa* (a commentary on the Mishnah and addition to the *Mishnah*) and the *Gemara* (further expansions of all). Stern also takes advantage of major rabbis and Jewish scholars in approaching a better understand of the sacred text.

The *Tanakh* is marked by a breadth of vision that includes both the individual and the collective; the full range of human activity; family life; class struggle; social concerns; commerce; agriculture; the environment, national identity; government; justice; repentance; forgiveness, social relationships; personal identity; gender issues; worship; prayer; physical health; emotional well-being; inner life; death; after death and the final judgment.

All Christian Bibles (or at least most) separate the Old Testament from the New Testament. Stern strongly disagrees. There is a process of the beginning of humanity in Genesis 1-2 of an abode of sinless Adam and Eve to its completion of a sinless paradise, and "new heavens" and "new earth" as recorded in Isiah 65:17 and Revelation 21:1. Stern argues for a seamless unity of *Torah*, prophets, writings, gospels, Acts of the Apostles, letters, and Revelation.

Names of God

Stern outlined twelve primary themes that speak to the heart of Judaism and the *Tanakh* for Christians. I am focusing on eight of these twelve. The first theme, the names of God, began in Genesis 1:1. The names of God in Hebrew thinking are many. Each name is like a curtain or a window. When the curtain is drawn back, depths of meanings shine forth. In this text, the name used is *Elohim* that indicates majesty, excellence, high dignity, greatness, creative power, authority, and sovereignty. The name also means the one who is the object of fear or reverence.

Elyon portrays the meaning of "the highest" or the "exalted one" In Genesis 14:18–20. In Genesis 15:2, the name used is *Adonai* that indicates "My Lord." A similar name is *El* that has a primary meaning of "a jealous God." It is used as a prefix to other titles such as *El'Elyon* (God most high), *El Shaddai* (God Almighty), *El 'Olam* (everlasting God), *El Hai* (living God), *El Roi* (God all seeing), *El-Elojei Yisra'el* (God, the God of Israel) and *El Gibbor* (Mighty God).

Of all the names given in the *Tanakh*, the name which appears most frequently is *YHVH*. It occurs 6,823 times and is roughly translated as "He who is self- existing self-sufficient, is He who lives" or "I am/will be what I am/will be". The Hebrew equivalent is *Ehyeh Asher Ehyeh* whose name was revealed to Moses in Exodus 3: 14.

Since the third century BCE, the name, (YHVH or *Ehyeh Asher Ehyeh*) or the *Tetragrammaton*, seems to have been regarded and the "unpronounceable name" and is said only once by the high priest in the Holy of holies of the temple. *El Shaddai* is indicative as God the nourisher or the one who imparts and provides life. *Tzva'ot* is added to *YHVH Elohim* to become "*YHVH Elomim Tzva'ot*" which means "The Lord of Hosts". This appears 240 times in the *Tanakh*. The actual meaning of *Tzva'ot* is "hosts" which, in prophetic usage, was transferred to the heavenly hosts joining the forces of God's people.

Frequently, the names of God are linked to what He does. He is one who leads, *El-beth-el* ('God of the God-house'), *El-olam* (God of the hidden time), *YHVH-nissi* (my standard), *YHVH-shalom* (peace), and *El-Elyon* (founder of heaven and earth).

MESSIANIC PROPHECIES

According to Stern, there are hundreds of texts in the *Tanakh* that refer to the coming of the Messiah. He selected those that provide us with the foundation of God's plan to bring blessings to His world through the Messiah. The first one is very early in the history of humanity. After this sin of Adam and Eve, God pronounces his judgement on the serpent (the Adversary). The text reads: "I will put animosity between you and the woman, and between your descendent and her descendant; he will bruise your head, and you will bruise his heel" (Genesis 3:15). A Rabbi wrote: "At his request, God showed Satan the Messiah; and when he saw him, he trembled, fell on his face and cried: 'Truly this is the Messiah, who will bruise me" (Stern, 2016:8).

Chapter forty-nine of the Book of Genesis is a record of Jacob blessing all of his sons. Judah has a special blessing that predicted that a scepter would never pass from him and that he would forever hold a ruler's staff from heaven between his legs (Genesis 49:10). Rishi, a prominent Rabbinic Jew of the Middle Ages, says that this verse refers to the Messiah to whom the Kingdom of *Adonai* belongs (Stern, 2016:66). Balaam, a soothsayer from the Moab, was asked to curse Israel who actually blessed her. Seeing what could have been an angel, he spoke prophetically and proclaimed: "A star will step forth from Jacob, a scepter will arise from Israel" (Numbers 24:17). The star was seen as a figure of the Messiah.

The second book of Samuel (2 Samuel 7:12-17) predicted that a descendent of David would sit on his throne in the future that would be forever. Psalm 89 celebrates this:

You said, "I made a covenant with the one I chose,
I swore to my servant David,
'I will establish your dynasty forever,
Built up your throne through all generations' (89:4–5).

This prediction extended to such promises as him being his first born, the most exalted of the kings of the earth and for whom God would be his father.

In a commentary on Isaiah 7:14, Stern quotes Rishi (2016:497): "Behold the *alma* (virgin) shall conceive and have a son and shall call his name Immanuel. This means that our Creator will be with us. And this is the sign: the one who will conceive is a girl who never in her life has had intercourse with any man. Upon this one shall the Holy Spirit have power."

A text that is so redolent of the coming Messiah is Isaiah 53:1–12– the suffering messiah. Several *Talmudic* sources refer to this text that the coming Messiah would suffer, be pierced, be a leper scholar and would be one who bore all the sins of Israel. This was the common Jewish understanding up until 500 CE. However, because Israel suffered so much from the hands of Christians, the suffering servant came to be known as Israel. Buber concurs.

Micah is striking in its specificity. "But you, Bethlehem near *Efrat*, so small among the clans of Judah, out of you will come forth to me the future ruler of Israel whose origins are far in the past, back to ancient times" (Micah 5:1). Among generations of Rabbinic scholars whose works are recorded in the Jerusalem Targum[21] and the *Talmud*, there is a common understanding of the meaning of this text. The future ruler of Israel is described as having origins or an existence 'back to Ancient times' (Micah 5:1) that precedes the creation of the world. This Messiah has existed since eternity.

In an extended text from Zechariah 9:9–10 and Zechariah 12–14, the Messiah is to come on two occasions. In the first occasion, he

---

[21] Originally spoken translations of the *Tanakh* that a professional interpreter would give in the common language of the listeners when that was not Hebrew.

is envisioned as a king but a king who is humble and is riding on a donkey. This prophecy has been already fulfilled with King *Yeshua's* triumphant entry into Jerusalem at the beginning of the last week of his life as recorded in Matthew (21:1-11).

The focus on the future coming of King Messiah is in Zechariah 12-14. Throughout these chapters, the phrase "When that day comes..." frequently occurs. Thus, this is indicative of a victorious return of the Messiah. This text begins each of the events and processes with the Messiah being central:

- "I will seek to destroy all nations attacking Jerusalem"
- "I will pour out on the house of David and on those living in Jerusalem a spirit of grace and prayer; and they will look to me, whom they pierced"
- "a spring will be opened up for the house of David and the people in Jerusalem to cleanse them from sin and impurity."
- His feet will stand on the Mount of Olive which lies east of Jerusalem"
- "*Adonai* my God will come to you with all the holy ones.'
- "There will be neither bright light nor thick darkness."
- "fresh water will flow out from Jerusalem half toward the eastern sea and half toward the western sea."
- "*Adonai* will be king over the whole world and will be the only one, and his name will be the only name."
- "Jerusalem will be raised up and inhabited."
- "*Adonai* will strike all the peoples who made war against Jerusalem."
- "Everyone remaining from all the nations that came to attack Jerusalem will go up every year to worship the King, *Adonai-Tzva'ot*, and to keep the festival of *Sukkot*[22]."

We look then to these passages from Zechariah that predicted that the Messiah would come, firstly, in a humble way (also prophesied

---

[22] The Feast of Booths, celebrating the forty years when the people of Israel in *sukkots* (booths or tents) in the desert between Egypt and Israel.

by Micah) and secondly, in triumph to reign as King with *Adonai*, His Lord.

The theme of Messiah as being the suffering servant from Isaiah 53 is revisited in Psalm 22. According to Stern, in this psalm, there is a remarkable similarity to how the evangelists describe *Yeshua* during his time of execution at the hands of the Romans. The Messiah's bones are pulled out of joint (verse 14) and his bodily water is dried up as recorded in verses 14-15. He is hemmed in by enemies. They gamble for his clothing during his death pangs (verses 16-18). To add to the shame, the Messiah is naked ("they gaze at me and gloat", verse 17). Stern's depiction is reinforced by some ancient rabbinic sources with these words: "The Holy One, blessed be he, began to tell him of the conditions, and said to him: 'Those who are hidden with you, their sins in the future will force you into an iron yoke and because of their sins your tongue will cleave to the roof of your mouth" (from *Pesiqta Rabbati*, the midrash on Psalm 22, and quoted by Stern, 2016:919). Stern adds to this and quotes a number of Rabbi's saying:

> The Rabbis said that when the son of David came, people would lay an iron yoke on his neck, so heavy he would bow under its weight. He would weep and cry: "My strength is as dry as a potsherd". Then God replied "Ephraim, my just Messiah, long ago you have taken it upon yourself, since the six days of creation. Now let your pain be as my pain".

The last Messianic prophetic text I will discuss comes from Daniel 9:24-27. It is unique and stands alone of all the prophecies in that it refers to the exact time of his arrival. Stern comments:

> This is the only biblical text that explicitly refers to the coming Messiah while specifying the exact time of his arrival. Josephus says that Daniel "was one of the greatest of the prophets for he did not only

prophesy future events but he also determined the time of their accomplishment" (2016:1257).

Daniel's text reads as follows:

> Know, therefore, and discern that seven weeks of years will elapse between the issuing of the decree to restore and rebuild Jerusalem until an anointed prince comes. It will remain built for sixty-two weeks (of years), with open spaces and moats; but these will be troubled times. Then after sixty-two weeks, Messiah will be cut off and have nothing. The people of a prince yet to come will destroy the city and the sanctuary, but his end will come with a flood, and desolations ae decreed until the war is over...he will put a stop to the sacrifice and the grain offering. On the wing of detestable things, the desolator will come and continue until the already decreed destruction is poured out the desolator (Daniel 9:25-27).

Stern calculates the time of his arrival and death in the following manner. He recounts two scholars, Doukhan (2012) and Rydelnik (2014) in interpreting the meaning of seventy-weeks. Daniel is verifying the fulfillment of this prophecy (made by Isaiah 44:28-45:4 of Jerusalem's restoration and the building of the temple). Seventy years would pass for the exile but through Cyrus, the Persian King, the people would return to Israel and would rebuild the Temple and the city of Jerusalem (circa 520-515 BCE). However, according to Ezra 7:7, a second return from Babylon occurred in 458 BCE under the authority of a new king of Persia, Artaxerxes (in Hebrew, *Artach'ashta*). If one takes a decree from him in 458 BCE, it would be 483 years (sixty-nine-week years) before Messiah's coming (483-458 or 30). This would be the approximate death ("the Messiah would be cut off and have nothing "of the Messiah. After his death, A prince (Could this be Titus [39 CE-81 CE]?), 70 CE, captures Jerusalem and burns the Temple on 9th of Av. This was in accord to Daniel: "The people of a prince yet to come will destroy the city and the sanctuary, but his end will come with a flood, and desolations ae decreed until the war is over...he will put a stop to the sacrifice and the grain offering" (9:27).

Scholars debate on the dates and the interpretation of the meaning of weeks and years. What can be concluded, though, is that the similarity between the prophetic predictions and the future events are remarkable.

THANKSGIVING FOR GRACES RECEIVED.

At the completion of each chapter, a section will be devoted to either give thanks to *Adonai* for the graces given to the people of Israel or to join with them in lamentations for the sufferings they have endured. In this chapter, lauds of gratefulness are to be offered for the amazing "Gift of the Jews" to God's plan for all of humanity.

Following are some praises and thanksgivings that come from *The Daily Prayer Book* (2008)[23] and from the Scriptures:

> You remember what has been done from eternity. Before you all secrets are revealed, as well as the multitude of things concealed from the very beginning. There is no darkness before the throne of your glory, nor is anything hidden from your eyes. Everything is revealed and known in your presence, Oh Eternal, our God! You look and you behold everything. From the very beginning have you made known and from the first revealed; that this day is the beginning (Daily Prayer Book).

> Blessed be you, *Adonai*, the God of Israel our father, forever and ever. Yours, *Adonai*, is the greatness, the

---

[23] This is commonly known as the Siddur.

power, the glory, the victory, and the majesty; for everything in heaven and on earth is yours. The Kingdom is yours, *Adonai*; and you are exalted as head overall. Riches and honour come from you, your rule everything, in your hand is power and strength, you have the capacity to make great and to give strength to all. Therefore, our God, we thank you and praise your glorious name. (From David's prayer, I Chronicles 29:10-13).

Yes, *Adonai*, you have given so much to us who are made in your image and likeness. All honour and praise rightfully belong to you for coming to us and given so much of yourself in the texts revealed from your heart.

CONCLUSIONS

On the theme of this document, remembering, repenting and reconciling, remembering the prophetic faith or the first testament is critical for the unity of the Jewish and Gentile believers in *Yeshua* or Jesus. The *Tanakh* is like a foundation stone to Judaism, Messianic Judaism and Gentile Christianity. It is as a fountain that has endless waters flowing from the throne of *Elohim* into the hearts of the believers. Thus, there is a call for repentance, as Gentile believers in *Yeshua*, have not looked at the text as a unique source of faith but only as a conduit to Jesus. Repentance is vital here. After this repentance, it paves part of the way for reconciliation of Jewish believers, Jewish believers of *Yeshua* and Gentile believers of Jesus.

The gift of, the inner mystery, the rich sap of Israel is only touched on in this chapter. The gems of truth abound abundantly in the *Tanakh*. So many are the challenges that face all of us in knowing more and more about our faith. Learning from the fountain of truth, righteousness, holiness, and love so very evident in Israel, we grow more and more into "Loving *Adonai* our God with all our hearts, all

our souls, all our minds, all our strength, all our resources, and all
our being" (see Deuteronomy 6: 4–5 and Matthew 22:37–38). The
bar is also so very high for us who are disciples of Jesus who asks us:

> I am giving you a new commandment: that you keep
> loving each other. In the same way that I have loved
> you, you are to keep on loving each other. Everyone
> will know that you are my disciples by the fact that
> you have love for each other (John 13:34–35)

References: Chapter One

Buber, M. 1949. *The Prophetic Faith*. New York: Harper and Row, Publishers.

Cahn, J. 2016. *The book of mysteries*. Lake Mary Florida: Charisma Media/Charisma House Book Group.

Daily Prayer Book. 2008. Tel-Aviv Israel: Sinai Publishing.

Doulkhan, J. 2012. *On the way to Emmaus: Five major Messianic prophecies explained*. Clarksville, MD: Messianic Jewish Publishers.

Finto, D. 2016. *Your people shall be my people*. Minneapolis, Minnesota: Chosen.

Heschel, A. J. 1951. *The Sabbath*. New York: Farrar, Strais and Giroux.

Rydelnik, M. and M. Vanlaningham, eds. 2014. *The Moody Bible Commentary*. Chicago: Moody Press.

Stern, D. H. 2016. *The Complete Jewish Bible*. Peabody Massachusetts: Hendrickson Publishers.

CHAPTER TWO

THE MOTHER OF ALL CHURCHES:
THE JERUSALEM CHURCH
REMEMBERING, REPENTING
AND RECONCILING

ORIENTATION

There appear to be three periods of the first Church that housed Jewish believers in Jesus: (1) the Church of Jerusalem (Pentecost to 70 CE), (2) The Church in the Galilee (70 to 135 CE), and, (3), the Church of the diaspora (100 to 400 CE).

The Essenes begin our discussion of the Church of Jerusalem that is followed by their link to John the Baptist and to *Yeshua*. Subsequent to this, is the presentation of central elements to the beliefs, rituals, ethos and organizational features of the community of Jewish believers of *Yeshua* in Jerusalem. The time period is from Pentecost to the Fall of Jerusalem and the destruction of the Temple.

THE ESSENES

From classical to contemporary and original documents, a fascinating story emerges about a renewal movement from about 150 BCE to 66-70 CE called the Essenes. Little was known about them until 1947 when a young Bedouin, Muhammad edh-Dhib, discovered scrolls in caves on the Western shore of the Dead Sea that was about eight miles from Jericho. Previously, according the scholarship of Vermes (1997/2000), three historians wrote about the movement: Josephus (37-100 CE), Philo of Alexandria (20 BCE-40 CE), and the Roman scholar, Pliny the Elder (23-79 CE). The story of the Essenes will be constructed from the classical work of Josephus, the scholarship of Vermes and the original scrolls. Using sociological categories developed in this chapter, I will be referring to the leaders of the Essenes as renewal prophets and *kenotic* leaders. The movement itself as a movement of renewal.

The years of the genesis of the movement are from the work of Vermes. Judea was ruled by the Greek Seleucids beginning in 200 BCE. Relations with the victors was relatively peaceful until Antiochus IV (215-163 BCE) began a persecution against the Jews and stole all the sacred artifacts from the Second Temple (one built from 520-515 BCE) and set up the idol of the Hellenistic god, Zeus. This was embraced by the Jewish elite, but was a scandal to the devout people. This sparked a revolt by the Maccabean family that brought an end to the Seleucid power in Jerusalem. Up until the time of the third Maccabean revolution, the priesthood in Jerusalem was a legitimate institution, after the tradition of the Sons of Zadok, the successor of the Aaronic priesthood having received divine legitimation from *Adonai*: "you will anoint and consecrate him (Aaron) and his sons, to serve me in the priesthood. Their anointing will confer an everlasting priesthood on them for their generations to come" (Exodus 40:14-15)[24].

In 173 BCE, Antiochus Epiphanes, the Seleucid king, deposed Onias III, the legitimate high priest of the House of Zadok. Then in 152 BCE, Johnathan, the Maccabean, took the High Priestly office to himself.

Thus, began a new dynasty of the high priests known as the Hasmoneans and ruled Judea until the Romans came in 63 BCE. They installed Herod the Great as monarch. It was at the time of the installation of Johnathan that a contemporary of his (unknown by name) who was called the *Teacher of Righteousness* and reacted not in revolt but in protest to the Hellenized and secular (control) kind of leadership exhibited by the Hasmoneans. Thus, begins the Essenes in about 150 BCE.

From the summary of Vermes (as he read the scrolls), from

---

[24] Zadok was appointed by Solomon to be the high priest: I Kings 2:35. See also Ezekiel 40:46: ".the priests responsible for the service of the altar. These are the sons of Zadok, those of the sons of Levi who approach *Adonai* to serve Him" and Ezekiel 43:19. Much earlier, a covenant was made to Levi, the predecessor to Zadok: This commandment is for you...you will know that I sent this commandment to you, to affirm my intention to maintain my covenant with Levi, says *Adonai* Sabaoth. My covenant was with him—a covenant of life and peace, and these were what I gave him—a covenant of respect, and he respected me and held my name in awe. The law of truth was in his mouth and guilt was not found on his lips, he walked in peace and justice with me and he converted many from sinning. The priest's lips ought to safeguard knowledge; his is where the law should be sought, since he is *Adonai*-Sabaoth's messenger.

Josephus and four original documents (*The Community Rule, Community Rule Manuscripts from Cave 4, The Damascus Document and the Messianic Rule*), I will construct an image of the Essene leaders as kenotic leaders and the community members as kenotic disciples using various themes. I will offer general characteristics of the community and then outline the themes. The themes consist of: the masters or guardians, the members or disciples, the images of God, images of evil and Belial (another name for the adversary or the devil), the novitiate, the Covenant, the disciplines, and the coming of the Messiah.

Before this begins, Josephus, Vermes and the Essene rules testify to two Essene branches. The most well-known is the community in the Qumran in the desert—north of the Dead Sea and east of Jericho. The second were town dwellers who shared the same beliefs, celebrated feasts together, and used a common library. Table 2:1 One indicates both the contrasts and the similarities.

Table 2:1: –The Qumran and Town Essenes	
The Qumran	**The Town Essenes**
Celibate	Married with Children sex only for procreation
Common Ownership of Property	Private Ownership
Ate, slept, prayed, counselled and worked together	Lived in Family Units
Worked in agriculture, pottery, curing of hides and writing of manuscripts	In agriculture but also in trades

Table 2:1: –The Qumran and Town Essenes	
The Qumran	**The Town Essenes**
Did not worship in the Temple	Did worship in the Temple
Similarities	

Similarities
• Made a Covenant with one another
• Renewed their Covenant together
• Elders or Guardians and members were accountable to them
• Very serious about keeping Covenant, obeying the law of Moses and the Prophets

General Characteristics

Josephus (93/1737) exhibits great admiration for the Essenes with a special reference to the Qumran branch. All members were celibate, held things in common, did not have servants and worked in husbandry for their livelihood. They manifested great affection towards one another and rejected pleasure and riches. He writes: "All one's possessions are intermingled with every other's possession" (93/1737:476). The members were hospitable and welcomed strangers and even supplied them with garments to wear. Every day they rose in prayer and worked until the fifth hour with great diligence. Their piety, according to the historian, was exemplary. He writes: "And as far as their piety towards God, it is very extraordinary" (93/1737:476). A last general characteristic is the charismatic nature of the Essenes who believed in prophecy. Josephus notes:

> There are also among them who undertake to foretell things to come by reading the holy books and using several sorts of purifications and being perpetually conversant in the discourses of the prophets, and

it is but seldom that they miss on their predictions
(93/1737:478)

Masters or Guardians

It is these men who are the shepherds of community members. They
are to teach the saints, hold them to accountability, bless the members,
study the Law, lead in prayers, be part of a twelve member "Council
of the Community" who judge infractions, welcome new members,
evaluate them to see if they are called to be permanent members (after
a novitiate) and be, especially, humble. In the *Damascus Document* (the
primary rule for those who live in the towns), it is written:

> He shall instruct the Congregation in the works of
> God. He shall cause them to consider His mighty
> deeds and shall recount all the happenings of eternity
> to them according to their explanation. He shall love
> them as a father loves his children, and shall carry
> them in all their distress like a shepherd his sheep. He
> shall loosen all the fetters which bind them that in his
> congregation there may be none that are oppressed
> or broken...And the Guardian shall instruct their
> sons and their daughters in a spirit of humility and in
> loving-kindness and shall not keep anger towards them
> (*Damascus Document,* Vermes (1997/2000:114-115).

The Spirit of the Disciples

Every member is to seek God with their whole hearts, are to be
humble, exhibit loving kindness and good intent to each other, abide
in contemplative prayer, abound in charity, show unending goodness
to others and are to be "Keepers of the Covenant." Congregationalists
are to pray frequent confessions of guilt by saying, "Truly we have
sinned, we and our fathers, by walking counter to the precepts of the

Covenant, thy judgements upon us are justice and truth" (*Damascus Document*, Vermes,1997/2000:107).

One striking behavior the disciples are to do is to be accountable to each other. They are to rebuke each other with loving-kindness and are not to do this out of anger or ill-temper. This rebuke is a process. One rebukes another personally, then in front of witnesses and, if this is not fruitful, to accuse him before the whole congregation[25].

Images of God

One section of the scrolls is devoted to hymns and poems. Here and in the rules (*The Community Rule Manuscripts from Cave 4* (Vermes,1997/2000:96), images of the divine are recorded. God is seen as: Abounding in Mercy, Prince of Light, having great loving kindness, Righteousness, the Author of Goodness, Fountain of Knowledge, Source of Holiness, Summit of Glory, Almighty, Eternal Majesty and Full of Wisdom. He is also characterized as loving knowledge, in love with His people, is a God of Glory, and is Most High.

Many more things can be said of the Essenes. Suffice it to say that the leaders (called Guardians) do exhibit a remarkable kenotic style of leadership and are also called renewal prophets, as they tried to renew the covenant that had been overshadowed by rebellion, both in the past and in the time of their existence. Further, the followers show a striking mirror of kenotic discipleship.

Images of Belial and Evil

An important task of all members in the Town and the Qumran Community is to discern between good and evil. Evil is personified in the person of Belial who is similar to the Adversary in the Christian tradition. He and his evil demons are characterized as angels of darkness, redolent with greed, wickedness, slackness, authors of lies,

---

[25] This is remarkably like the admonition that Jesus gives to his disciples (Matthew 18:15).

cruel, and full of lust. Men and women who follow Belial are called *sons of the pit*. When this spirit rules, men are envisioned as:

> They are all of them rebels, for they have not turned from the way of traitors but have wallowed in the ways of whoredom and wicked wealth. They have taken revenge and borne malice, every man against his brother, and every man has hated his fellow, and every man has sinned against his near kin, and has approached unchastity, and has acted arrogantly for the sake of riches and gains. And every man has done that which seemed right in his eyes and has chosen the stubbornness of his heart (*Damascus Document*). (Vermes (1997/2000:105).

The Covenant

A central feature of the community was its Covenant commitment. The founder (*Teacher of Righteousness*) and the Guardians took very seriously the covenant made by Yahweh, the God of Israel, and the people of Israel. In fact, one of the main reasons why the Essenes came to be was to live out the covenant that had been broken so many times by the Israelites of old and the priests of Jerusalem under the leadership of the Hasmoneans. The covenant was twofold: a primary covenant to God and a secondary one to each other. From The Community Rule: "He shall undertake by a binding oath to return with all his heart and soul to every commandment of the Law of Moses in accordance with all that has been revealed of it to the sons of Zadok, the priests, Keepers of the Covenant who together have freely pledged themselves to His truth and to walking in the way of His delight" (Vermes, 1997/2000:77-78).

Josephus outlines the essential features of this covenant:

- Piety towards God
- Observe justice towards all men

- Do no harm to anyone
- Hate the wicked
- Assist the righteous
- Show fidelity to all people, especially to those in authority
- Never abuse authority
- No stealing or doing unlawful gains
- Not to reveal your inner life to non-members
- Honor the angels (93/1737:477)

Both Josephus and Vermes call the Essenes a sect. The only evidence that I can see is that they did exhibit a sectarian attitude to non-members and to the Jerusalem authorities, "Everlasting hatred for the men of the pit" (*Community Rule Manuscripts from Cave 4.* (Vermes, 1997/2000:95). However, more significant are the elements of a movement of renewal. The Essenes sought to renew the observance of the Law of Moses and the Prophets, they gave their whole hearts to live the covenant, they were committed to live the ancient tradition of the *Torah,* and they lived a life of simplicity as a mark of their total commitment.

Links between the Essenes, John the Baptist and Jesus

There is much speculation on these links by Biblical scholars and historians of early Christianity. I will offer some evidence that these links are plausible and they will enable us to have a fuller understanding of the central elements of community life. Farnes (2011: spring), a Near Eastern studies student will provide us with a potential link with John the Baptist and Meier (2011: Volume III), a Biblical scholar, informs us of Jesus' possible link to the Essenes. Added to this will be the work of Schmalz and Fischer (1999).

Both Farnes and Meier agree that there is no textual evidence, either in the New Testament or in non–Biblical authors such as Josephus, for the link between the Baptist and Jesus with the Essenes.

What both authors do is to identify similarities and commonalities between the Essenes-John the Baptist and the Essenes-Jesus. Thus, the evidence is only plausible and suggestive.

The similarities arise from common sacred views, behaviors and messages. In regard to John and the **Quarantines**[26] Farnes quotes a scholar (Charlesworth,1999) who noted these commonalities:

1. Both John and the members of the Qumran come from similar geographical locations. John was said to be east of Jerusalem, in the wilderness of Judea, close to the River Jordon and only a few kilometers from the Qumran monastery. It would have been possible that he had some contact with them.
2. The Community of the Qumran and the Baptist shared a preference for using prophecies, especially, Isaiah in the text: "A voice cries, 'Prepare in the desert a way for *Adonai*. Make a straight highway for our God across the wastelands'" (40:3).
3. Water was used by both as a means of cleansing and purification. However, John only baptized his disciples and others once but the Essene monks bathed several times a day.
4. Eschatology was common to both. They gave warnings of judgement that was coming.
5. Asceticism was especially a hallmark of John and the monks of the Qumran. All were celibate and avoided marriage, they fasted frequently and, like the Nazarites, refrained from strong drink.

Farnes affirms that it was possible that John was adopted by the Essenes (a common practice among them) and lived with them and, then, after a novitiate, left. He concludes his article: "In conclusion, there is strong evidence that John was indeed a Uranite, brought up at Qumran after being adopted ... he then lived on his own in the Judean wilderness on the east side of the Jordon River making his own clothes and eating whatever he could find" (Farnes, 2001).

---

[26] The name of the Essenes who live in the desert monastery in the Qumran.

Schmalz and Fischer support these authors by indicating that John was an Essene who likely grew up in the Qumran monastery. Their evidence is that he and the Essenes taught the imminence of the kingdom of God, both used baptism as a remission from sins. The Baptist and the Essenes offered similar moral teachings and they frequently used the text from Isaiah 40:3-5 that later became part of Matthew's gospel rendition in Matthew 3:1-3.

Meier is much more elaborate in his discussion of the relationship between Jesus and the Essenes. He is modest in his claims in using data that describes similarities and differences in thought, language, and social structure. He subdivides his discussion under three headings: (1) eschatology, (2) attitudes toward the Temple, and (3) rules governing behavior.

The Essenes interpreted their eschatology in a similar way that did Jesus. The final reign of God, or the Kingdom of God is both a current reality and a future event. In the Qumran liturgy, led by a priest, they believe the reign of God comes with a whole host of angels. The end times will be dramatic in the eyes of Jesus and the Essenes. In the present kingdom of God, both for Jesus and the monks, there will be the saving acts of God such as healing the wounded, sight to the blind, the raising of the dead and the Good News to the poor. Meier concludes this section with: "All in all, the parallels are remarkable" (2001:498).

Around the time of the Essenes and Jesus, the Jerusalem Temple and the *Torah* were the central religious symbols of Late Judaism. However, as we saw above, and according to the Essenes, the temple was polluted and the priesthood corrupted because in 150 BCE, the **Hasmoneans** took control of the priesthood breaking from the traditional line of The House of Zadok. Thus, the Essenes dissociated themselves from both the Temple and the Priesthood and longed for the day of the restoration of the Temple. They created for themselves a spiritual temple.

The third category of similarities had to do with rules governing behavior. In regard to divorce and illicit sex, Jesus and the Essenes were on the same page. The Essenes, however, were more stringent.

Lusting after another was considered sin from both Jesus and the Qumranites. Celibacy was the chosen life-style for both. It was seen by Jesus and the Essenes to be signs of the future kingdom where there would be no more need for children being physically born (and thus no sex). Wealth and property were suspect as a distraction from lives totally dedicated to God and the coming kingdom. The celibate monks renounced all wealth and property while their town counterparts did work, used money but were not to become wealthy. They, in turn, combined monies to be given to the poor and the sick. The poverty-wealth divide was not present among them. This was similar to the teaching of Jesus and practiced by the Post-Pentecost Church in Jerusalem (see Acts 2:44–45).

Schmalz and Fischer also substantiate what Meier has documented. These authors argued that Jesus proclaimed the Gospel of the Kingdom that is similar to that of the Essenes. Other commonalities included the fact that both rejected the compromised temple and both offered an alternative to atonement that did not involve sacrifice but mercy (Matthew 9:13 and Hosea 6:6).

One strong similarity not referred to by Meier was the intense ethic of love among the Essenes. Every member was to seek God with their whole heart, were to be humble, were to exhibit loving kindness and good intent to each other, living in contemplative prayer, abound in charity, show unending goodness to others and were to be "Keepers of the Covenant." This is reflective of Jesus who spent so many of his months teaching his disciples to love each other: "My command to you is to love one another" (John 15:17) and "This is my commandment: love one another, as I have loved you" (John 15:12).

De Salvo (2011) adds that there is evidence of a suffering Messiah who was also crucified. He cites a scroll fragment called 4Q285 and is this fragment it was written:

> Isaiah the prophet: And there shall come forth a
> shoot from the stump of Jesse—the branch of David
> and they will enter judgement and the Prince of the

Congregation will kill him with strokes and wounds (De Salvo, 2011:156).

Beliefs, Rituals, Ethos and Organizational Features of the First Community of believers in *Yeshua*.

This section focuses on the nature of the Community of *Yeshua* believers before 70 CE when they were scattered away from Jerusalem and Judea to Galilee and Pella, north and east of upper Galilee. The following section outlines theological reflections on the beliefs of these first Christians who were known as messianic believers in *Yeshua* while maintaining essential elements of Judaism.

Features of the Jerusalem Church.

The vital presence of the Essenes did not end with John the Baptist and the Messiah. Schmalz and Fischer have provided us with several names: the Judeo-Christian Church, the Church of the Circumcision, The Nazarene Synagogue of Mount Zion or the Nazarene Church. It had the following characteristics:

- A Qumran–like Essene commune.
- A strict discipline and hierarchy[27] (see Acts 2:42–45).
- Called Nazarenes of Mount Zion. Many of them were Essenes before they received *Yeshua* as Messiah.
- Following a Jewish liturgy that included worship on the Sabbath, having teachings and readings from the Scripture (including parts of the New Testament), the use of Davidic music and dancing, and the celebration of the Lord's Supper (see Acts 2:46–47).

---

[27] It was a "reverse hierarchy" meaning that those who serve or the least are on the top of the hierarchy.

- Celebration of Baptism (archeological findings reveal a Qumran like baptismal font near Mount Zion.
- Adhering to and living the Great Feasts of Israel.
- Practicing circumcision.
- Holding the Law of Moses in high esteem and following the *Torah*. They reflected the words of the Messiah: "Do not imagine that I have come to abolish the Law or the Prophets. I have come not to abolish but to complete them" (Matthew 5:17-19).
- Their belief system: belief in the resurrection of the dead, the divine creation of all things, the unity of God and that *Yeshua* is the Son of God.
- Also called the ***Ecclesia ex circumsione***:

Quoting a Messianic Rabbi, Schmalz and Fischer (Stern,1998:588) noted:

> The Nazarenes of Mount Zion, like their contemporary Messianic Jewish progeny, elected to keep their Jewish religious and cultural identities because they were and are convinced that this was what both the Old and New Testaments required of them. The Jewish Messiah did not come to save Jews from their Jewishness: He came to save them and all mankind from its sin (1999: v and http://www.biblesearchers.com/hebrewchurch/ synagogue/seal.shtml#Oteeoos).

Not indicated by these authors, I suggest that there is a strong likelihood that the Jerusalem Church had a covenant or that this community was a covenant community. I say this by way of inference. It is documented that the Essenes had a covenantal relationship not only with *Adonai* but with each other. Since a significant number of them were part of the first believers of the Messiah, *Yeshua* or Jesus, it stands to reason that they also had a covenant not only with Jesus but also with each other.

Schmalz and Fischer, referring to the Franciscan archeologist, Pixter (1999) claim that the first congregation of Jewish believers was in the upper room where Jesus celebrated his last supper, the gathering place where the disciples went after the Ascension, and where the Holy Spirit descended on the disciples on Pentecost Sunday. It was in the Essene Quarter of the city of Jerusalem (of which there was an Essene Gate (Raniey and Notley, 2006) and was constructed near to or on the tomb of David. From the Jerusalem Church, the Nazarenes would go to the Temple courts, other synagogues and to their private homes where the Eucharist was celebrated

Of special interest to these authors is the earliest symbol of the Jerusalem Church-the Messianic Seal of the Jerusalem Church that is relevant today as a significant symbol of unity. Figure 2: 1 depicts the image:

Figure 2:1: The Messianic Seal of the Jerusalem Church[28].

In the 1960's, a Greek Orthodox Monk by the name of Tech Oteeoos, told a German man by the name of Ludwig Schneider that he had excavated and found thirty to forty pieces bearing the

---

[28] Drawing by Janet Hatfield of the Alleluia Community. Used with permission.

three-part symbol. The monk gave Schneider eight artifacts of the Seal. Also, etched into a wall in an ancient *Mikveh* (cleansing font likely a baptismal font) was another rendition of the symbol1.

Schmalz and Fischer (1999) offer the following interpretation of the Seal. The Seal is a symbol of unity of Judaism, Messianic Judaism, and Gentile Christianity. As one can see, the symbol is composed of three parts. The top is a Menorah, in the middle, The Star of David and on the bottom, a fish. In some versions, there is a *tau* or *taw* symbol in the eye or in the center of the fish. These authors claimed that the heart of the symbol is unity. All three symbols are molded together—to symbolize the heart of unity through *Yeshua,* the Messiah.

The Menorah is a symbolic representation of *Adonai,* the God of Abraham, Isaac and Jacob. It was made of pure gold that reflects how precious, sacred, and incorruptible is God. The seven branches represented a mystical number implying divine perfection. It burned always to signify eternal light for God is light (I John 1:5) and he wraps Himself in light as a garment (Psalm 104:2). The sacred object also represents Jesus (The Light of the world [John 8:12]) and the church united under the Lordship of Jesus and radiating Light to the world (Matthew 5:14-16).

The Star of David is the symbol of Judaism, the State of Israel, King David, and Zionism. There are many sub-symbols: it represents the six attributes of God (power, wisdom, majesty, love, mercy and justice), the six days of creation, and the Messiah, Jesus. Several Scriptures give evidence to the importance of Jesus being the star: "A star shall come forth from Jacob and a scepter shall rise from Israel" (Numbers 24:17); "I am the root and the offspring of David, the bright morning star" (Revelation 22:16). In references to Messiah's birth, it was a star that guided the wise men from the East to Bethlehem (Matthew 2:2).

The fish is representative of individual believers, a community of believers, churches, groups of churches, the Universal Body of Christ, and of Jesus Himself. Schmalz and Fischer (1999) provided evidence that a Church Father, Clement of Alexandria (150-215 CE), encouraged his readers to include the sign of a fish around the year 150 CE. On at least one of the artifacts (depicted in Figure 2:1), the *taw* or *tau* is over the eye of the fish that symbolized the cross of Jesus.

Remarkably, the Seal is joined together in a seamless link. The Menorah's base is part of the Star of David and the bottom of the Star of David is the tail of the fish. This is a powerful symbol of unity between the believers of Jesus-both Messianic and Gentile. Unity emerged during the first and the second centuries.

According to Danielou (1964), the first three centuries of the Christian faith developed into three cultures, three visions and three expressions of faith: Jewish, Hellenistic and Latin. Since that era, the emphasis has been on Hellenistic and Roman theologies of the faith with the marginalization of the Jewish expression of the faith. This chapter's focus is on restoring the rich heritage left by the Jewish believers of *Yeshua* as Messiah.

DATA FROM EXTANT WRITINGS ON THE NATURE OF THE COMMUNITY OF BELIEVERS.

Danielou (1964) relies on data from the Jewish and Christian apocrypha from these sources emerge the richness of the life of the early Jewish believers. I present a sample of them that focus on various elements of the faith.

The Cardinal frequently refers to a definition of Late Judaism to indicate that it was the Judaism of the early first century CE that was contemporary with Jesus, the Pharisees, the Sadducees, the Essenes and the Zealots. It is in this setting that various writings were constructed. I will use Danielou's categorization and present the central elements of this first expression of the Christian message: the Sibylline Oracles, the apocalypse of Peter, the Didache, Odes of Solomon, Epistle of Barnabas, Shepherd of Hermas, and the Epistle of Clement.

The Sibylline Oracles

Composed likely in Antioch of Syria, the central teaching of this document is the divinity of *Yeshua*. It accents the powerful event of the Baptism of *Yeshua*, his descent into hell, and that the cross is a glorious event which broke the power of evil and set the saints of the Old Testament free with his descent.

The Apocalypse of Peter

Written in Ethiopia, this work amplifies the importance of the transfiguration, the centrality of the return of the Messiah, the punishment of the damned, the descent into hell and the ascension. The authors wrote of the communication of *Yeshua* to the disciples' deep mysteries of his message.

The Didache

This text is acclaimed as the most important extant document of Jewish Christianity that was designed to teach a Gentile believer the fundamentals of the faith. It is very similar to the Rule of Life of the Essenes that celebrates the ritual of Baptism, prayer three times a day, the prayer of *Maranatha* (Come) that is described by Danielou (1964: 29) as "The most precious relic of the primitive Aaronic liturgy of Jerusalem". It is stamped with Essenism in the same way all of early Christianity. Danielou wrote: "it is possible the most venerable surviving document of the Jewish Christian literature" (1964:30).

The Odes of Solomon.

This document was also likely to have been written in Syria. Its elements of the Jewish dimension of the Christian faith includes: the descent of *Yehsua* into hell, the symbol of the cross, baptism in living water (not from a font but a stream or a river), the coronation of the baptized, the feminine imagery of the Spirit of God, the virginal motherhood of Mary, a theology of paradise, and a liturgy that celebrates the nuptial nature of the wedding of Messiah to his bride, his church.

Epistle of Barnabas

This is the first of early documents that take on the tone of antisemitism that teaches that the Jews put *Yeshua* to death, and that the *Torah* is not important. Other elements of the document teach that *Yeshua* is the Beloved, that there will be a millennial, that all Jews should become believers in *Yeshua* as the Messiah, and that the first three chapters of Genesis became a paradigm on *Yeshua's* life and teaching.

Shepherd of Hermas

The uniqueness of this document is that the author was asked by the Bishop of Rome to write the text. Danielou believes that the author was likely a prophet mentioned in the Didache and that he wrote it in the city of Rome. It contains many of the earliest characteristics of Jewish Christianity: discernment of spirits, the two-way teaching, an elaborate angelology (to be discussed later), the descent of *Yeshua* into hell, and accenting the ethics of the Essenes.

The Epistle of Clement

Clement, the third pope after Peter and an early Bishop of Rome, (around 96 CE) had a theological setting that was Jewish Christian. He speaks of *Yeshua* as the "Name," and "the Beloved." Much of his writings relied on the *Targum* (ancient Jewish commentary on the Scripture) and honored many of the saints of Israel: Enoch (a model of obedience), Noah (a model of fidelity), Abraham (faith), Lot (hospitality), Rahab (also of hospitality), and a long list of those who were marked by great humility (Elisha, Elijah, Ezekiel, Abraham, Moses and David). He exalted Abraham, Isaac and Jacob as models of those who walk with God.

In summary, these writings give us a remarkable insight into the roots of the Christian faith. They present us with the image that *Yeshua* is the Beloved, the Father is a gardener, and that His church is His planting. They teach us that Isaiah was ascended and that *Yeshua* descended into hell. Further, the transcendence of God is accented and that there are holy mysteries of the faith still to be understood.

THE THEOLOGICAL ELEMENTS OF THE JEWISH EXPRESSION OF THE FAITH:

Danielou (1964) expands on the images of the Church of Jerusalem under the following headings: angelology, the Son of God, the *Torah*, the Cosmic Ladder, Demons, Heavenly Books, the Incarnation, the Redemption, the Mystery of the Cross, the Church, Baptism-Eucharist, and personal holiness.

Angelology

First century Jewish Christianity was redolent with the supernatural and the transcendent. Angel and demons abound who are in constant battle with the demons whose goal is destruction: first to Israel, second to the Church and third to all humanity. Their image is being immense transcendent, glorious and colossal. One image is that one was so tall he/she was as tall as the earth is from the heavens.

This section outlines the names of the various angels, their nature and their functions. All constitute a supernatural world of intermediaries between God and humans.

They have names (some of which appear in Scripture) such as Raphael, Michael, Uriel, Gabriel, Renel, Azael, Gabriel, and Israel (meaning the man who sees God). Two of them are accented Michael and Israel. Michael has many functions:

1. He governs the people of Israel.
2. He brings His people before the Face of God.
3. Believers, at his hand, are brought into the Holy Place.
4. He carries on combat against the kingdom of the enemy.

So also, is Israel. He is the angel who appeared to Jacob and gave him his new name, Israel (Genesis 32:27-30). Philo, the Jewish Alexandrian sage, mentions this and Origin, a Christian Patristic scholar, wrote of him: "I, Israel (the one who sees God, Genesis 32:31), the Archangel of the power of the Lord and the *archistrategos* among the sons of God" (Danielou, 1964:133). The angel is one who sees God.

Another angel, of importance is Gabriel who is described as an angel of the Holy Spirit and transcends other angels. He presented Enoch before the face of God and is known as the comforter and sits at the right hand of God. From the Gospel according to Luke, we read that he came to Zechariah to announce the birth of John the Baptist (Luke 1:18) and of the Messiah, *Yeshua*, his word to Miriam (Luke 1:26)

The functions of angels are many. They guarded the Temple (before its destruction in 70 CE) and acted as intercessors as well as giving the *Torah* and the Hebrew language to Israel. They stood before *Adonai*, giving endless praise (as the two seraphim of Isaiah 6) to Him and were behind every righteous act of God's people. They also had a role in nature and human civilization for they preside over the movements of the stars, watch over the rivers and the streams, protect harvests and protect human institutions, nations, cities. A special role, however, is to join Michael in protecting Israel. One remnant is the function of the guardian angels for all believers in *Yeshua* (Matthew 18:10).

Danielou concludes his discussion on angels with this: "It may justly be said that in the domain, Jewish Christianity left a heritage of major importance to later theology, liturgy, and spirituality" (1964:187).

Son of God.

The theology of the Mother of all Churches is richly focused on *Yeshua*, Messiah. He is called "The Name," "Most Holy," "Glorious," "Most Excellent," "Majesty," "the beginning," "first-born," "Day,"

"Image of the primordial Day," "Morning star," and the "Word." These names are linked to the Tabernacle in the desert, to the Ark of the Covenant in the Temple, to being a tower of the Church, the Creator of the cosmos who is above all every power and principality, and is the image of the Father.

Torah

Despite what *Yeshua* said: "Don't think that I have come to abolish the *Torah* or the prophets. I have come not to abolish but to compete. Yes, indeed! I tell you until heaven and earth pass away, not so much as a *yud* (like a comma) or a stroke will pass from the *Torah*—not until everything that must happen has happened" (Matthew 5:17-18). Many Gentile believers in Jesus have not obeyed him. They have thought that the "New Law" in the New Testament has replaced the old. We have been guilty of replacement theology which teaches that nothing in the first covenant matters anymore, and that the *Torah* has been replaced. Jewish Christianity teaches something quite differently.

They believe that, in the mind of *Adonai*, the *Torah* pre-existed creation and will continue until, as *Yeshua* has said, "When everything that must happen has happened." It is seen to be the "first incarnation" or "*Torah* is so to speak the visible sacrament of the presence of the divine word" (Danielou, 1964:163). The *Torah* was not only given to Israel but to the whole world through the Son of God, *Yeshua,* the Messiah.

Cosmic ladder

This is truly a fascinating teaching that is not present in Gentile Christianity. There are various versions of this ladder but this one seems to be a combination of all of them. Figure 2:2, called the "Cosmic ladder", depicts this:

Figure 2 : 2 The Cosmic Ladder

One: Resides the Glory of God.

Two: The Higher Angels- Seven Archangels, seven cherubim., seven seraphim and seven phoenixes

Three: the Heaven of the Watchers; Angels caring for creation.

Four: the sun and the moon and the angels that preside over them.

Five: **Paradise**: Souls of the Just awaiting resurrection. **Sheol**: the Souls of the impious awaiting punishment.

Six: The abode of demons who war against the Angels and the Messiah's fight during his passion

Seven: Hell: the Abode of Satan and the Demons

Several Patristic Fathers side with the imagery of the seven heavens. Irenaeus (130-202 CE) in describing the creation of the cosmos, wrote that the earth is encompassed by the seven heavens in which dwell Powers, Angels, and Archangels giving homage to God. He relates the seven heavens to the seven-branched candlestick (the menorah) so central to Judaism. Clement of Alexandria also acknowledges the image of the seven heavens.

The heavens are also linked to the mystery of the incarnation, the descent to hell, the ascension to heaven. *Yeshua* came from the first heaven and descended to earth through all the heavens. No angels or demons were aware of this descent. However, after the passion, death, and resurrection of *Yeshua*, he went back to the first heaven to sit at the right hand of the Father. During this passage, all the angels and the demons became aware. The Angels rejoiced while the demons fled in terror.

Demons

Demonology also plays an important part of Jewish Christianity. It was conjectured that the angels were all created before the cosmos as discussed in the chapter entitled The Prophetic Faith. After the creation of the cosmos, *Adonai* charged all the angels to take charge of it and care for it. However, under the power of Satan (also called the prince of the world, king of the world, prince of darkness *Beliar*, and god of the world), many reneged and rebelled at God's order. One version was that after *Adonai* created humans and He favored them; Satan became jealous and then fell from glory. He, however, hated God so much that he tried to destroy humans who are made in the divine image.

These Jewish believers in *Yeshua* also linked vices with demons and argued that behind every vice, every sin was a demon. Sometime, if given access, they entered into human bodies and attempted to plunder, do violence, stirred up disorderly attacks, perpetuated agitation and temped to do sin. The good news, however, is that their end is destruction in hell forever.

Heavenly Books

In heaven, it is written, that all of men and women's action are written in a "book" to be produced on the Day of Judgement. This book, also called "the book of destiny" or "the book of life," contains the whole of God's design in nature and in history. The deeds of the children of Israel are also written in it. From the prophet, Daniel, it is noted that at time of the end, Israel will be delivered, everyone whose name is found written in the book will be delivered (12:1). To his disciples, *Yeshua* promised that their names have been recorded in heaven (Luke 10:20). Paul also proclaims a similar promise to his co-workers in the faith whose names are in the "Book of Life." John, in the Book of Revelation speaks of those who have endured a great persecution will have their names written in the "Book of Life" (Revelation 3:5).

The Incarnation

Jewish believers in *Yeshua* are very much Christocentric. *Yeshua* as the Son of God has already been discussed. Danielou adds to this the mysteries of the incarnation, redemption, and the cross.

A Jewish Christian way to understand the incarnation is to accent the hidden descent from the highest heaven of *Yeshua* with his Father, down through all the heavens into the womb of Miriam. This descent was hidden from nearly all of humanity (Miriam being the exception), all the angels and the demons. He came "clothed in the wisdom of the Father" (Danielou, 1964:213). Three mysteries converge into one: the nativity, the visit of the Magi, and *Yeshua's* baptism. All are surrounded with intense glory and the heights of the supernatural. With the coming of the Messiah, every sorcery and spell is dissolved, ignorance of wickedness is vanished and the ancient kingdoms of evil are torn down.

Also, of special notice is the Baptism in the Jordan. It is here where the dragon (Satan) is crushed, Israel and the Gentiles are saved, and the waters, once the abode of evil, are sanctified. Light and fire are made visible that effect not only the Jordanian region of Judea but the whole of the cosmos.

The Redemption.

The passion, death and resurrection of Messiah were first a foremost a battle against all the powers of evil, demoniac forces, diabolical strongholds, death, and Satan (the dragon) himself. The setting of this battle is *Yeshua's* descent into hell where he engaged in a spiritual and victorious battle. The second purpose of this descent was to free those faithful saints of the first covenant, the people of Israel. Justin Martyr (100-165 CE), quoted by Danielou, wrote: "The Lord God remembered his dead, the saints of Israel that had fallen asleep" (1964:235). It was said that *Yeshua* spoke to Abraham, Isaac, and Jacob: "with my right hand I gave them the baptism of life, and the pardon and remission of all evil."

However, the redemption was not quite complete until the ascension. This was also a glorious event for an angel, higher than the sky, carried Messiah from earth into the highest of heavens beside his beloved Father. It is said that divine chariots of fire carried him through all the seven heavens to the Father where "He sits at the right hand of the Highest." The chariot was accompanied with thousands and thousands of angels. This is not esoteric language for comparable language is in Origin (184-253), Gregory of Nazianzus (329-396), St. Ambrose (340-397) and Gregory of Nyssa (335-395). Danielou calls this *hyper cosmic imagery.*

The Mystery of the Cross.

The cross is redolent with mystery and glory. It was thought that the cross came out of the grave with *Yeshua* and a great angel carried it. It is not to be thought of as "dead wood" but wood that is spiritual, mysterious, and living. The Messiah carries this cross in his descent into hell. Several names are given to it: a mast of a ship, a wheel, an axe and a rock. Other images speak of the depths of the mystery of the cross: a desired horn, life of the devout, scandal to the world, enlightening waters, and rod of iron. Indeed, the cross is a cosmic cross. Its beams symbolize the embrace of all creation. Its pole reaches down to the depths of hell (for defeat) to the highest of the heavens (for glory). It is the source of unity to all of humankind, all of nature, and all of the universe. Indeed, Jewish believers of *Yeshua* envision the cross as a cross of glory and victory and not one of death.

The church.

The counterpart to Messiah is his church. Two images of the church capture Danielou's attention: the Aged woman and the Bride of the Messiah.

Why aged? For she is ancient and the second great creation of *Adonai*, the nation, the people of Israel. One early document stated: "I created the world for the sake of Israel." She is a "great tower,"

founded on the divine word and water. This tower is not restricted
to the earth but is a cosmic tower that reaches to the first heaven. In
the mind of *Elohim*, she existed before the creation of the heavens
and the earth.

Of special note, she is also the Bride of the Messiah. The
prototype is the creation account of Genesis chapter two. Man was
created and joined to his wife, also created. The man is a symbol
of Messiah and the woman, the church. Just as Adam and Eve were
joined together and become one flesh, so also is the Messiah with
his bride, the church.

Baptism and Eucharist

Baptism was mandated by the Savior (Matthew 28:19). Its imagery
was profoundly influenced by the Essenes who used running water
for cleansing. The Jewish followers of *Yeshua* developed a ritual of
Baptism that was: (1), preparatory and, (2), the immersion in living
(running water).

The preparatory period was intensive. The Neophyte was taught
the Two Ways, the Golden Rule and the two great commandments.
They were to renounce any and all idols, Satan, and their own sin.
They were to submit to the *Torah* and make a covenant. They were
too fast and to make a complete break with their old way of life.

The rite involved the following:

1. Immersion in living water.
2. The proclamation of the Father, the Son and the Holy Spirit.
3. The anointing with oil.
4. Putting on a garment.
5. Being crowned.
6. Linked to the Feast of the Tabernacles.

The Eucharist was connected to a meal where milk and honey
was consumed. It was the bishop who blessed the bread and the wine.
The rite involved the following:

1. Thanksgiving prayers over the bread and the wine.
2. The doxology.
3. Prayer of gathering together.
4. The blessing of the "name" on each person.
5. A kiss of shalom given to one another.

Personal Holiness.

This was central and vital to the first congregations. The teaching of the two ways was a focus on the growth into holiness. Because there is a dual reality in the human person, a propensity to evil and a propensity to good, it is of great importance that the way of holiness was spelled out.

Behind every sin and vice is a demon. So, "Spiritual life is thus seen first as a fight against demons" (Danielou, 1964:361). Besides this battle, the battle against the seven principal vices needs to be fought: slander, stubbornness, vain confidence, anger, temper, double-mindedness and lack of sorrowfulness.

The seven vices are balanced with the seven virtues: simplicity, seeking the good, fidelity to the *Torah,* living the divine will, accenting wisdom, being open to cosmic mysteries, and awaiting the return of the Messiah.

This completes the presentation of the central beliefs of the Church of Jerusalem. This covered the organizational features of the new congregation, images of some of the Jewish Christian writers, and the theological elements of the Jewish believers in Messiah, *Yeshua.*

The Nazarenes or The Jewish Believers in *Yeshua* within Israel

Four sources capture the essence of Jewish followers of *Yeshua* after the destruction of the temple in Jerusalem and the dispersion both of these disciples and Jews after 70 CE (Danielou, 1964, Pritz, 1988, Sanders 1993 and Skarsaune, 2002). Danielou and Pritz agree that the first Jewish disciples of *Yeshua* were called Nazarenes not until after many were forced to leave because of the Roman invasion and the destruction of the Temple[29]. Indirectly so does Sanders. Danielou does not focus on them and, consequently, I will focus on Pritz and Sanders. Pritz offers us information of the kind of people the Nazarenes were while Sanders accented the conflict between the Jewish believers in *Yeshua* and the Jews.

Justin Martyr (100-165), Origin (185-254), Eusebius (264-380), Epiphanius (315-403), and Jerome (342-420) all knew of the Jewish believers in *Yeshua*. A combined image of them is as follows:

1. They believed that *Yeshua* was not only the Messiah but also the Son of God.
2. The Nazarenes followed the *Torah* and observed the Mosaic institutions.
3. There were two kinds:
   a. Orthodox believers who believed in *Yeshua* as divine and the Son of God.
   b. Ebionites who believed in the Messiah ship of *Yeshua* but not in his divinity and the who was born of a natural birth through Joseph and Miriam (thus heretical).
4. Submission to circumcision.
5. Honouring the Sabbath and all the Jewish feast days.
6. They used both the Old Testament (the *Tanakh*) and the New Testament writings. They also accepted the canonical scriptures from Judaism
7. The Gospel of the Hebrews was an important document to them.
8. The Gospel of Matthew was of central importance.
9. A belief in the resurrection of the dead.
10. All of creation has its origins in God.

---

[29] Schmaltz and Fischer (1999) used the title Nazarene applied to the Church of Jerusalem. The evidence, however, seems to side with the theory that the Jewish believers in *Yeshua* were not called the Nazarenes until after the exile and dispersion of 70 CE.

✧ DONALD SWENSON ✧

11. They prayed three times a day.
12. They were the true heirs of the Jewish believers in *Yeshua* from Jerusalem.
13. Had a positive view of St. Paul
14. Refused to demand that when the Gentiles became believers in *Yeshua* they need not be circumcised.
15. Practiced Baptism as entrance into the Community.
16. They used their Hebrew tradition to understand their new relationship with *Yeshua*. This was in contrast to the Gentile believers in *Yeshua* who used Greco-Roman world views and philosophies to interpret their belief.
17. They were universal in wanting the Good News to be taken to the whole world and longed for their fellow Jews to accept *Yeshua* as Messiah.

Other church fathers wrote impressions of them. Pritz estimates that the early Church Fathers were, generally, positive towards them and accepted them as another expression of the Christian faith. However, later patristic fathers, being immersed in anti-Semitic ideologies, rejected them and considered them to be heretical. For example, Epiphanius (315-403) and Augustine (354-480 CE) wrote critically about them. They saw them as heretical and from the time of Augustine, the Church rejected them as not being authentically Christian.

The focus of Sanders was on the relationship between the Nazarenes and the Jews of Galilee between the two revolts of the Jews and the Romans (70-135 CE). It was during this period that there were major changes such as the formation of Rabbinic Judaism (in contrast the Judaism of the priesthood and the Temple). It was also witness to the growth of *Tannaism* (the first midrash of an interpretation of the Jewish Bible) to form classical Judaism. It was also during this time that the New Testament was canonically constructed along with the dynamic presence of the Nazarenes in Galilee. Jewish believers in *Yeshua* attended synagogue and considered themselves good Jews.

During this same time, some Jewish believers of *Yeshua* experienced persecution at the hands of Jewish leaders. Sanders documented many of the characteristics of the Nazarenes that Pritz had presented: they followed the ritual of circumcision, honored the Sabbath, celebrated the Jewish feast days, had a heart to share their new faith with fellow Jews and they did not require that Gentile believers in *Yeshua* needed to become Jews following the edict of the First Council of Jerusalem in Acts 15.

However, it was during this period that Gentile Christians and the Jews slowly excluded the Nazarenes from the Jewish synagogues and Gentile Christian churches. The exclusion from the synagogue culminated in 135 CE with the revolt of *Bar Cochba*. Many Jews claimed that he was the messiah but the Nazarenes refused on the grounds that *Yeshua* was believed to be the Messiah. Consequently, the Nazarenes were excluded even more.

Evidence for this exclusion came from the extant Jewish literature. On the positive side, the Nazarenes and the Jews did have some social intercourse but increasingly this became conflictual. Midrash documents testify that the Nazarenes ate the flesh of meats from the Gentiles, were called idolaters, not acknowledging *Adonai*. These Jews spoke falsely of *Yeshua*, that the Nazarene books (some of the Gospels and Paul's writings) are to be destroyed and were even more hated than were the Gentiles. The Rabbis argued that *Yeshua* was cursed, hung on a tree, practiced magic and lead Israel astray.

Along with these stereotypes was a prayer of a curse called *birkat ha minim*[30]. This became part of the Jewish Synagogue ceremony. One document discovered in 1898 reads: "For the apostates may there not be hope if they do not return to Your laws. May the *nosrim* (could read Nazarenes) and *the minim* (heretics) perish in a moment" (Sanders, 1993:59). Sanders estimated that the invocation began to be read about 80 CE.

Skarsaune (2002) builds on the presence of the Nazarenes in the

---

[30] *Birkat haminim* is a Jewish curse on heretics. It included Jewish Christians before Christianity became markedly a Gentile religion.

Galilee in Capernaum and Nazareth. His evidence is the presence of a large room dating to the first century that may have been the "House of Peter"– a house that was frequented by *Yeshua* as recorded in Mark 1:29-34 and 2:1-12. Skarsaune wrote: "So perhaps this is the house used by the earliest Christian community of Capernaum as their place of meeting? No doubt this community was mainly Jewish" (2002:191). Franciscan archaeologists discovered graffiti on a building under the Churches of the Annunciation and St, Joseph that are of Jewish Christian origins.

Outside Christian sources reveal, in Rabbinic literature, the active presence of Jewish believers in *Yeshua* in the second century CE. Skarsaune commented more on the effects of the curse on these believers. Its usage in the synagogue services indicated that the Jewish believers were still in the habit of visiting the Jewish synagogue and that they were so numerous that the rabbis had to take them seriously.

According to Jerome (342-420) and Epiphanius (315-403), there is solid evidence that the Nazarenes still existed in the fourth century. They recognized *Yeshua* as the Son of God, believed in the virgin birth, recognized the apostolate of Paul and the Gentile mission, had the gospel in Hebrew, continued to keep *Torah* along with circumcision and the honoring of the Sabbath.

All in all, even though there was some social interaction between the Nazarenes and the Jews in Galilee, the former was eventually considered pariah and excluded from normal daily life and the celebrations in the synagogues.

THE DIASPORA: THE CHURCH OF THE JEWS AND THE GENTILES.

The distinguished mark of the Christian assemblies of the period of time between 70 and 150 CE is that they were mixtures both of Jewish believers in *Yeshua* and Gentile believers in Jesus. Using a modern word like ecumenism, these early congregations lived ecumenism. Skarsaune constructs images of this community using the prominent writers and documents of that time: *I Clement* (96 CE), the *Didache* 100 CE), Ignatius (110 CE), Barnabas (130 CE), *II Clement* (125 CE), Hermas (140-145), *the Letter of Polycarp* (156 CE), the *Martyrdom of Polycarp* (156 CE) and the *Letter to Diognetos* (170 CE). Ecclesial historians type these writings and authors as the Apostolic Fathers who focused on internal matters of their communities. Skarsaune describes I Clement, the Didache, Ignatius, and the Epistle of Barnabas.

I Clement   The author envisioned the church as a direct continuation of both biblical Israel as well as Israelite history. He honored the *Tanakh* for there are an abundance of quotes which appeared in the document. Pius men of the First Testament are considered to be the author's own ancestors and the prayers recorded resemble a striking parallel to Jewish prayers of antiquity. The document exhibits a high Christology that was inspired by the Letter to the Hebrews in the *B'rit Hadasha*. The whole of the document presents a friendly, positive, and grateful attitude towards biblical Israel and the Scriptures of Israel.

Didache   This is an entirely Jewish document as an in structural tool for would-be converts to the Way of Messiah, *Yeshua*. Much of the work is dedicated to church order with prescriptions for baptism, prayer, fasting and the Eucharistic celebration. All have a Jewish foundation that is explicit. Skarsaune combines his impression of I Clement and the Didache with this statement: "The deep familiarity with Jewish traditions we have met in I Clement, as well as in the Didache, is hardly conceivable unless we imagine Jewish believers as the theological tutors of the authors and/or communities behind these documents" (2002: 214).

Ignatius   Skarsaune begins his discussion of Ignatius by writing: "In Ignatius, the Jewish context of Christianity seems much more remote than in any Christian writing before him"

(2002:214). There is in Ignatius a distancing process away from the rich Jewish tradition. One statement by him is "It is monstrous to talk about Jesus Christ and to practice Judaism". For Ignatius, his link to the *Tanakh* was a literary one. It was a book, not a living past which through traditions, customs, and observances influenced his life. There grew from his theology Skarsaune calls his "a New Testament orthodoxy but not a Jewish orthodoxy". It maybe from Ignatius that two world-views emerged that increasingly divided Jewish belief in *Yeshua* and Gentile belief in Jesus. Yes, for both groups, the *Tanakh* was an authoritative book. However, for the Gentile believers the *Tanakh* remained a book, describing history that was past and finished. However, in contrast to Jewish believers in *Yeshua,* the *Tanakh* was made of innumerable cords of tradition, festivals, daily practices, religious concepts, and worldviews. It patterned their lives and intricacy connected them to an 1800-year history of *Adonai* revealing, guiding, listening to, ordering, directing and loving a people, Israel, whose destiny was to bless the nations. It does seem that there was sown at his hand seeds of replacement theology so prominent in what is known among the Apologetic Fathers (circa 150–200 CE).

The Epistle of Barnabas   The focus of this author (unknown) was how Christians should understand the *Tanakh*, especially the ritual commandments. He makes what seems to be a contradictory statement that the ritual commandments are valid for Christian but that they were never taken to be literal. Their value is spiritual and the Israelites were misled by an evil angel. Barnabas went further to argue that Moses withdrew the covenant. It is the Christian who can understand the *Torah.* Skarsaune comments: "This same covenant is now offered anew in Christ, and Christians are the ones who understand the true meaning of the Old Testament Law, while the Jews continue in their tragic misunderstanding" (2012:218). Indeed, the Jews were never the people of God and the Christians are the real people of God.

This author's theology of interpretation was the beginning of jettisoning the literal and historical meaning of the *Tanakh* and to spiritualize it. This is still common today in many Christian circles. Indeed, the Epistle of Barnabas, along with Ignatius, sets the groundwork of a replacement theology so common throughout Christian history.

Skarsaune sums his discussion with these words:

> There can be no doubt that the biblical scholars of the early church were almost without exception Jewish believers or God-fearers with a good "Jewish "education—people who from their childhood had known the sacred Scriptures and had learned the appropriate methods of interpretation in the synagogue. This they liberally passed on to the church at large, so that much of their exegetical work with the Old Testament later turned up in typically Gentile Christian writings (2002:222-223).

THANKSGIVING FOR GRACES RECEIVED.

Grace flowed abundantly to the new assembly that was created by the hands of *Adonai*, the Ecclesia composed of Jewish believers. This was the beginning of the fulfillment spoken of by Amos (9:11) and James (Acts 15: 16): "When that day comes, I will raise up the fallen hut of David". These men and women brought with them centuries of treasures and gems from the words of *Adonai* and through the voice of Miryam: "He has taken the part of His servant Israel, mindful of His mercy which He promised to our fathers, to Abraham and his seed forever" (Luke 1:54). Following are some excerpts from Jewish tradition:

> Blessed are you, O Eternal! Our God and the God of our fathers, the God of Abraham, the God of Isaac, the God of Jacob and the God of Messiah Jesus, the

God who is great, mighty and tremendous. The Most-
High God, who gives gracious favours, possessor of
all, who remembers the pious deeds of the patriarchs,
and of Our Messiah. Remember us unto life, Oh
King, who delights in life! Inscribe us in the book
of life for your own sake, O ever-living God! King,
Helper, Saviour and Shield. Blessed are you, Eternal!
The shield of Abraham. (Daily Prayer Book).

You remember what has been done from eternity.
Before you all secrets are revealed, as well as the
multitude of things concealed from the very
beginning. There is no darkness before the throne of
your glory, nor is anything hidden from your eyes.
Everything is revealed and known in your presence,
Oh Eternal, our God! You look and you behold
everything (Daily Prayer Book).

CONCLUSIONS

The glory and the demise of the Church of Jerusalem, the Nazarenes
and the church of the diaspora has been traced in this chapter. The
focus of the study has been on the origins and the identity of three
moments of Jewish believers in *Yeshua*: those of Jerusalem, of the
Galilee and of the diaspora. We have learned of the beauty of the
first disciples of *Yeshua* whose witness began a process of a change
in world history. Much time was spent on the theology of the new
expression of Judaism that was rooted in its past and in the newness
of incarnation, life, baptism, ministry, passion, death, resurrection
and an ascension of *Yeshua*, the Messiah and Son of God. This young
but dynamic movement evolved into an institution of great influence
but later met challenges from the Jews of the first century and, later,
from the Gentile believers of *Yeshua*. This latter challenge will be the
topic of the next chapter.

Again, it is vital to remember the beauty and richness of this Mother of all Churches, the Nazarenes and those of the diaspora. We have rejected much of this richness and need to repent. This repentance is a prelude to reconciliation between Jewish believers of *Yeshua* and Gentile believers of Jesus.

REFERENCES-CHAPTER TWO

Charlesworth, J. 1999. "John the Baptizer and Qumran Barriers in Light of the Rule of the Community." In *The Provo International Conference of the Dead Sea Scrolls*, p. 356. Edited by D. Parry and E. Ulrich. Leiden: Brill.

Daily Prayer Book. 2008. Tel-Aviv Israel: Sinai Publishing.

Danielou, J. 1958. *The Dead Sea scrolls and primitive Christianity*. Translated by S. Attarisio. Baltimore, Marland: Helican Press.

Danielou. J. 1964. *The theology of Jewish Christianity. Volume one of A history of early Christian doctrine before the Council of Nicea*. Translated by J. Baker. London: Darton, Logman and Todd.

Farnes, A. 2011. "John the Baptist and the Qumran Connection". Studia Antiqua: 9 (no1) Spring.

Janicki, T. 2017. Editor, translator and commentator. *The Way of Life: The rediscovered teachings of the Twelve Jewish Apostles to the Gentiles. Didache: A new translation and Messianic Jewish Community*. Vine of David: Marshfield, Missouri.

Josephus, F. 93/1737. *The works of Flavius Josephus*. Translated by W. Whiston. London, UK: William P. Nimmo.

Cahn, J. 2016. *The Book of Mysteries*. Lake Mary: Frontline: Charisma Media. The day of this mystery is 324.

Oteeoos, http://www.biblesearchers.com/hebrewchurch/synagogue/seal.shtml#Oteeoos

Meier, J. 2001. *A marginal Jew: Rethinking the historical Jesus*. Volume III. New York: Doubleday.

Pixner, B. 1990. "Church of the Apostles found on Mt Zion". *Biblical Archeology Review*. May/June.

Pritz, R. 1988. *Nazarene Jewish Christianity*. Leiden: Brill.

Raniney, A. and R. S. Notley. 2006:364. *The Sacred Bridge: Carta's Atlas of the Biblical World*. Carta: Jerusalem.

Sanders, J. 1993. *Schematics, sectarians, dissidents, and deviants.* Trinity Press: Valley Forge, Pennsylvania.

Schmaltz, R. E. and R. R. Fischer. 1999. *The Messianic Seal of the Jerusalem Church.* Tiberias, Israel: Olim Publications.

Skarsaune, O. 2002. *In the shadow of the Temple: Jewish influences on early Christianity.* IVP Academic. An imprint of Intervarsity Press: Downers Grove, Illinois.

Stern, D. 1988. *Messianic Jewish Manifesto.* Jerusalem: Jewish New Testament Publications, Inc.

Vermes, G. 1997/2000. *The Dead Sea Scrolls.* London: Folio.

CHAPTER THREE

THE FIRST WOUND OF DIVISION-THE SEPARATION OF GENTILE BELIEVERS IN JESUS FROM THE JEWISH BELIEVERS IN *YESHUA*: REMEMBERING, REPENTING AND RECONCILING

OVERVIEW

In this chapter, I focus on The Apostolic Era (time of *Yeshua* to the end of the first century) and The Late Classical Era (100 CE to 475 CE) that is the period of the height of the Roman Empire until its collapse in 475 CE. The accent will be on the first wound of division, the separation of the *Yeshua* believing Jews and Jesus believing Gentiles.

To better understand the roots of the division between Gentile believers in Jesus and Jewish believers in *Yeshua,* several concepts and theories from the sociology of religion will be used. Outlined in the Introduction, they consist of ideal types and secularization theory. These two will assist us to better interpret the causes of this first division.

After these types, concepts and theories are presented, topical headings consist of the Anti-Semitic cultures of ancient Egypt, Greece and Rome, secularization processes in the social construction of Christian antisemitism and the division between Jewish believers in *Yeshua* and Gentile believers in Jesus.

In the light of our subtheme, remembering, repenting and reconciling, it will be seen that it is vital to remember the age-long presence of antisemitism and the reasons for the first wound of division. Following this is to take responsibility for much of this and repenting collectively that will form a basis for reconciliation. Texts from the *Tanakh* will illustrate repenting.

Several ideal types are used in this presentation: the *stranger, Adversos Judaeos* and *Ecclesia et Synagoga.* The ideal type, stranger, will assist us in understanding antisemitism in the ancient cultures of Egypt, Greece and Rome. *Adversos Judaeos* informs us of the background to antisemitism in Early Christianity (from the Apostolic Era to the end of the Roman Empire) and Ecclesia *et Synagoga* is best applied to the relationship of the Christian Church to Judaism from the time of the Council of Nicaea to modern times.

The term *stranger* comes from the work of the sociologist, Georg Simmel (1858-1918), one of the founders of the discipline, himself of Jewish background, provides us with the meaning of stranger from which we arrive at strangeness. He argues that a stranger is a psychological-cultural-geographical matter. The stranger, to the host society, is a contradiction: he is within and without, an outsider and a counterpart, close and distant, attached and detached, inclusive and exclusive, and shared commonality and unique commonality. Simmel offered an example in European history about the Jews being strangers: "The history of the European Jews offers a classic example." He concludes his article by writing:

> Despite his peripheral status, the stranger remains an essential part of the community. Communal life envelops the position of the stranger, consisting as it does of a particular mix of closeness and distance also inherent to human relationships generally. Our relationship to the stranger is molded by this unresolved reciprocal tension between distance and closeness. (Simmel,1908/2016:176).

The term *Adversos Judaeos* refers to a series of homilies preached at various times and places in the Late-Classical Era. These texts, which go back to the second century, are directed against the Jews, Judaism and "Judaizing" Christians, i.e., members of the Christian communities who espoused Jewish beliefs or participated in elements of their religious practice. The contents, which were initially presented as polemics and later settled into convention formed a repertoire for anti-Jewish and later Anti-Semitic ideas (Rainer,2011-2017)

The ideal type, *Ecclesia et Synagoga,* refers to symbolic representations in Christian art of the Medieval Era (375 CE to 1500 CE) depicting the victorious Church and the defeated Synagogue, symbolizing the triumph of Christianity. The Church is shown erect and triumphant, bearing a cross. The Synagogue is usually blindfolded and dejected, carrying a broken staff and sometimes decorated with the Commandments symbolizing the Old Testament, or, Israel (Seiferth, 1964).

The Anti-Semitic culture of the ancient societies of Egypt, Greece and Rome.

Very prominent was the Anti-Semitic culture of the civilizations of the Egyptians, the Greeks and the Romans. This forms a baseline of a theory in the subsequent section of why antisemitism became part of the culture of Early Christianity at the hands of some Church Fathers.

Simmel's concept of the stranger assists us well in interpreting the relationship between the Jews and the peoples of ancient Egypt, Greece and Rome. Three scholars provide us with the content of antisemitism in the Ancient world: Sevenster (1975), Feldman (1993), and Schafer (1997). The Jew as stranger without, wherein antisemitism is abundant, is documented well from the works of Sevenster and Feldman while, at least during the Roman Empire, the Jew as insider and who bears an admirable or welcome presence, is illustrated through Schafer's analysis.

Sevenster (1975), constructs a theory of why antisemitism was so common in the ancient world of Egypt, Greece and Rome. He provides us with important facts and definitions to set the stage for his analysis of the roots of antisemitism in the ancient world. First of all, the term antisemitism was not used in the scholarly literature until 1880 CE. Semites were a group of people in the Middle East included those who were not Jews. Judaism is the word used to describe a way of life, thought and belief that focuses on religion while the term "Semite" is applied to a people group of a Semitic culture especially applied to Jews and Arabs. The verb to *judaizse* means to conform to certain Jewish customs. The title "Israelite" is tied to the Hebrew Bible when a new name Israel, to the son of Isaac, Jacob (Genesis 35:10). The land of the Jews, which now has a political entity, is also named Israel.

Sevenster counters two theories of why there was a culture of antisemitism: race and social status. Race was used to be linked to some physical characteristics, stock or kin. He argues that this was not the base of this prejudice but had more to do with differences in cultural values, customs and laws. A second theory, exhibited in much of Western history, was the economic position of the Jews. Is it accurate to say that antisemitism exists because Jews have been the envy of other peoples because of their high social status? Sevenster says no. He indicates there is no evidence that its source was rooted in jealousy for the economic success of the Jews. He actually says that they were despised for their poverty and not their wealth Two papyri documents from Egypt state that an official of a synagogue stole cloth while three different Jews raided a vineyard. This is evidence that if they were wealthy, why would they engage in thievery?

Yes, there were wealthy Jews in the Ancient World attested to by the Jewish historian, Josephus (also reinforced by Schafer). In Egypt, there were some who were tax collectors, inspectors, soldiers, policemen, physicians, lucrative farmers, traders and educated scholars such as Philo (20 BCE-40 CE). The majority, however, were hard-working, ordinary people who made their living in the same way the Gentiles exercised their livelihood. Sevenster concludes this section of his work with: "The most fundamental cause of antisemitism in the ancient world must be sought elsewhere" (1975:88).

His key thesis was: "The most fundamental reason for pagan antisemitism almost always proves to lie in the strangeness of the Jews amidst ancient society" (1975:89). There is much in Sevenster that corresponds to this ideal type provided by Simmel: their way of life and customs at once unique but common with the host society; own belief (especially monotheism and the Law or the *Torah)* living in a belief system foreign to them; living morally sexual lives in contrast to promiscuity and loose sexual mores; and being apart from the Gentiles but exercising good-will towards them (Philo) and genuine piety towards outsiders. The most fundamental element of the uniqueness (and strangeness) of the Jew, attested by Philo and Josephus, was the love for the *Torah.* Sevenster writes:" Essentially the conflict with the ancient world was always centered on the Law" (1975:108). The core contrast from the *Torah* was: (1) repudiation of any form of image worship; (2) to worship only One God, *Adonai*; (3) abstention from pork; (4) circumcision; and (5), Sabbath observance.

Frequently, the fact that the Jews obeyed these injunctions, the ire of many arose and accused them of irreverence to the gods and treason towards the state (for in Ancient Egypt and Rome, the head of the state was considered to be divine).

Schafer augments Sevenster's interpretation of strangeness (and, by deduction, the Jews as a stranger) in his discussion of monotheism. He wrote that to these ancient peoples "strangeness was the idea of a God who is not only unique but also aniconic[31]" (1997:35).

Many of the ancient writers documented their profound Anti-Semitic ideologies and practices. Pliny (23-79 CE) acknowledged Jewish contempt of the divine powers; Tacitus (55-120 CE) wrote that the Jews were the basest of all people and they regarded profane what Roman called sacred and regarded sacred what the Jews call profane; Juvenal (55-140 CE) argued that Shabbat rest was an indulgence of human laziness, that they were miserable people, beggars, fortune tellers and that they flaunted the laws of the Romans; Seneca (4 BCE-65CE) believed the Jews were a damned people, spread pollution, and that because of them, the innate character of the Roman society was in constant danger; Manetho (Egyptian historian of the 3rd century BCE) argued that the Jews did not worship the gods of Egypt and that they were "haters of men" and had "outlandish" laws; Diagoras of Melos (Greek poet and sophist of the 5th century BCE) jeered at any who believed in deity or deity which would have included Jews; Namatianus (5th century CE court poet) exaggerated that the root of all folly was of the Jews; and one of the worst of accusations was that every seven years, a Greek was abducted and sacrificed in the form of a ritual murder by the Jews (Apion 30-20 BCE – c. 45-48 CE), an Egyptian grammarian and sophist). Several other stereotypes were circulated. Jews were prone to lust, were sexually promiscuous, and had too many children. In Egypt, they were blamed for a leprous pestilence and that they were exiled for this reason. Sevenster summarizes the above: "In this seldom disowned

---

[31] The term refers to images of deities, symbols, and the like) not portrayed in a human or animal form.

strangeness, emanating from the way of life and thought prescribed by the *Torah,* lies the profound cause for the antisemitism of the ancient world" (1975:144).

This outline gives evidence for the Jew as being an outsider, outside the ancient societies, a counterpart, distant, detached and having a unique commonality. However, this is only one side of the meaning of a stranger. As depicted by Simmel's ideal type, the Jew as a stranger is an intricate part of the host society, he is within, close, and has a shared commonality with his neighbors.

Josephus reminds his readers that there is a long tradition within Judaism of welcoming the outsider. Some scriptural bases consist of: "You are not to oppress a foreigner, for you know how a foreigner feels, since you were foreigners in the land of Egypt" (Exodus 23:9); "You will not molest or oppress aliens, for yourselves were once aliens in Egypt" (Exodus 22:20); "If you come on your enemy's ox or donkey straying, you will take it back to him" (Exodus 23:4) and "You must not exploit a poor and needy wage-earner, be he one of your brothers or a foreigner resident in your community" (Deuteronomy 24:14). Philo counsels his fellow Jews to engage in fellowship and good will towards Gentiles and to offer prayers for them. Several Roman leaders honored and gave privileges to the Jews. They were allowed to observe their customs according to their ancestors and to practice their sacred rites. The Greek king in Syria, Antiochus III (224 BCE-187 BCE) exempted Jews from paying tax, gave monies to the Jews for their worship services, and offered payment to a damaged synagogue

A special organization in the Roman Empire was the *collegia licita* which was an institution where people of like mind, were involved in a common trade, or a kind of fellowship. The members had some level of self-government and were given permission to manage their own affairs. The Jewish synagogue, known in Alexandria and Sardinia, had this privilege. The Jews were allowed to collect their own taxes to support the Temple in Jerusalem and were allowed to minister their own justice. Relations with Rome and Judaism reached a high when Julius Caesar (100 BCE–44 BCE) called the Jews "our friends and allies."

In regard to Egypt, evidence of Anti–Semitic attitudes and discrimination of the Egyptians is documented in the Hebrew Bible. On the eve of the Exodus, it was written:

> Yes, the cry of the people of Israel has come to me, and I have seen how terribly the Egyptians oppress them (Exodus 3:9) and the Egyptians treated us badly; they oppressed us and imposed harsh slavery on us. So, we cried out to *Adonai*, the God of our ancestors. *Adonai* heard us and saw our misery, toil and oppression (Deuteronomy 26:6-7).

Schafer grounds some of the discussions of the relationship between the Jews and the Egyptian Gentiles with an analysis of two events of major conflict between the Egyptians in the military colony of Elephantine (about 400 BCE) and among the Hellenized Egyptians of 40 CE in Alexandria.

Elephantine was a military garrison which was home to a significant Jewish population in the southern part of Egypt and on an island in the Nile River. Jews had settled there long enough to have a temple built for them to adhere to their Jewish heritage. The Persians attacked the nation and conquered the Egyptians. It was thought that the Jews were allies with the Persians and in 400 BCE, the Egyptian priests destroyed the Temple. Further, the lamb was a sacred animal to the Egyptians and the Jews sacrificed lambs which was an affront to the Egyptians. In addition to this, the Jews continued to celebrate the Exodus that was a success story of the Jews but chagrin to the Egyptians. The locals were further aggravated when the Persians destroyed the Egyptian temples but not the Jewish Temple (which had been rebuilt). Schafer (1997: 135) argues that the "mother" of antisemitism was not from Alexandria but from the heart of Egypt.

Jews had lived in Alexandria for many years with relatively peaceful relationships to the Hellenized Egyptians. Things changed, however in 37 BCE when Caligula (12- 41 CE) became the Roman Emperor and demanded that his image was to be erected in the synagogues. A local elite, Flaccus, was appointed as the governor of the Roman Colony. He went with Philo (20 BCE-50 CE) in a delegation to Rome to discuss with Caligula the situation of the Jews in Alexandria. Philo documented that Anti-Semitic accusations flowed out of his mouth: "You Jews are god-haters, foolish, unfortunate, and non-eaters of pork (which was the most common meat among the Romans)". After the return of the delegation, mobs (made not only of Alexandrian but also naturally born Egyptians) perpetrated violence against the Jews. Synagogues were destroyed, the Jews were thought to be aliens and foreigners. The first pogrom was created when all the Jews were forced to live in one section of the city. Schafer (1997:140) writes: "It was the first known ghetto of the world." Not only that, homes, shops and businesses were pillaged. Worse than that, if they left the ghetto, they were stoned, beaten, slain and burnt. Degradation went further when the mobs dragged the bodies of the slain and mutilated them in the streets of the city. All this was under the eye of the governor, Flaccus who did not offer protection from Rome.

Before a discussion on the specific phenomena of antisemitism are presented, it is well to know, from the pen of Schafer, what some of these ancient writers' thought was the origin of the people of Israel. Tacitus, who has given the most detailed account of the history and religion of the Jewish people, believed that the Jews were expelled from Egypt because they caused a plague and King Boccharis was told by an oracle that the land of Egypt must be purged of the Jews who were led by their leader, Moses. These people were opposed to all people, were lustful, base, abominable, depraved and the men were forbidden to have sex with foreign women. Schafer acknowledged that because Tacitus was such an influential writer of his time that "through him it (these stereotypes) became common property of the Western civilization" (1997:33).

Both Feldman and Schafer have organized the evidence of

antisemitism under the following headings: misanthropy, monotheism, dietary laws, the Sabbath, circumcision and proselytism.

Misanthropy and Human Sacrifice.

Schafer (1997) noted that the Jews were accused as hating all of humankind. So very powerful were the negative stereotypes that these ancient writers believed that the people of Israel committed moral infractions of brutality, contentiousness, and were prone to flattery. However, the most horrific stereotype was the accusation of human sacrifice based on the mythology that Seth killed Osiris. One origin of the myth was given by Apion (30-20 BCE −45-48 CE), and documented by Josephus. During the occupation of Jerusalem by the Greeks, the Syrian King, Antiochus IV, (215 BCE - 164 BCE), was a Seleucid king of the Hellenistic Syrian kingdom said to have entered the sanctuary of the Temple. There he saw a statue of a pig, a head of an ass, and a Greek young man being "fattened up" to be sacrificed. It was said that this was an annual Jewish ritual and which Josephus regarded as a malicious slander against his people. To this, Schafer wrote:

> The Jews are a secret confederacy which conspires against foreigners and whose worship consists of a ritual (the supposed human sacrifice) that enforces this conspiracy (1997:64).

This horrendous accusation could have been a recall of the ritual sacrifice of Osiris by Seth and a false prelude to the medieval ritual myth of the sacrifice of a Christian boy.

Monotheism

To these ancients, the concept that there was only one god and that he could not be seen was considered irrational. The Jews were aniconic in that no images of God were possible as he was above all images. Livy (59 BCE-17 CE) noted that in the Temple of Jerusalem, there were no images (recalling the first commandment Exodus, 20:3-6). However, this belief was very costly for the Jews. Some of the authorities of these ancient worlds accused them of being atheists and against the State (because the state was dedicated to a variety of gods and goddesses).

These negative images or stereotypes were only the beginning of the Anti-Semitic attitudes. The God of Israel was relegated to being a god of the Egyptians rooted in their mythology. Schafer argued that two of the major deities of ancient Egypt were the god of fertility or life named Osiris and the god of destruction, Seth (known also as Typhon), who represented the power of death, evil, chaos, and disorder. In the Egyptian story, Seth kills and dismembers Osiris. Further, this god was thought to be the god of the foreigners, the Hyksos, who were expelled from Egypt. Seth was connected to the God of the Jews, a foreign god whose intent was destruction and not life.

Along with these stereotypes of the God of Israel, there emerged a strange belief that the Jews worshipped an ass. Tacitus explains. On the journey away from Egypt, Moses and the people suffered from a lack of water. Moses, it was said, followed a herd of ass which led him and the people to water. Subsequently, the Jews worshipped the ass who had delivered them from thirst and possible death. It is also interesting to know that Seth was depicted as an ass in Egyptian mythology.

Schafer wrote it well: "It must be regarded as another piece of evidence of Anti-Jewish sentiment rooted in early Egypt which was adopted by the Greeks writers and became efficacious in the course of history (1997:58). Could Marcion[32] have adopted his image of the God of the Hebrew people as being malicious, vengeful and autocratic come from these images?

---

[32] Born in 85 CE and died in 160, Marcion was an important figure in early Christianity who rejected the Deity in the Hebrew Scriptures and in distinction affirmed the Father of Christ as the true God.

Dietary Laws

Another source of contention between the peoples of these civilizations and the Jews concerned with dietary laws that focused on prohibitions against the eating of pork. Why would these ancients take such offense? One reason, documented by Epictetus (50 CE to 130 CE), was that pork is holy and needs to be eaten for it belongs to the proper worship of the gods. For the Jews not to eat pork was believed to be apostasy, an affront to and a hatred of the gods. The religious connection in Greece to eating pork is that pigs were sacrificed to the gods and to eat of the food was to partake of the being of the gods.

Feldman adds further insights to the reason why the Jews did not eat pork beyond the prohibitions recorded in Leviticus 11:2 and Deuteronomy 14:3). The pig is covered on the underside by scaly eruptions and lives off dirt and abides in unclean places. The practice of the Jews of not eating pork becomes a critical mark of them in antiquity. Porphyry (234 – 305 CE), a Neoplatonic philosopher who was born in Tyre, in the Roman Empire, wrote: "Once more the absence from pork is singled out as the most characteristic and the most important of the Jewish customs" (quoted in Schafer, 1997:76). It was so important a law that many Jews gave up their lives rather than to eat of pork (See II Maccabees 7:1-42).

The Sabbath

Feldman wrote of the first pagan scholar to mention the custom of honouring the Sabbath was Agatha chides of Cnidus (208 BCE-?) in Asia Minor who was an historian during the second century, BCE. Agatharchides listed the Jewish customs of abstaining from work on the seventh day, prohibiting bearing arms, not engaging in agriculture and not doing any public service. It was during this day that the Jews prayed with outstretched arms. However, as recorded by Josephus, he saw the Jews also as being superstitious, engaged in folly, and foolish not to take up arms when attacked.

The most common accusations against the Jews regarding them keeping the Sabbath was that the people were targeted as lazy and indolent[33]. According to Plutarch (45 CE-127 CE), the Jewish keeping of the Sabbath was a "barbarous custom". This writer associates keeping the Sabbath with the Jews being smeared with mud, casting oneself face down in filth and participating in an abhorrent superstition.

Feldman adds to the pagan interpretation of the Jewish Sabbath from several authors. A number of stereotypes consisted of: the Sabbath being cold, flat, lifeless and insipid; the participants being fanatics; bizarre and a day of commemoration for when the people were expelled from Egypt, developed tumors in the groin and rested to relieve the pain.

Although there is evidence that some of these ancient writers spoke well of the Jew who kept the Sabbath, there is overwhelming evidence that this custom was abhorred by these scholars. Their image of the Jew as being a stranger is reinforced by their stereotypes of the Jewish Sabbath.

Circumcision

Feldman posits that the most outstanding mark of being a Jew in this ancient world was being circumcised. Several pagan scholars attest to that: Horace (65 BCE-8 BCE), Persius (34 CE-62 CE), Petronius (27 CE-66 CE) and Sallustius (86 BCE-35 BCE). The language against the Jew was he was circumcised. Both the Greeks and the Romans exalted the male body to such a degree that any form of mutilation was anathema. Circumcision was considered to be a mutilation.

Several negative stereotypes became associated with the practice such as it was shameful, disgraceful, ugly, crude, barbarous and foreign to the culture of the Greco-Roman world. Schafer's research

---

[33] The Egyptians accused the Hebrews of being lazy and the Pharaoh demanded that they gather straw for the building of bricks (see Exodus 5:8 and 17). Pharaoh said: "Lazy! You're just lazy! That why you say, 'Let us go to sacrifice to *Adonai* (verse 17).

adds other stereotypes that the Jewish men were more prone to lust than other men, guilty of misanthropy, and more sexually potent than other men. All together, these images symbolized Jewish degeneracy.

Proselytism.

Several Latin scholars including Tacitus, Jevenal, Seneca and Rutilus were terribly annoyed over the large numbers of Romans who became Jewish and argued that proselytism was a menace to the unity of the state. Feldman argued that much of the hatred of the Jews in Egypt was that the Jews were accepting many proselytes and that if this number began to increase, they wound dominate the world. Why, Feldman asks: the religion has a claim to antiquity, having leading intellectuals along with high levels of education, a pure monotheism, a high regard for the Law code of Judaism, a love for books and military prowess and the fact when women became Jews, they had a much higher status than they did as Egyptians, Greeks or Romans.

According to Schafer, there appears to be a pattern: Anti-Semitic attitudes began a series of discriminatory practices and laws against the Jews. Horace accused the people of compelling Romans to convert to Judaism. Seneca called them an "accursed people". These prejudices gradually developed into three forms of discrimination: (1), laws against proselytism, (2), expulsions, and (3), taxation.

Septinius Severus (193-211 CE) forbade the conversion of Romans to Judaism. If a Roman was known to have converted, he was to be banished to an island, have his property confiscated and scourged. To convert was considered to be a crime—the crime of atheism (not believing in the deities of Rome). The prohibition was declared to be enforced by Constantine in 328 and Christian emperors from his time at least up to the time of Theodorius II (408-450 CE).

Two significant expulsions occurred in the Late Classical Era: Jews were expelled from Rome in 139 BCE and 19 CE. The primary reason given was that the Jews shared their faith with the Romans and by doing so were undermining Roman society, rules, and culture.

The third consequence of antisemitism was the imposition of

extra taxes to Jewish believers. This happened after the first revolt that was led by Domitian, emperor from 81-96 CE and Vespian (9-79 CE). The tax, termed *Fiscus Judaicus,* was imposed on all Jews including women, children and slaves. Previous to this, Roman law allowed a tax to be given to the Temple in Jerusalem. Now, the revenue from the tax was to support the temple to Jupiter in Rome. The effects of this on Gentile believers in *Yeshua* and Jewish believers in *Yeshua* will be discussed later in the document.

In summary, many of the stereotypes, prejudices and discriminatory actions against the Jews were socially constructed in the Ancient world and became a paradigm throughout Western history up until the time of the holocaust. Examples are: the Jews are the basest of all people; miserable and beggars; damned; tend to flaunt social laws, spread pollution and caused a plague in Egypt; hateful of others; involved in ritual murder and prone to lust.

In addition to these attitudes, the Jews were subject to cruelty. The first ghetto and pogrom were constructed in Alexandria around 50 CE. As indicated above, homes and businesses were destroyed. Many were beaten, stoned and killed. They were forced to live in ghettos with the loss of any trace of citizenship.

History after the genesis of Christianity documents well that that so many of these stereotypes, prejudices and discriminatory laws and actions of the Ancient world of Egypt, Greece and Rome were repeated over and over again throughout the West from the first centuries of the Christian tradition through to modern times.

SECULARIZATION PROCESSES IN THE SOCIAL CONSTRUCTION OF CHRISTIAN ANTISEMITISM

An adaptation process or secularization of the Gentile believers to Hellenism commences early. Many of the Patristic Fathers assimilated to their surrounding Greco-Roman culture. Part of this assimilation was their receptivity to the inherent antisemitism within that culture. A plausible vehicle of this assimilation were the schools established in Rome and Greece. There is evidence that these Patristic Fathers were educated in these schools and would have learned Latin, and Greek—enabling them to think like an educated Roman or Greek[34].

A theme is that many of these theologians socially constructed a cultural motif called *Adversos Judaeos*, or *Against the Jews* that formed the basis of "Replacement Theology" or "Supersessionism." These special terms will be presented followed by a selection of Church Fathers illustrative of *Adversos Judaeos*, replacement theology, and supersessionism.

Special Terms

Supersessionism.   An etymological meaning of the term connotes something coming later supersedes something that went before. An example from the book of Genesis illustrates the process. Isaac had twin sons by his wife, Rebekah. Esau was the first born while Jacob the second. As adults, Esau sold his birth right to his brother Jacob. He usurped the right and he superseded Esau (see Genesis 25:29-34).

Krewson (2017:2-3) provides us with a definition as applied to Judaism and Christianity:

> Christian supersessionism is the belief that the Jewish people and religion have been entirely replaced by the Christian people and religion, and that divine favor rests only with those (both Jew and Gentile) who follow Jesus as God's Messiah. Jews therefore can find religious legitimacy only as members of the Christian church.

This has several elements:

---

[34] Basil the Great, 1949. (329-379 CE). He was educated in Caesaria, Constantinople and Athens, addressed young men and taught them that they need to read the Greco-Roman authors in their growth in virtue. He recommended reading Hesoid, Homer, Plutarch, Cicero, Xenophon, Plato, Euripides, and Aristotle.

- It looks at the Old Testament as foundational and temporary, divinely intended for replacement by the New Testament message.
- God has judged the Jewish people because of their rejection of Jesus as Messiah. The Gentile believers now enjoy God's favor but the Jews, his disfavor. This is the heart of the literary genre, *Adversos Judaeos*.
- The third element, is the elimination of the Jews completely in the emergence of the Church. The historical plot line is creation, fall from sin, redemption in Jesus and the consummation of all things at the end of times—bypassing the Jewish history and heritage.
- To this is added from Finto (2016:104): "Supersessionism essentially nullifies the promises of God to the previous group."

Replacement Theology   Some scholars consider replacement theology to be a synonym to supersessionism. In contrast, McDonald (1993) nuances the term with the following elements: God has ceased to be the God of the Jews who have forsaken Him but now the God of the Christians; since the Jews have failed to recognize Jesus as Messiah they shall now recognize their own demise; they are condemned and rejected by God; God has rejected their ritual practices; they are obdurate and blind; Scripture does not belong to them but to the Christians and it is they who have the gift of understanding the text and not the Jews; and the Christian Church has inherited Israel's promises.

According to Fichtenbauer (2019), this theology brought two very tragic consequences. The first was the persecution of the Jews in general and the demise of the Messianic Jewish presence in the Church. He writes:

This was catastrophic, not only for the Jewish church, but also for the Gentiles. The Gentile Church became disorientated and incomplete. This was the churches first division. Numerous others followed. It worked like a virus and contaminated the church. It was perpetuated according to the model of replacement theology. Even though it may not be apparent at first. This replacement strategy is fundamental characteristic of every division (2019:42–43).

Adversos Judaeos. The term *Adversos Judaeos* refers to a series of homilies preached at various times and places in the Late-Classical Era. These texts, which go back to the second century, are directed against the Jews, Judaism and "Judaizing" Christians, i.e., members of the Christian communities who espoused Jewish beliefs or participated in elements of their religious practice. The contents, which were initially presented as polemics and later settled into convention formed a repertoire for anti-Jewish and later Anti-Semitic ideas (Rainer, 2011-2017).

This theology, in the mind of Jerome (347 –420 CE), goes beyond theology to the typology of the land of Israel. All the major sites in the history of Israel, especially Jerusalem, Bethlehem, Judea and Galilee, are replaced with Christian meaning. The original Hebraic meaning of the Exodus, the giving of the *Torah* at Mount Horeb, the journey in the desert, the crossing of the Jordon, the establishment of the Davidic kingship, the settlement of Jerusalem, the many battles, the sacrifices in the temple, and the Jewish feast days were deliberately stripped of their historical and Jewish meanings and replaced by Christian themes. The literal meanings became allegorical meanings. In a word, the sacred land of Israel becomes the holy land of the Christians.

Selective teachings of the Patristic Christians[35]

The literature of Patristics and their interpretations of the Jews and Judaism is vast. I will present only a few of them. It should be

[35] Montgomery and O'Dell (2019:54-55) add several earlier Christian patristic fathers and writings: The earliest *Books of Testimonies*, The *dialogue of Jason and*

understood, however, is that this literature is common to all the major fathers of the Gentile Christians. All adhere to supersessionism, replacement theology and the *Adversos Judaeos* teachings.

These teachings grew only gradually. The first target was not the Jews themselves but the *Yeshua* believing Jews and the Jesus believing Gentiles who were attracted to Judaism. Even though the Jewish Christians were orthodox in their theology they were judged as heretics because they honored the Sabbath, practiced circumcision, held the *Torah* in high honor, celebrated the Jewish feasts, kept the Resurrection feast during the week of the Passover, and were open to the *Midrash* literature of classic Judaism[36]. This is the heart of the ancient wound of division.

The Letter to Barnabas was written by an unknown author around 100 CE. It taught that the Jews lost their birthright and they were excluded from the people of God and the Church (Fichtenbauer, 2019).

Ignatius of Antioch (35-107 CE) was one the earliest leaders of the Church who accused the Jewish Christians (called the Nazarenes at that time) of heresy and judged them because they kept the Sabbath and not the "Lord's Day" (Sunday). He claimed it was the Catholic Christians (the first to use the term Catholic) who live according to Jesus and not according to Judaism (Guston, 1986).

Ireneaeus of Lyon (135-202 CE) strongly believed that Christians should avoid any kind on social contact with the Jews in order not to be confused in their faith. He argued that the Church should be cleansed from all Jewish elements (Fichtenbauer, 2019).

Marcion (85-160 CE), although not a Patristic writer, was radical in his understanding of Judaism and left a deadly mark in first and second century Christianity. He considered the god of the Old Testament to rule through the law and did not love humanity. Another god, the God of the Christians, was loving and forgiving.

Papiscus, The Dialogue of Timothy and Aquila, Celus, Aphrahat, Pseudo-Ephraim, and Dionysius Bar Salibi.

[36] Biblical exegesis by ancient Judaic authorities using a mode of interpretation prominent in the *Talmud* (Midrash).

Further, he outright rejected the Old Testament as being canonical. Both of his teachings were rejected by the Gentile Church but still he left his mark in the Anti-Jewish thought of the church (Wilson, 1986a).

Justin Martyr (100-165 CE) was famous for his dialogue with Trypo-a "strawman" Jew who Justin Martyr challenged. In this document, he taught the mutual exclusivity of Judaism and Christianity and denied the theological validity of Judaism apart from Jesus. He is the first to outline a replacement theology: *Torah* is replaced by the new law of Christ, Moses is replaced by Jesus, Israel is the old people of God, and the Christian Church was the new people. The Jews are being punished for their rejection of Jesus as Messiah. They lost the share in the *Torah* and the promises given to them (Remus,1986).

Arguments against the Jews and the Jewish Christians were at the polemical level until the coming of Melito (died in 180 CE) when they became morbid. He was of Jewish background but steeped in Greek philosophy and was an advocate of supersessionism. Wilson (1986b) noted that his most famous work was *Peri Pascha* of which most was directed to his interpretation of Israel. In his interpretation of the Old Testament, all things Jewish were expunged that has a literal meaning and only what was symbolic and allegorical was maintained. In classic terminology of replacement theology, "the once chosen people have been superseded by the church and the law by the gospel" (Wilson, 1986b:89). What distinguishes Melito from earlier supersessionists is that he accused all Jews of killing Jesus and were judged guilty of *deicide*. It is from him that later anti-Judaism rhetoric uses the phrase *Christ-killers*. Melito defended the Romans and blamed the Jews which cast a dark shadow on subsequent Christian vilification of the Jews.

Tertullian (150-225 CE)[37] adds another dimension to replacement theology by introducing the literary genre *Advesos Judaeos*. Because

---

[37] See Chapter Four for an extended analysis of this Church Father

his writings were so influential in early Christianity, a whole chapter (Chapter Four) is devoted to him.

Hippolytus (1986) and lived 170-235 CE continues in the construction of negative stereotypes against the Jewish people. He accuses them of condemning Jesus to death; that Jesus' forgiveness on the cross was not directed to the Jews but to the Gentiles. Speaking to a person who was a representative of all Jewish people, he judged them: you have darkened the eyes of your soul, you wander in darkness, indulge in vain hopes, beat the Messiah, and experience divine hatred. Hippolytus concludes his diatribe by calling down curses on them so they be blotted out of the book of life.

Ambrose (1993) lived 337-397 CE adds further to the *Adversos Judaeos* genre. A Jewish synagogue in Asia Minor had been burned down n by the local Christians. The Emperor, Theodosius I. (347-395 CE) ordered the Christians to rebuild the place of Jewish worship. Ambrose objected and said that Christians should not be punished for burning a Jewish synagogue. The synagogue, according to the Saint, is a home of unbelief, a house of impiety, a receptacle of folly which God himself has condemned. He wrote, speaking to one Jew: "the instances of his unbelief ought to be done away with together with the unbeliever himself." He was convinced that the more suffering imposed on the Jews, the humbler and open they would be to the Gospel of Jesus.

Ambrose is classic in his replacement theology. He wrote (1983:444): "For the Church shut out the Synagogue". He called the Jews liars, Arians who denied the divinity of Christ and who killed Jesus.

Of all of these fathers of the Christian faith, it was Chrysostom (347-407 CE) who spoke so violently against the Jews and the *Yeshua* believing Jews. While he was the bishop of Antioch, he preached a series of homilies in the genre of *Adversos Judaeos*. His language is vitriolic: the synagogue is like a theatre and a whorehouse, a den of thieves, and a haunt of wild animals. The inhabitants live by the rule of debauchery. These sermons resulted in Christian violence against the Jews: assaults on synagogues, the exclusion of Jews from public offices and expulsions. An early example of the complete annihilation of Judaism occurred in Alexandria in 414 CE (Carroll, 2001).

St. Augustine (354-430 CE) continued the *Adversos Judaeos* tradition. He wrote:

> If they had not sinned against Him with impious curiosity, which seduced them like magic arts, and drew them to strange gods and idols, and at last led them to kill Christ, their kingdom would have remained to them and would have been, if not more spacious, yet more happy than that of Rome (413-426/1952).

Carrol (2001:215) quoted him as writing: "and the Jews are the House of Israel which God has cast off. They themselves are the builders of destruction and rejecters of the cornerstone." But there is another side to Augustine. The Jews have a role in the salvific plan of God. Their prophecies about the coming of Jesus the Messiah are true and Israel continues to be a witness of the Christ. They are allowed to survive but not to thrive.

The last Patristic scholar to be presented is St. Jerome (347-420). Krewson calls Jerome's version of supersessionism "innovative supersessionism." The rationale for him using this term will be discussed in the next section. Here I will expand the saint's continued accent on the *Adversos Judaeos* genre. He adheres to the theology that the Christians have superseded the Jews who are rejected and that their religion is obsolete and even pernicious. He is especially against the Jesus believing Jews and rejected Jesus believing Judaism teaching about the millennium. We have already seen above in the discussion of the term replacement theology of how Jerome engaged in typological transfer of the sacred sites of Israel to the holy sites of Christianity.

In some of the letters of Jerome that Krewson had access to reveal a substantive replacement theology in the *Adversos Judaeos* tradition. The Jews are forsaken by God and the ceremonies in the synagogues are without life. Jerome rejected any Jewish customs such as circumcision, keeping the Sabbath, and following dietary laws.

Further, he exaggerated the threat of Jews against Christians and claimed that they tampered with the Scriptures. Krewson (217:84) quoted Jerome as writing: "the whole cult of Jewish observances was destroyed, and they offer all manner of sacrifice not to God but to fleeting angels and unclean spirits."

Archdeacon Fichtenbauer, comments on these Patristic Fathers:

> All of these theologians had great revelations concerning the Kingdom. But, concerning the role of the Jews in God's plan for Salvation, they were more or less blind. The devil fomented it, knowing that as long as Christians do not fail to understand the 'mystery of Israel', he would remain dominant in the world. The same blindness is found among Christians today. Very often individuals who are very dedicated to God also have a blind spot when it comes to the Jewish issue (2019:38).

From Adversos Judaeo to Antisemitic Politics

Fichtenbauer (2019:38-39) refers to secular authorities, synods and councils which not only adhered to the *Adversos Judaeos* theme but added laws and policies affecting the Jews in a negative way. Following is some:

Synod of Elvira, Spain: Conducted in 306 CE, it banned social discourse between Jews and Christians. Marriages between Christians and Jews were outlawed.

Emperor Constantine[38]: He forced all the Gentile bishops at the Council of Nicea (325 CE) to cleanse the Church from all things

---

[38] A great historical irony is that he was not even a Christian during his reign. The author of a well-known book, *The Age of Constantine the Great*, makes a cogent argument that he lived a pagan life up to his last days when he was baptized (Burckhardt, 2007).

Jewish. He ordered the Sunday and not the Shabbat as the holy day of the week. He further changed the dates of Easter to not to coincide with the Hebrew Feast of Passover.

The Synod of Laodicea (365 CE): If any Christian kept the Shabbat in their homes, they were to be excommunicated and even face death.

Council of Chalcedon (451 CE): Jews who became Christians had to renounce everything Jewish in their lives. Church authorities were allowed to take children from Jewish families and have them raised as Christians in monasteries.

Emperor Theodosius II (438 CE): He legalized the transformation of synagogues into Christian churches.

Council of Nicea II (787 CE): Those Jews who became Christians, if they kept the Shabbat, circumcised their boys, or encouraged the children to live the *Torah*, they suffered terrible persecution.

To summarize this section, I offer an extended quote from the Franciscan archeologist, Mancini. He indicated not only a division between *Yeshua* believing Jews and Jesus believing Gentiles but also a dissolution of the former not to be revived until modern times.

> Judeo-Christians began to decline when a new mentality and a new culture penetrated the Church. In other words, they started to disappear when what is called the "Great Church" began to make itself felt in Palestine. Their extinction was in sight when the new movement gained undisputed dominance. Its intolerance and its passion for unifying everything are the basic reasons for the decline. It meant, first, the reason for cutting off Judeo-Christianity from the vital trunk of Christianity and, in the end, its total disappearance (1970:173-174).

Indeed, it is the loss to the Gentile Church for now not sharing "in the rich sap of the olive tree" (Romans 11:17). Also, many of the promises given to Abraham have been lost to the Gentile Church. She did not bless the descendants of Abraham (in fact cursed them) and thus did not enjoy the abundant blessing promised from the mouth of *Adonai* (Genesis 12:3). As part of the Gentile Church not being blessed, I would contend that some of the effects of this cursing are: disunity among Christians and the Gentile Church continuing to be independent of the Church of the Circumcision. Could this have been a distal cause of the independent ecclesial movements in the Post-Reformation era; the evaporation of the charismatic dimension of the church (see Swenson, 1972[39]) and the radical dishonoring of women by some of the Church Fathers (see Swenson, 2009[40]?

---

[39] Swenson D. (1972). He documented evidence of the wide use of the charismatic gifts, especially prophecy from the Apostolic era until around 250 AD. His evidence included the writings of the Church of the Circumcision or the Nazarenes such as the *Didache, The Epistle of Barnabas,* and *The Shepherd of Hermas.* Early Gentile Christian writings such as the *Pseudo-Clementine Writings* and *The Constitutions of the Holy Apostles* attested to the vitality of these gifts. Many authors also documented to the vital place of these gifts: Clement (?-101 AD), Ignatius of Antioch (35-107), Tertullian (160-220), Eusebius (264-340), Iraneus (130-200), Origen (185-254), Hippolytus of Rome (170-235), Gregory Thaumatungus (205-265). During the period before the Council of Nicea (325 AD), many writers attested to the decline of the gifts in the Christian Communities. Some of these writers were John Chrysostom (347-407), Basil (329-379), Cyprian (200-258), Athanasius (296-373), Anthony of the Desert (251-356), Pachomius (4th century), Ambrose (339-397), Jerome (342-420), and Augustine (354-430). He quoted a church historian, Walker, as saying: "The gifts of the Spirit, which had been very real to the thought of Christians of the Apostolic and sub-Apostolic ages, and which might be possessed by anyone, were now a tradition rather than a vital reality" (Walker, 1959:81)

[40] Swenson, D. 2009. *Society, spirituality and the sacred. A social scientific introduction.* Second edition. Toronto: University of Toronto Press. He made his case of the radical marginalization of women in third and fourth century utilizing the scholarship of Torjesen (1993:114)), who noted "the enormous extent to which the Christian Church allowed Greco-Roman social dogma to pervade its teaching" (p. 114). Part of the changed image of women consisted of fears of feminine sexuality and of an emphasis on female shame: "woman" was made to feel that she was the source of sin and evil in the world. Torjesen (1993:7) wrote

THE DIVISION BETWEEN *YESHUA* BELIEVING
JEWS AND JESUS BELIEVING GENTILES

This is the second division that the young faith endured. The first one was the separation of Rabbinic Jews and *Yeshua* believing Jews. This was documented in Chapter Two under the sub-title *The Nazarenes or The Jewish Believers in Yeshua within Israel*. This section of the text is an outline of this division that some have termed it the separation of all separations.

Two primary sources of a theory of the separation between *Yeshua* believing Jews and Jesus believing Gentiles are one, a social-scientific study of ancient Antioch by Zetterholm (2003) and, two, Sanders (1993). Zetterholm engages sociology with ancient texts to tell the story of the division in Antioch while, Sanders, also using sociological language, expands the phenomenon and the reasons why there was the division of the Roman Empire of Asia Minor and Rome. Zetterholm begins his study with an outline of the city of Antioch, then continues with an overview of Judaism in the city that will be followed by his historical theory of the division.

Antioch was founded in 300 BCE by Seleucus Nicator (358–281

"Although these notions about female shame and women's sexuality have their roots in the social order of ancient Greece, they have had a profound effect on the Christian understanding of women, sexuality, and sin throughout the history of the Church—they are foundational to the Western doctrine of sin, the church's theology on sexuality, and the Christian concepts of self and even of God. Ide (1984) and Cole (1993) document some of the sayings of a selection of Church Fathers such as: Clement of Alexandria (150–215): "His characteristic is action; hers, passivity ... the mature, then the immature"; Epiphanius, Bishop of Cyprus and Salamis (315–403): "... the female sex is easily seduced, weak, and without much understanding. The Devil seeks to vomit out this disorder through women" (Ide, 1984, p. 68); Tertullian "You [women] are the devil's gateway; you are the unsealer of that forbidden fruit; you are the first deserter of the divine law; you are she who persuaded him whom the devil was not valiant enough to attack. You destroyed so easily God's image, man. On account of your desert–that is, death–even the Son of God had to die" (Ide, 1984, p.77); and Ambrosiaster (4th century) and John Chrysostom both taught that man, not woman, was made in the image of God (Cole, 1993, pp. 121, 162).

BCE) as a Greek political center and, during the Roman times, an important metropolis in the East and a capital of Syria. By the first century CE, it had a population of 300,000 inhabitants who experienced a high degree of density, low age expectancy, and had few personal attachments.

Zetterholm estimates that the Jewish community may have been between five and ten percent of the population and the supported as many as thirty synagogues which were given legitimacy by the Romans as *collegia*. A "common Judaism" was present that consisted of the acceptance of the Bible as God's word, a study and the observance of the *Torah*, an awareness that the Jews were a unique people different from Gentiles, monotheism, Sabbath Rest, and the vision that the Temple in Jerusalem was central to their lives. Zetterholm identified four kinds of Judaism: (1) fringe Jews, (2) religious traditionalists or *Torah* observant, (3) Jesus believing Jews (or Messianic Jews), and (4) Hellenistic Jews who adapted themselves to Greek culture.

There appears to be no evidence that the *Yeshua* believing Jews had any intention of leaving Judaism and that Jesus-believing Gentiles should subordinate themselves to synagogue authorities who were also Jesus believing. The Jesus movement (consisting both of Jews and Gentiles) had at least one synagogue that consisted of both Jewish and Gentile Messianic believers. Among the Jews (not Jesus believing) there were two eschatological images: that the Gentiles would all be destroyed in contrast to the view that they would come to Judaism.

The acceptance of Gentiles into Israel was a central issue of the new Jesus movement. Elders of the movement sought how the Gentiles could be "brought in"? Thus, the Jerusalem Council was called as recorded in the Books of Acts, chapter 15. No, the elders said, a Gentile does not need to become a Jew (to be circumcised and follow the kosher laws). They were required to adhere to four laws some of which were found their origin in Noah (see Genesis 9:4): that they abstain from meat sacrificed to idols, refrain from consuming blood, not to eat the meat of a strangled animal and to refrain from fornication. Although there was a unanimous decision by the elders in Jerusalem, the issue was not totally settled in Antioch and did become an issue among the Jesus believing Jews and the Jesus believing Gentiles.

Central to Judaism in Antioch as well as throughout Israel and the diaspora was the centrality of the covenant: the relationship between Israel and God. Part of joining the Jesus believing Jewish Community was having an equal status of the covenant that seemed to be applied in the council statements. In Galatians, Paul is emphatic about the Gentile believers being equal to the Jewish believers in Jesus. However, Zetterholm contends that James, the head elder of the congregation in Jerusalem, mandated that the Jesus believing Gentiles needed to become Jews or, at least, have the status as *God-fearers*. Thus, seeds of division were sown from this controversy.

What were some of the other sources of division? One set of external factors were political in nature while the other set was ideological. Politically, tides of awkward acceptance of the Jews in Antioch changed to a rejection of them by the Antiochan Gentiles. The Jewish revolt of 66-73 CE led to laws and restrictions against all Jews that included *Yeshua* believing Jews and Jesus believing Gentiles. As discussed in the section on the Anti-Semitic culture of the ancient world, the Romans imposed a punishing tax called *Fiscus Judaicus*. Jesus believing Gentiles began to distance themselves from *Yeshua* believing Jews and Jews in general. Further, the government in Antioch made Sabbath observance illegal. This was a further move of the Jesus believing Gentiles to isolate themselves from their Jewish brothers and sisters and Jews in general. Eventually, the Jesus believing Gentiles chose to have Sunday as their day of rest so as not to be guilty of observing the Sabbath.

The second set of factors that led to division was ideological and the genesis of the genre *Adversos Judaeos* that was detailed above under the section of the social construction of Christian antisemitism. The author of this genre was Ignatius of Antioch (referred to in the same section above) who sought strip everything Jewish in the new faith except Jesus and the Scriptures. He taught that for Jesus believing Gentiles to embrace a Jewish world-view was "monstrous." Zetterholm comments further:

The conflict that emanated from the formation of the new Gentile movement was certainly a means towards a specific result: namely, the separation from every kind of Jewish influence. At the same time, it meant maintaining some specific Jewish religious traits as the Holy Scriptures and the concepts of covenant and the Messiah, while certainly "de-Judaizing" them and transforming them into a new Gentile religion—Christianity (2003:208).

Except for the theory of James demanding conversion to Judaism for the new Jesus believing Gentiles, it appears that the Gentile part of the early congregation was schematic and broke away from its Jewish roots. Relying more and more on Hellenistic culture and philosophy, the eventual Latin and Greek trajectories were created. I do find it very interesting that these early Christian leaders sought to understand their Jesus faith not in the richness of Judaism but in the polytheistic world of Hellenism.

Sanders does well to expand the problems and issues beyond Antioch between the two forms of early Christianity. His sources include Ignatius, Deutero-Pauline epistles, Pliny the Younger (a Roman lawyer and author, 61-113 CE), Clement and Justin. One common focus of these writers and writings was the prospective of division between these two forms. The genesis of the issue was the initial expansion of the young faith from Judaism to the Gentile world. In the book of Acts (10:1-48), Peter responds to a dream where he heard a voice asking him to consume animals that were unclean in Jewish tradition. He was a reluctant prophet like Jonah and refused by saying they were unclean. The voice continued and said that he was not to call unclean that which God had made clean. It did not refer to food but to the sharing of the message of Messiah to Gentiles. He was then obedient and the first believers, a Roman army officer and his family, believed in *Yeshua*.

The issue continued to be a problem, for some Jewish believers still wanted the Gentiles to become Jews. However, this was not common for Sanders noted, from Ignatius, that there was strong evidence that the Jewish believers did not try to impose their Jewishness upon the Gentile believers.

Sanders looked at a set of epistles that were written to the same congregations that Paul wrote to but were not canonical. In an epistle to the Colossians, the author spoke against Jewish believers who desired the Gentiles to follow Jewish traditions. There seemed to be some debate that these Jewish believers were heretical but the author denied that.

The issue in Ephesus was different. There was a move by Gentile believers to encourage the Jewish believers to forsake their commitment to Judaism in the matter of circumcision, Sabbath observance, adherence to dietary laws, honoring the Torah, and the continued celebration of the Jewish feasts. Sadly, the Gentile position held sway. Sanders wrote:

> While the Epistle to the Ephesians therefore gives no direct information about Jewish–Christian relations, its theological position is such that the implication for the development is clear; those Jewish Christians who continue to be *Torah*-observant (regarding such requirements as Sabbath and circumcision, of course) are now regarded as having opted out of the body of Christ. Observant Jewish Christians have become, for the author of Ephesian, relics hindering the effecting of the Christological unity. Thus, we may say that the situation of Ephesian is one in which Gentile Christianity has evolved was from relations with Jewish Christians (1993:201).

Sanders cites a Roman author, Pliny the Younger, on some of the situation in Bithynia and Pontus. Here, the Roman author noted, that many of the people had become Christians who were of Gentile descent and not Jewish. Sanders noted: "This does not mean that no Jews in the area became Christians but it does mean that we have no evidence of such" (1993: 202). Further, it seems that there is no evidence that the Jews were denouncing these new believers to Roman authorities.

Clement I (35-88 CE) was the fourth bishop of Rome whose letter, Clement, reveals how profoundly Jewish he was. This letter has one-half of the quotations from the Old Testament. In it, he refers frequently to the basis of the faith was the Torah followed by the Prophets and then to Messiah, *Yeshua*.

Justin Martyr, during his time, identified three kinds of the followers of *Yeshua*. Figure 3:1: indicates this:

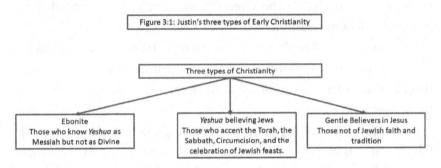

Regarding the Ebionites, Justin did not consider them to be Christian. He also had many doubts about Jewish believers in *Yeshua* that became a central part of the Gentile Christian critique against the Jewish segment of the young faith.

Sanders accounts for the strength of Jewish believers in *Yeshua* in Rome from archeological and other sources. Early Roman Christianity was closely related to Roman Judaism and that the Christians of Rome, during the first century, were of Jewish origins. Evidence comes for hagiography, burial sites, churches named after Jewish traditions, and that many believers in *Yeshua* lived in predominately Jewish quarters in Rome. Sanders wrote: "there was a preponderance of Jewish Christians in the first century—the majority of believers were Jewish Christians" (1993:228).

Sanders completes his study of the first century of Christianity with using the sociological concepts of sect and new religious movement. When Christianity was an extension of Judaism, one could categorize it as a sect within Judaism. However, as it migrated more and more to the rest of Asia Minor and Rome, it could be called a new religious movement.

How can we evaluate Jewish believers in *Yeshua* as a sect? Not all the characteristics of a sect can be applied but the essential features of the type can. The sect has a strong sense of doctrine and morality, that the leaders were not likely to be professionally trained, that it stood strong against secularization tendencies and was not over accommodative to the external environment and was organizationally precarious. By not tending to be secularized and non-accommodative to the Greco-Roman culture, it tended to be in a high-tension relationship.

Because it stood in sharp contrast to this culture it was embedded in, its continuity was in jeopardy. It was precarious. One could consider this to be another reason for the slow demise and marginalization of the movement.

Sanders (1993:242) presented several characteristics of Gentile Christianity as being a new religious movement in the environment of Asia Minor and, eventually, throughout the Roman Empire:

1. The religious economy of the Greco-Roman world was quite unregulated and allowed for new religious expressions to enter into the main culture.
2. The conventional faith had weakened. This was observed by Pliny the Younger.
3. The young movement had high levels of individual commitment.
4. It deviated from the doctrine and the morality of the host society.
5. Gentile Christianity had a strong social network of support. This was noted by Stark (1997) in his study of early Christianity.

With the use of these two typologies, we are in a better position to understand why Jewish believers in *Yeshua* and Gentile believers in Jesus parted company. However, the primary reasons are that the

Gentile believers distanced themselves from their brothers and were the primary reason for the first division and the first major wound in the genesis of the world religion we know today as Christianity.

LAMENTATIONS FOR THE SUFFERING THE FIRST- BORN SON OF GOD, ISRAEL.

This chapter, as presented in the Introduction, by Kinzer (2018). He compares the crucifixion of *Yeshua* to the suffering of Jerusalem (and all of Israel) from the destruction of the city and the Temple in 70 CE to the termination of the *Shoah* in 1945. As *Yeshua* did suffer in his passion and death, so did the people of Israel suffer over these long centuries. His crucifixion can be compared to the *Shoah* with the death of six million European Jews. As did the Jewish people suffer, so did *Yeshua* weep along with the millions of cries of *Adonai's* people in the death camps of the Nazi's. As we journey through the historical eras, we will find that Christians have not joined themselves with *Yeshua* in this regard, but many have, sadly, rejoiced in the suffering of the Jewish people. The call, then, is that Christians lament and cry with *Adonai's* original people who lived in exile and suffering.

Chapters five, six, and seven will be a documentation of theses sufferings, horrors and tragedies to the people of Israel that has been a constant presence in the world and in Christianity from the second century to the middle of the twentieth century. This is a cause for deep lamentations and repentance that antisemitism that has been inflicted on the First-Born of *Adonai*. The suffering of the people of Israel is illustrated by the destruction of the First Temple (587 BCE) and the Second (70 CE) through the Tanakh and the work on the first century Jewish historian, Josephus (37 CE–100 CE).

The Second book of Kings, the Second book of Chronicles and Josephus (76-77 CE/1999)[41] well document the destruction both of

---

[41] The prophets Jeremiah and Ezekiel also inform us the capture of Jerusalem, the burning of the Temple and the deportation of the people to Babylon (Jeremiah

Jerusalem and the First Temple[42] in 587 BCE. The narration appears like this. In 589 BCE, Nebuchadnezzar king of Babylon advanced on Jerusalem with his entire army. According to Josephus, the city was under siege for eighteen months during which famine flooded the city[43]. After this, the Chaldeans broke through the wall burned down the palaces and homes of the royalty and killed many, young and old, male and female. Josephus wrote:

> The general of the Babylonians now overthrew the city to his very foundations and removed all the people and took for prisoners the high priest Sariah and Zephaniah the priest that was next to him and the rulers that guarded the temple. They were three in number and the eunuch who was over the armed men and seven friends of Zedekiah. Sixty other rulers all of which together with the vessels which way they which they pillaged he carried to the King of Babylon in Riblah the city of Syria (76-77/1999:346).

The temple was then burned to the ground and the only people left were the poor and common people. The temple burned for twenty-four hours on the ninth day of the month of Av (*Tisha B'Av*). In Jewish tradition, this day was to be remembered as a day of mourning and lamentations. In this section of the chapter, as well in chapters four to six, I would like to continue this tradition.

In much more detail did Josephus outline the destruction of the city of Jerusalem and the second temple in 70 CE by Titus (39 CE–81 CE). Extensive was his recording in minute detail of the events for

---

39, 40, 52 and Ezekiel 4 and 6).

[42] This is the temple built by Solomon that was completed in 1000 BCE.

[43] Ezekiel prophesied the famine: "Son of man, I am going to cut off Jerusalem's food supply, in their extremity, the food they ate will be weighed out; to their horror the water they drink will be rationed, until there is no food or water left, and they fall into a stupor and waste away because of their guilt (Ezekiel 4:16-17).

he devoted two books (5 and 6) that covered 64 pages in his section entitled *The Jewish War*.

The historian lays much blame on the Jews themselves for the destruction of their city and their temple. As the Romans were approaching the city to lay siege to it, Zealots and their opponents were fighting with each other. Josephus made a bold statement: "I venture to say that the rebellion destroyed the city, and the Romans destroyed the rebellion, which it was a much harder thing to do than to destroy the walls so that we may justly ascribe our misfortunes to our own people, and the just ventures taken on them to the Romans" (76-77/1999:859).

Over a period of several months, the Romans constructed banks to climb and gain access to the city. There were three sets of walls that they had to traverse. Along the way, many Romans were killed but, finally, they entered the centre of the city where they massacred many, captured others and sold them as slaves. The Romans left behind themselves carnage and a ravaging famine left thousands of corpses (numbering 115, 800) in the streets of the city. Josephus described the utter tragedy of death, fratricide, victims of the Romans, cannibalism, and the burning of the city and the temple. So much was the tragedy that homes were burned which housed residents and blood was poured that it quenched the fires. Referring to the destruction of the Temple, much lament ensued:

> Now although anyone would justly lament the destruction of such a work as this was, since it was the most admirable of all the works that we have seen or heard of both for its curious structure and its magnitude, and also for the vast wealth bestowed upon it, as well as it had such a glorious reputation it had for its holiness (76-77/1999:897).

The historian observed that it was this day and month (*Tisha B'Av*) that the first temple was destroyed by the Babylonians in 586 BCE. He called this fate, but one may argue it was providential. This comes the setting of the mourning and lament that is encircled by remembering and repenting of the sin against the Jews even though one may see that their suffering was redemptive and refining to, eventually, create a new Israelite who is purified and cleansed to "be a blessing to the nations" (Genesis 12:3).

Relying on the spiritual insights of Kinzer (2018), I offer to the reader that *Yeshua,* the Messiah, walked and suffered with the Jewish people from this era through to the *Shoah.* To make this evident, I will quote from the *Tanakh* that refers to the suffering of *Yeshua* from Isaiah well as from the Book of Lamentations that reflect the suffering of the Jews.

I have categorized Isaiah 52:13 to 53:12 into four sections that will introduce the mournful reflections of the sufferings of Messiah *Yeshua.* Selections from Lamentations that reflect the suffering of the first- born Son of God, Israel will be given in each historical era. Following are the texts that reveal the First Wound of Division.

Of Messiah: See how my servant will succeed! He will be raised up, exalted, highly honored! Just as many were appalled at him, because he was so disfigured that he didn't even seem human and simply no longer looked like a man, so now he will startle many nations because of him, Kings will be speechless for they will see what they had not been told they will ponder things that they never heard (Isaiah 52:13-15).

Of Jerusalem: How lonely lies the city that once thronged with people! Once great among the nations, now she is like a widow! Once princess among the provinces, she has become a vassal. Bitterly, she weeps at night, tears running down her cheeks. Not one of her lovers is there to comfort her. Her friends have all betrayed her. They become her enemies. Judah has fled into exile from oppression and endless slavery; she lives among the nations but there she finds no rest;

her pursuers have all overtaken her in the midst of her distress. The roads to Zion are morning because no one comes to the festival. Her gateways are all deserted her priests are groaning, her unmarried girls are grieving-- how bitter it is for her! Her foes have become the head, her enemies relax, for *Adonai* has made her suffer. because of her many sins. Her young children have gone away captured before the full. All splendor has departed from the daughter of Zion. Her princes have become like deer unable to find pasture running on, fleeing from the hunter in the days of affliction and anguish, Jerusalem remembers all the treasures that were hers ever since ancient times. Now people fall into the power of the foe and she has no one to help her, her enemies are gloating over her mocking her desolation. Jerusalem sinned grievously; therefore, she is become unclean. All who honoured her now despise her because they have seen her naked. She herself also moans and turns her face away (Lamentations 1:1-8).

The reader is encouraged to identify with the suffering Israel and Messiah *Yeshua* who walks and weeps with her. Vivid in both readings is a recollection of this suffering. Mourning and lamentation are to be part of the repentance theme so prominent in this document.

CONCLUSIONS

For many reasons, this outline has been extensive to provide evidence that the young faith, during the decades of the first century could be called "The Jesus Movement." However, it suffered division contrary to the mind of its founder, Jesus, The Messiah who prayed for unity (see John 17:17). Much of the source of the division was ideological in nature influenced by the antisemitism of the ancient world. This prejudice was translated into the literary genre, *Adversos Judaeos* in the minds of some Patristic Fathers. It was argued that second-fourth century Patristic Fathers absorbed this ideology because of their being educated in Greco-Roman academes. A section of the paper was devoted to the many factors that influenced the division. The final section, on identifying with the suffering of Messiah and Israel, is a call to a radical repentance. In the seventh chapter in this text, hope for renewal and reconciliation will be outlined.

REFERENCES: CHAPTER THREE

Ambrose, St. 1983. "Letter XL: to Theodosius on the burning of the Jewish Synagogue," p. 440–445. In *Nicene and Post-Nicene Fathers of the Christian Church,* edited by D. Schafff and H. Wace, Volume X, *St. Ambrose, selected works and letters.* Grand Rapids MI: Wm B. Eeerdems Publishing Co.

Augustine, St. 413–426/1952. *The city of God.* Chicago: The University of Chicago.

Basil the Great in Pegis, A. (Editor). 1949. "Address to young men on reading Greek literature." In *The Wisdom of Catholicism,* p. 8–26, New York: The Modern Library.

Bowker, J. 2000. "Secularization" *The Concise Oxford Dictionary of World Religions* Edited by J. Bowker. Oxford University Press. *Oxford Reference Online.* Oxford University Press. Mount Royal College. 13 September 2006<http://www.oxfordreference.com/views/ENTRY.html?subview=Main&entry=t101.e6503.

Burckhardt, J. 1949/2007. *The age of Constantine the Great.* London: The Folio Society.

Carroll, J. 2001. *Constantine's Sword: The Church and the Jews.* Boston: A Mariner Book. Houghton Mifflin Company.

Cole, J. K. 1993. "The fathers on women and women's ordination". In *Studies in early Christianity,* edited by E. Fergusan, D. M. Scholer and P. Corby-Finney, pp. 117–167. New York: Garland.

Danielou. J. 1964. *The theology of Jewish Christianity. Volume one of A history of early Christian doctrine before the Council of Nicea.* Translated by J. Baker. London: Darton, Logman and Todd.

Feldman, L. 1993. *Jew and Gentile in the ancient world: Attitudes and interactions from Alexander to Justinian.* Princeton, NJ: Princeton University Press.

Fichtenbauer, J. (Archdeacon). 2019. *The Mystery of the Olive Tree: Uniting Jews and Gentiles for Christ's Return*. Luton, Bedfordshire: New Life Publishing.

Finto, D. 2016. *Your people shall be my people*. Minneapolis, Minnesota: Chosen.

Guston, L. 1986. "Judaism of the uncircumcised in Ignatius and related writers." In *Anti-Judaism in early Christianity*, edited by S. Wilson, p. 33–44. *Volume II: Separation and Polemic*. Montreal: Wilfred Laurier University Press.

Hippolytus, 1986. "Expository Treatises against the Jews." In *Fathers of the Third Century: Hippplytus, Cyprian, Novatian*, edited by A. Roberts and J. Donaldson, p. 219–221. Grand Rapids Michigan. Wm B. E. Eeermens Publishing.

Hood, J. Y. B. 1955. *Aquinas and the Jews*. Philadelphia: University of Pennsylvania Press.

Ide, A. F. 1984 . *Woman as priest, bishop and laity*. Mesquito, Texas.

Ide House and Cole, J. K. 1993. "The fathers on women and women's ordination". In *Studies in early Christianity*, edited by E. Fergusan, D. M. Scholer and P. Corby-Finney, pp. 117–167. New York: Garland.

Josephus, J. (76–77 CE/1999). *The New Complete Work of Josephus*, Translated by W. Whiston and commented on by P. Maier. Grand Rapids, MI: Kregel Publications.

Kinzer, M. 2018. *Jerusalem crucified, Jerusalem risen*. Eugene Oregon: Wipf and Stock Publishers.

Krewson, W. L. 2017. *Jerome and the Jews: Innovative supersessionism*. Eugene Oregon: Wipf and Stock Publishers.

Mancini, I. OFM. 1970. *Archeological discoveries relative to the Judeo-Christians*. Franciscan Printing Press. Jerusalem Fortress.

McDonald, L. 1993. "Anti-Judaism in the early church fathers." In *Anti Semitism and early Christianity*, edited by C. Evan and D hanger, p. 215–252. Minneapolis: Augsburg Fortress.

Midrash. https://en.wikipedia.org/wiki/Midrash

Montgomery, R. and B. O'Dell. 2019. *The List: Persecutions of Jews by Christians throughout history.* Israel: Root Source Press.

Niebuhr, H. Richard. 1951. *Christ and culture.* Harper and Row: New York, New York.

Osiris. https://en.wikipedia.org/wiki/Seth

Rainer, K.(2011-2017) Berlin, "Adversos Judaeos Homilies", in: *Encyclopedia of Jewish History and Culture Online,* Original German Language Edition: Enzyklopädie Jüdischer Geschichte und Kultur. Im Auftrag der Sächsischen Akademie der Wissenschaften zu Leipzig herausgegeben von Dan Diner. © J.B. Metzler, Stuttgart/ Springer-Verlag GmbH Deutschland 2011–2017.. Consulted online on 17 January 2018 <http://dx.doi.org/10.1163/2468-8894_ejhc_COM_0003>

Remus, H. 1986 "Justin Martyr's argument against the Jews." In *Anti-Judaism in early Christianity,* edited by S. Wilson, p. 59-80. *Volume II: Separation and Polemic.* Montreal: Wilfred Laurier University Press.

Sanders, J.1993. *Schismatics Sectarians, Dissidents, Deviants. The First One Hundred Years of Jewish-Christian Relations.* Valley forge, Pennsylvania: Trinity Press International, 1993.

Schafer, D. 1997. *Judeophobia. Attitudes towards the Jews in the Ancient World.* London: Harvest University Press.

Seth: https://en.wikipedia.org/wiki/Seth

Sevenster, J. N. 1975. *The roots of pagan Anti-Semitism in the Ancient World.* Leiden: E. Brill.

Simmel, G 1908/2016. "The Stranger". Translated by R. Mosse. *The Buffler:* no. 30:176-179. Originally published as Soziologie. Untersuchange uber die Formen der Vergesellschaftung. Berlin: Dunckcker and Humbolt.

Seiferth, R.W.S. *Synagoge und Kirche im Mittelalter* (1964); B. Blumenkranz, *Juden und Judentum in der mittelalterlichen Kunst* (1965). In *Encyclopaedia Judaica*. © 2008 The Gale Goup.H

Stark, R. 1997. *The rise of Christianity*. New York: HarperCollins.

Swenson, D. 1972. *The charismatic movement within denominational Christianity*. A thesis submitted to the Faculty of Graduate Studies in partial fulfilment of the requirements for the degree of Master of Arts. The Department of Sociology, The University of Calgary. Calgary Alberta, Canada.

Swenson, D. 2009. *Society, spirituality and the sacred. A social scientific introduction*. Second edition. Toronto: University of Toronto Press.

Torjesen, K. J. 1993. *When women were Priests*. San Francisco: Harper: San Francisco.

Troeltsch, E.1931. *The social teachings of the Christian churches. Vols I and II.*

Walker, W. *A history of the Christian Church*. New York: Charles Scribners Sons.

Weber, M. 1922/1978. *Economy and society*. Berkeley: University of CA Press.

Wilson, S. 1986a. "Marcion and the Jews." In *Anti-Judaism in early Christianity*, edited by S. Wilson, p. 45-58. *Volume II: Separation and Polemic*. Montreal: Wilfred Laurier University Press.

Wilson, S. 1986b "Melito and Israel." In *Anti-Judaism in early Christianity*, edited by S. Wilson, p. 81-102. *Volume II: Separation and Polemic*. Montreal: Wilfred Laurier University Press.

Zetterholm, M. 2003. *The formation of Christianity in Antioch: A social-scientific approach to the separation between Judaism and Christianity*. Kindel edition. Routledge: London

CHAPTER FOUR

ADVERSOS TERTULLIAN'S THEOLOGY[44] FROM THE SEVERANCE OF THE ROOTS OF CHRISTIANITY FROM JUDAISM AND ISRAEL TOWARDS A NEW IDENTITY OF THE CHURCH: REMEMBERING, REPENTING AND RECONCILING

---

[44] This is a play on words as Tertullian is against the Jews, I claim the opposite to be against his theology

INTRODUCTION

Great harm has been done to the Christian Church, and its witness to the world, because of the original wound and division of the Body of Messiah. Yes, from its genesis in the first and second centuries of the common era this harm has continued. This harm was self-inflicted and did not arise from external enemies. As indicated in previous chapters, it took on these themes: (1) The social construction of the culture of anti-Semitism focusing on the genre *Adversos Judeaos*; (2) the creation of the great wound of division between Gentile Christianity and Jewish Christianity; (3) the severance of the primary roots of Christianity from Judaism, Israel and the Torah; and (4) the social construction of supersessionism and replacement theology. In our times, since the end of the Shoah (1945) and the establishment of the state of Israel (1948), new theologies of the relationship between the two Abrahamic religions have risen from the ashes. Some of these are the rise of Messianic Judaism, and reconciliations between Jewish believers in *Yeshua* and Gentile believers in Jesus, Messiah.

Why should Tertullian (155-221 CE) be so accented? Because his influence on Latin Christianity, according to Danielou (1977), Dunn (2006), Lieu (2006), is major and he had a profound influence on his successors. Danielou (1977:231) wrote of him: "Tertullian was the greatest intellect of his time." I am selecting to challenge the theology of Tertullian which I consider to be a foundation of early Christian anti-Semitism. This is followed by a summary of Tertullian's imagery of the Jew. After this, I will outline Tertullian's meaning of *Adversos Judeaos* and will respond to his theology. I will conclude the chapter on the hope for unity and reconciliation in the body of Messiah.

THE LIFE AND THEOLOGY OF TERTULLIAN

Dunn (2006) acknowledges that little is known about the life of the theologian. What Dunn has done is to glean information about his life from Tertullian's many treatises. It is known that his literary career was spent in Carthage and that he grew up as a non-believer in Christ, but it is not known how or when he converted to Christianity. He was a married man and joined with his wife (her name is not mentioned) in Christian service. There is no evidence that they had children, and he was remorseful that he committed adultery.

He reached the maximum level of education at the schools of higher learning in Carthage and was familiar with the classical literature of Greece and Rome. Little is known of his appearance except that he taught against shaving which indicates he wore a beard. There is some controversy about him leaving the Catholic Church and joining himself to a movement called Montanism which was charismatic, ascetic, enthusiastic, innovative, spiritualist, ecstatic and rigorous. The members practiced asceticism in the form of rigorous fasting, forbidding remarriage and did not believe in the possibility of post-baptismal reconciliation of Christian sinners. Women were given leadership responsibilities especially in the role of prophecy. Tertullian agreed to all of these practices but the evidence that he was schematic is sketchy. Barnes (1985), a well-known scholar of Tertullian, argued that as he aged, he became more and more enamored over Montanism, but he never left the Catholic church and was not heretical nor unorthodox.

He was a prolific scholar and author. There are at least thirty-one extant treatises attributed to him. He was a writer whose thinking about issues changed over the years with an increasing emphasis on Montanism. A common feature of his writing was of a particular controversial issue such as his relationship to Judaism, remarriage after the death of a spouse and the possibility of post-baptismal reconciliation of Christian sinners. His style of writing was a form of argumentation taken from the Latin tradition of rhetoric which was structured to create an environment of debate to win.

His legacy continues to the present. He was the first Latin-speaking Christian author who was responsible for much of the theological vocabulary of Western Christianity and to have contributed on nearly every sector of early Christian life and thought. Dunn writes:

In a most articulate manner that has rarely been surpassed since, Tertullian represents a strand of Christianity that endures to this day and continues to exert a powerful influence over many (2006:11).

Tertullian was not primarily a systematic theologian but rather a moralist. Yet, much of his theology formed a basis for later theological discourse in the Latin Church. He was the first to use the language of three persons in one God, Father, Son, and Holy Spirit. Each is distinct but in total unity together. Creation is out of nothing, and the Genesis One and Two texts are to be taken literally. Humans were:

Born of the breath of God; immortal, corporeal, having shape, simple in substance, susceptible of the functions proper to it, developing in various ways, having freedom of choice, affected by external events, mutable in its facilities, rational, dominant and capable of presentiment (Quoted by Danielou, 1977:372).

Of central importance for the theologian is that humans are free to choose. This gives him (her) power to choose and power to act for him (her) self. This freedom was manifested in the lives of Adam and Eve. Both were given the grace of freedom to choose to eat of the knowledge of good and evil (Genesis 2;15–17). Both chose to disobey and incurred the effects of this disobedience in pain of women in childbirth, suffering for men for they had to work hard for sustenance, and, so tragically, the absence of the divine presence which was with the couple in Eden.

Tertullian thought theologically on topics such as life after death, Christology, ecclesiology, demonology, the secular state of society, sacraments, eschatology, and especially, morality. As referred to above, this Church Father was less of a theologian and more of a moralist. Baker (1977) expands on this. Faith is very much reduced to morality and Christian life is expressed almost exclusively in moral conduct. This moral conduct, though, according to Baker owes more to Stoic philosophy and less to the Scriptures. Mysticism or meditation are largely ignored. All of theology gets drawn into the one frame of reference of right behaviour. The role of the bishop is not to encourage an increased relationship to Jesus but to correct wrong behavior and to impose penance on those who transgress. Baker writes: "There is no need to spell out how this has been a salient feature of Western Christianity, both Catholic and Protestant, ever since" (1977:476). This also left a mark on Christian spirituality with an emphasis on the passion and death of Messiah and less on his Resurrection and Lordship. Humans are defined more as sinners and less as made in the divine image. There is more of an emphasis on sin and less on righteousness. Christian life is more about striving to be morally correct and less on receiving grace to live the moral Christian life.

In addition to these contrasts, Tertullian, according to Danielou, believed that Tradition trumps Scripture. He claims this because before the canon of the New Testament, there was a tradition that carried the essential message of the New Testament. This is another legacy of the man who was a founder of Latin Christianity in that Tradition plays an important role in the whole history of Catholicism.

There is a debate in the scholarship about Tertullian. Some knew him as adjusting to the Roman culture represented by Danielou (1977) and Baker (1977) while others, represented by Gilson (1983), envisioned him as an opponent to philosophy.

They who argue that he was this opponent of any kind of philosophy quote Tertullian:

> What indeed has Athens to do with Jerusalem? What concord is there between the Academy and the Church? …. Away with all attempts to produce a mottled Christianity of Stoic, Platonic, and dialectic composition! We want no curious disputation after enjoying the Gospel! With our faith, we desire no further belief. For this is our primary faith, there is

nothing which we ought to believe besides (1986, p. 246).

This understanding of the Church Father is accented by the philosopher, Etienne Gilson (1938) in his study of Medieval theology. He comments that Tertullian's position of "faith alone" has come to be known as "The Tertullian family" where there is an absolute opposition between faith and reason, of faith in the word of God and the use of natural reason in matters relating to revelation. In modern times, fundamentalist Evangelisms would fit this category.

The great irony, however, is that Tertullian did use philosophy— the philosophy of Stoicism[45] as perceived through the eyes of Danielou and Baker. Danielou writes: "Tertullian's knowledge of philosophy was enormous, and he was particularly influenced by Stoicism" (1977:214). His philosophy corresponds to the Stoic theory of the existence of God, the absolute existence of an objective reality, the harmony of the human body and society, the unchangeability of God, and his theory of history by using Stoic categories.

Tertullian uses the analogy of a tree that grows from a seed to full maturity. The process is righteousness that is based as a seed in the beginning of humanity that accented the human's natural fear of God. The second stage, righteousness comes through the Law and the Prophets and is the advancement towards Christian maturity. Stage three is the arrival of the Gospel as a focus on righteousness while the last stage, is characterized as the coming of the Holy Spirit.

Baker (1977) agrees and notes that Tertullian owes a great deal to both the Roman and the Greek mental pictures of human life. The

---

[45] A Greek philosophical system founded by Zino of Citium (334-265 BCE) around 300 BCE and developed by him and his successors into the most influential philosophy of the Hellenistic age. It views the world as permeated by rationality and divinely planned as the best possible organization of matter. Moral goodness as the best possible organization of matter. Moral greatness and happiness are achieved, if at all, by replicating the perfect rationality in oneself and finding out and enacting one's own assigned role in the cosmic order of things (Sedley, 1998:141-161).

accent is on morality that holds a primary place in Stoic philosophy. Several quotes from Baker are in order: (1), "Their faith (Tertullian and other Latin fathers) is very much reduced to morality and nothing more", and (2), "Christian faith is expressed almost exclusively in moral conduct" (Baker, 1977:476).

The purpose of this excursion is to indicate that the underlying theme of the Church father is not Judaism, the riches of Israel, and that Jesus was a very observant Jew. It was this Jewish Messiah who gave to humanity a divinely inspired morality that has its origin in the revelations of the Torah, the Prophets, and the Writings. His theme of morality is from Stoicism in its various dimensions. If Tertullian was open to the riches of the First Testament, he would have discovered myriads of gems that go beyond morality to include faith, the Divine presence, and, with St. Paul in his praise of his own people:

> The people of Israel were made God's children, the Shekinah has been with them, the covenants are theirs, likewise the giving of Torah, the Temple service and the promises, the Patriarchs are theirs and from them, as is his physical decent is concerned, came the Messiah (Romans 9:4-5).

TERTULLIAN AND THE JEWS

Scattered throughout the massive writings of this Early Church Father are many references to the Jews, Israel, and Judaism. The research from Danielou (1977), Fulton (2001) and Dunn (2004) form the basis of coming to an understanding the inherent adversarial spirit that Tertullian exhibited not only to the Jewish people but also to those Jews who believed in Jesus as the Messiah that was at the substance of Judaeo-Christianity.

Danielou documented how he wanted to dissociate the Christian message from the Jewish roots. He begins by showing that Tertullian objected to and denied the apocalyptic teaching[46] of Judaeo-Christianity, the angelology developed by Judeo-Christians and a disbelief in the teaching of millenarianism where Messiah, from the land of Israel, would reign on earth for one-thousand years. New Jerusalem as depicted by John the Evangelist in Revelation (21:10-27) was not to descend to Judea. There was no renewal of the heavens and the earth, and that Paradise was to be in heaven and not on earth. The kingdom of God was to be a heavenly kingdom and not one on earth. Danielou wrote: "We may therefore conclude that Tertullian's rejection of these themes was the result of a conscious attitude on his part of opposition to Judeo-Christianity" (1997:145) and "His attitude towards Judeo-Christian teaching was one of rejection" (1977:343).

Fulton was interested in the treatise of *Adversos Judeaos* as an exercise of literary criticism. I will not present this critique but use his work to illustrate how much Tertullian was against the Jews. In Tertullian's treatise text called The Apology (or *Apoligeticum*) there are many quotes having adversarial statements against the Jews. Here is a sample of them (Fulton 2011:60-61).

The Jews, once loved and cared for by God, are now unworthy of His love. They have rejected the Law (the Torah) and have followed ways of the ungodly. For this, and many other infractions, they were rejected by God and have fallen into ruin. All over the world, they have strayed, and, especially, have not God as their king or ruler. The *Tanakh*, in the words of the prophets, have warned them many times and have taught that there would be a time in the future when God would choose another people from every race and people who would be more faithful. All the gifts given to the Jews would be transferred to these peoples. They, the Gentile Christians would supersede the Jews who would obey God and follow all His ways. Tertullian claimed that the Jews knew that Christ would come but their sin prevented them from believing that Jesus was the Messiah. Fulton wrote of the audacity of Tertullian: "In short, the Gentile

---

[46] To understand more of this literature, see Swenson (2021), pages 52-60.

Christians would supersede the Jews in God's favor was foretold in sacred Scripture" (2011:60).

Tertullian accented the claimed divine rejection with these words:

> But how deeply they have sinned, puffed up to their fall with a false trust in their noble ancestors, turning from God's way into a way of sheer impiety, though they themselves should refuse to admit it, their present national ruin would afford sufficient proof. It was the merited punishment of their sin not to understand the Lord's first coming...they themselves read how it is written of them that they are deprived of wisdom and understanding—of the use of eyes and ears (Apology (p.35).

Dunn (2004)[47] presented several descriptions of the Jews from a variety of Tertullian's treatises. They are the seed plot of all the calumny against us (the Gentile Christians) and their synagogues were fountains of persecution. Of all peoples, the Jews are the most difficult and God's action in the Old Testament was inferior to what He is depicted as doing in the New Testament. They became a symbol of all that was wrong, and their love of gold (money) came from their abandonment of God.

In Tertullian's *Apology* (p. 17-55) and *Against Marcion* (p. 269-474), there are an abundance of references to Scripture. Selected references that are given as "proof texts" that are chosen to undergird his primary theses against the Jews. Following are some excerpts from these treatises.

Several references to the killing of Jesus by the Jews are presented. A summary quote captures the essence of his teaching: "so they not only rejected him as a stranger but slew him as an enemy "(*Against Marcion*, pages 325, 326, 341). It seems that he is not original in his

---

[47] *To the heathens, Against Marcion,* and *On the Apparel of Women.*

accusation of slaying *Yeshua*. Melito (died in 180 CE) had already argued the same. Danielou (1977) claimed that some of Tertullian's sources were Melito, the Epistle of Barnabas and Justin.

Another theme from these two treatises is that Israel is not unique in having the Law to guide them. Before Abraham and Moses, the peoples of the earth had the Law in their hearts. What this claim does is to challenge the Jewish tradition that they are a unique people, chosen by Adonai, to bring light and a blessing to all the nations.

Texts from the *Tanach* are chosen that the ceremonies and sacrifices presented in the *Torah* are empty of meaning and are creations of the Jews and not commanded by Adonai. These sacrifices and rituals are socially constructed by the Jews and are not divinely inspired.

A further theme: the Jews are "deprived of knowledge and understanding to realize that Christ was predicted" (*Against Marcion*, 314 and 325). Scripture scholars call these texts "Messianic prophesies" and what Tertullian calls "the Jewish error" for not accepting them and believing them.

Sometimes he is vitriolic in his stand against the Jewish people. It is well known in Christian scholarship of the blatant heresy that Marcion taught about there being two gods: the god of wrath from the Old Testament and the god of mercy of the New Testament. Marcion also denied the divine inspiration of the Old Testament. Tertullian claimed that Marcion "drank the poison from the Jews" and that the Jews were partakers of the heresy of Marcion (*Against Marcion*, p. 327 and 334).

A further theme the founder of Latin Christianity taught was the total abrogation of anything Jewish in the Christian faith. The Old Law (the Torah) is gone and is replaced by Christ. Moses has no more impact on the Christian faith for he, as one of the original founders of the Jewish faith, has no relevance to the Christian message.

Beyond this, God's grace has been forfeited by the rebellion of the Israelites. Tertullian commented (*Against Marcion*, p. 341):

- God's grace has failed among them, and no fruit has been produced, only thorns.
- Dews of divine grace were withdrawn from the nation.
- They blasphemed their God and forsook Him.

With the coming of the Messiah, Jesus, three main pillars of Judaism have been abolished and replaced by Him: The Shabbat, circumcision, and the Torah. Indeed, all three were interpreted as old wine skins that could not contain the new wine, the Gospel message.

By way of summary, Tertullian rejected Judeo-Christianity on several fronts: the apocalyptic teachings, the belief in the millennium, and that there is no renewal of the heavens, or the earth were removed.

To the Jews in general, many are the accusations and rejections of them as God's people. Because they had rejected Jesus as Messiah, God rejected them. All the gifts that were originally given to them have now been transferred to the Gentile believers (replacement theology) who have superseded (supersessionism) . It was they who killed Jesus and are guilty of deicide.

The people of Israel are a seed plot of all the calamity that the Gentile believers endured. They are the symbol of all that was wrong, and they are totally abandoned by God. Their god is not Adonai of Israel or the Lord of the universe but money. Further, they are not unique in having the law. The law had been given to people before Abraham. Their festivals, celebrations and rituals are without substance. Another claim that Tertullian presented is that Marcion is not unique in his rejection of the God of the *Tanakh* for he drank the poison of the Jews. Indeed, in every way possible, divine grace has been taken away from them.

ADVERSOS JUDEAOS.

This treatise, written in approximately 197 CE, is, according to Dunn (2004), an argument about whether the Christians are the beneficiaries of God's plans or not. Tertullian searches the *Tanakh* to say yes. In fact, Dunn commented that this treatise is one of the most scripturally based treatises he wrote.

Tertullian begins this treatise with the story of the birth of twin sons to Rebecca, the wife of Isaac (Genesis 25:19-33). The text reads that the older son (Esau) will serve the younger (Jacob). He reverses the text. Jacob, the father of the Jews, was to serve Esau, the father of the Gentile Christians. He wrote: "the first, the elder people, namely the Jewish, inevitably will serve the younger. The younger people, namely the Christians, will rise above the elder.... the Jewish people—that is the more ancient—were devoted to idols, as they had deserted God, and were addicted to images, as they had abandoned the divinity" (Tertullian in Dunn,2004:69). Tertullian's anti-Jewish rhetoric continues throughout the text. If there is a prophetic indictment against Israel (as was common in the prophetic literature), he considers it to be a permanent rebuke of the people of Israel and not specific to an historical period or place.

Several critiques are to be highlighted. Israel is a stubborn people, for she has forgotten Adonai. Israel was not unique in having been given the Law for all peoples before Abraham had also received the Law. One accusation is a distortion of the *Tanakh*. From Genesis 4:1-16, Abel represented the Gentiles who was murdered by Cain who represented the Jews. So, from the very beginning, Tertullian discovered a precedent for the latter judgement that the Jews killed their Messiah. Referring to his execution, he stated: "So the entire synagogue of the children of Israel killed him" (Tertullian in Dunn,2004:84 and 94).

Several passages are highlighted that do refer to the Messiah, but the Jews did not receive them as referring to Jesus: the coming of Immanuel (Isaiah 7:13-18); the root of Jesse (Isaiah 11:1-3); the suffering servant (Psalm 22, Isaiah 42:2-3, Isaiah 53) and that he received the gifts of the Holy Spirit (Isaiah 11:1-3). Because the Jews did not accept Jesus as Messiah, their synagogues are scattered among the Gentiles, the Holy Spirit does not dwell in them as He used to dwell in the Temple.

An extended quote from him illustrates his anti-Semitic theology:

For the Lord of hosts has taken from the Jews and from Jerusalem—among other things-the wise architect who is building the Church, the temple of God and the home of the Lord. From then on the grace of God has ceased among them, and the commandments have been given to the clouds that they do not release rain upon the vineyard of Sorech, which means that heavenly benefits have been commanded not to spring up for the house of Israel. In fact, it had brought forth thorns, some of which made a crown for the Christ, had brought forth not righteousness but the cry it had extracted from him on the cross. Thus, the showers of spiritual gifts were withdrawn, and the law and the prophets ceased with John... After that, by the continuation of their own rage, the name of the Lord was blasphemed through them as it is written.... (Tertullian in Dunn,2004:100-101).

Tertullian ends this treatise by musing on the two advents of Jesus. The first coming, he came in humility and suffering. This was best illustrated from Isaiah 53. When he returns a second time, he will come in glory as depicted in the Book of Daniel: "..like a son of man, He approached the Ancient One and was lead into his presence. To him was given rulership, glory and a kingdom... his rulership is an eternal rulership that will not pass away (Daniel 7:13-14).

It was with Tertullian as the Founder of Latin Christianity, along with other Patristic followers that these traditions (replacement theology, super secessionism, and the genre *Advesos Judeos* became the DNA of Christianity. Eventually, according to Krewson, some Reformed Protestants, Evangelicals and Orthodox Christians adhered to this anti-Semitic tradition.

A Response to Tertullian and the Patristic Fathers from Cardinal Lustiger[48].

The primal tragedy of the Church started with her genesis. This was several-fold: the decline and eventual loss of the Jerusalem Church or *ecclesia ex circumcision*, the severance of Gentile Christianity from its Jewish roots and the division between Gentile believers in Jewish believers in *Yeshua*. Shortly after the second Jewish revolt of 135 CE, the city of Jerusalem was trampled on by the Romans. It was later claimed by the Byzantine Church and after it, became the victim of Islam in 638 CE. The second reason is documented in this paper through the work of Tertullian and the last through the work of Swenson (2021).

Another factor of increased distancing was the increased Hellenization of the Gentile believers in Jesus. The Cardinal wrote of the early church relying more on Hellenistic philosophy and culture rather than on Israel. This was a migration from Jerusalem to Athens that is also documented in this chapter on Tertullian.

The present task is to recognize the amazing gifts of the Jews not only to the Christian Church but also to all of humanity. Lustiger (2007:101) lists ten gifts of which many not recognized by Tertullian and other Patristic Fathers:

1. **Sacred history** is central to Judaism. Historical events are part and parcel of the theology and morality of the faith. Key events are the call of Abraham, the Exodus, the entry into the promised land, the exile, the return to the land and the future coming of Messiah.

---

[48] He was a Jew who became a Catholic Christian in his youth. He was later ordained a priest and a bishop. His last main position was the Cardinal and Archbishop of the Archdiocese of Paris. On a pillar of Notre Dame Cathedral is written of the Cardinal: "I was born Jewish. I received the name of my paternal grandfather, Aaron. Having become a Christian by faith and baptism, I have remained Jewish as did the Apostles" (Quoted by Kinzer 2015: 188-189).

2. **The Torah**. Not only for Israel but also for the Christian Church and all of humanity. It has been at the core of Western values with a focus on justice and peace.

3. **The Tanakh** or the inspired word. Christians and Jews share most of the Bible and believe that it is not humanly made but divinely given.

4. **Israel's liturgy and prayer**. In the case of Catholicism, the liturgy took as its model the Shabbat Service. The Catholic Mass is heavily dependent on the Passover meal, the Psalms and the readings from the Torah, the Prophets and the writings. The establishment of Christian feasts are modelled on the feasts of Israel.

5. **The Land of Israel**. The land, the country, the people are sacred not only to Judaism but also to Christianity.

6. **Reign.** Both Judaism and Christianity are engaged in bringing the kingdom of God to the earth. Both believe that God is the King not only of Israel and the Church but also to all of humanity.

7. **Redemption**. The original meaning of Israel was that of animal sacrifice for redemption and the forgiveness of sin. Jesus, in Christianity, became the living sacrifice for the removal and the forgiveness of sin.

8. **Repentance**. Humans, says Lustiger, have "homicidal tendencies". This is so very evident in the history of Israel as well as in the secular world. This was epitomized in the Shoal. There is need, in both Abrahamic religions to repent not only of personal sin but also corporate sin. This was illustrated by Pope Paul II when he asked forgiveness of all Jewish people of the sin of the Roman Catholic Church at the Holocaust Museum of Jerusalem.

9. **The richness of the Talmudic tradition**. This has almost been lost among Christians and needs to be resurrected.

10. **Focus on Eschatology**. Both traditions are messianic. Both long for the coming of the Messiah. The only difference is that Jewish believers are waiting for the coming of the

Messiah for the first time while Christians long and hunger for the second coming.

The Cardinal ends his work with reflections on the common destiny of Judaism and Christianity. Both reject absolutism, the fascism with tyranny and setting oneself up to judge what is good and evil.

Because both have a common bond with the Torah, both are to use it for humanity. The image of servanthood is at the core of Judaism and Christianity. The goal is to create a space of justice, safety, and compassion for all humans.

The demands of relativism are strong in the secular culture of the West. There is a call to be vigilant not to change the Torah and the Ten Commandments to suit the whims of humans and egotistic desires.

Both traditions have a mission to the unity of humanity. Humans were made in the divine image (Genesis 1:27) who is supremely one. Lustiger (2007:163): writes: "To convey to divided men the call to a unity that is greater and stronger than their enormous divisions". Together, this vision and goal is more possible to be accomplished.

CONCLUSIONS

The initial part of this conclusion is to highlight the many facets of Tertullian's anti-Semitism. It should be recalled that theologians consider him to be more of a moralist then a doctrinal theologian. He seemed to draw more on Stoicism then on the Hebrew and Christian scriptures. As a doctrinal theologian he emphasized more the passion and death of the Messiah than on His resurrection, ascension and the gift of Pentecost.

It is within this context that his many themes against the Jews emerge. He considered them to be unworthy of divine love and followed the ungodly Gentiles. They are rejected by God because they have rejected Jesus as Messiah while the Gentile believers are accepted. They believed that He was the Messiah. The Gentile Christians replaced and superseded the Jews for the latter have deeply sinned. They are "the seed plot" of all the calumny levelled against the Gentile Christians. It is they who killed Jesus and engaged in persecution against the Christians of Gentile origin. The Hebrews are not unique in receiving the Law of God. Previous peoples had the Law of God written in their hearts from creation. Stereotypes against the Jews abound in Tertullian's treatises. According to him, the Jews are stubborn, selfish, lovers of gold, recalcitrant, hard-hearted, egotistical, and legalistic.

All the rituals and ceremonies of the people of Israel were not divinely given but were humanly created. The synagogue is the fountain of all persecutions against the Christians of Gentile background, and it is there that the false rituals are practiced.

Likely, hidden away in his many treatises are more accusations, stereotypes, prejudices, exaggerations, and discriminations. The good news is that the Catholic Church, has officially repudiated these themes of the *Adversos Judeaos* tradition. Imagine, these themes have been present not only in the Catholic Church but in other Christian traditions for centuries and have become the DNA of so many believers in Jesus. It is very important to remember them, to repent, and to seek reconciliation. We are now in a new era. In the words of Kinzer (2015:8):

> This is a theological revolution. Formerly, perverted expressions of Christian devotion to Jesus[49] had inspired hatred of Jews and Judaism. According to the theological bombshell planted by Pope John XIII and ignited by Pope John Paul II, this ancient reflex of contempt had been disrupted and even reversed. New Christian devotion to Jesus was to become the

---

[49] Cardinal Lustiger calls this the creation of an idol. He also makes a note that in denying the Jewish connection to Jesus is to deny something of Jesus himself.

source of love for the Jewish people and appreciation
for Judaism.

The future is hopeful. Many meetings of Gentile believing
theologians and Messianic scholars have engaged in dialogue and
are coming to a closer sense of unity that reflects the ultimate goal of
the Emissary, Paul: "For he (Messiah) is the peace, to create a single
New Man out of the two of them, and through the cross, to reconcile
them both go God in one Body…" (Ephesians 2: 15-16).

CONTINUED LAMENTATIONS FOR THE SUFFERING OF THE FIRST BORN SON

This lamentation theme continues in this chapter. Here the focus was
on how antisemitism had its genesis in the Latin Church, primarily,
in the works of Tertullian. Antisemitism did not begin with him,
but his pen contributed much to the Latin Church's theology. I
would argue that much of his theology was tainted with this ethos.
Reviewing his works helps us to remember. Repenting of his errors
and the error of the Latin Church leads to reconciliation. The theme
of reconciliation is documented in chapter six. So very vital is this
reconciliation for if it is not forthcoming more and more, the Body
of Messiah will continue to suffer.

References to Chapter Four

Primary Sources

Tertullian. 175-220 CE "The Apology." Pages 17-55. In Volume III. 1986. Coxe, A. Cleveland, ed., *The Ante-Nicene fathers. Translations of the writings of the fathers down to A.D. 325.* The Rev. Alexander Roberts, D.D., and James Donaldson, LL.D., editors. American reprint of the Edinburgh edition. Revised and chronologically arranged, with brief prefaces and occasional notes, by A. Cleveland Coxe, D.D. (Buffalo, The Christian literature publishing company, 1885-96. 10 volumes).Grand Rapids Michigan: WM. B. Eerdmans Publishing Company.

Tertullian.175-220 "An Answer to the Jews or *Adversos Judeaos.*" Pages 151-173. In Volume III. 1986. Coxe, A. Cleveland, ed., *The Ante-Nicene fathers. Translations of the writings of the fathers down to A.D. 325.* The Rev. Alexander Roberts, D.D., and James Donaldson, LL.D., editors. American reprint of the Edinburgh edition. Revised and chronologically arranged, with brief prefaces and occasional notes, by A. Cleveland Coxe, D.D. (Buffalo, The Christian literature publishing company, 1885-96. 10 volumes).Grand Rapids Michigan: WM. B. Eerdmans Publishing Company.

Tertullian.175-220 CE "Against Marcion." Pages 269-474. In Volume III. 1986. Coxe, A. Cleveland, ed., *The Ante-Nicene fathers. Translations of the writings of the fathers down to A.D. 325.* The Rev. Alexander Roberts, D.D., and James Donaldson, LL.D., editors. American reprint of the Edinburgh edition. Revised and chronologically arranged, with brief prefaces and occasional notes, by A. Cleveland Coxe, D.D. (Buffalo, The Christian literature publishing company, 1885-96. 10 volumes).Grand Rapids Michigan: WM. B. Eerdmans Publishing Company.

Tertullian. 175-220 CE "On the apparel of women.." Pages 14-25. In Volume IV. 1986. Coxe, A. Cleveland, ed., *The Ante-Nicene* fathers. *Translations of the writings of the fathers down to A.D. 325.* The Rev. Alexander Roberts, D.D., and James Donaldson, LL.D., editors. American reprint of the Edinburgh edition. Revised and chronologically arranged, with brief prefaces and occasional notes, by A. Cleveland Coxe, D.D. (Buffalo, The Christian literature publishing company, 1885-96. 10 volumes).Grand Rapids Michigan: WM. B. Eerdmans Publishing Company.

Tertullian. 175-220 CE "To the heathen or *Ad Nationes.*" Pages 129-147. In Volume III. 1986. Coxe, A. Cleveland, ed., *The Ante-Nicene fathers. Translations of the writings of the fathers down to A.D. 325.* The Rev. Alexander Roberts, D.D., and James Donaldson, LL.D., editors. American reprint of the Edinburgh edition. Revised and chronologically arranged, with brief prefaces and occasional notes, by A. Cleveland Coxe, D.D. (Buffalo, The Christian literature publishing company, 1885-96. 10 volumes).Grand Rapids Michigan: WM. B. Eerdmans Publishing Company.

Tertullian. 175-220 CE "The prescription against heretics", Pages 243-265. In Volume III 1986. Coxe, A. Cleveland, ed., *The Ante-Nicene fathers. Translations of the writings of the fathers down to A.D. 325.* The Rev. Alexander Roberts, D.D., and James Donaldson, LL.D., editors. American reprint of the Edinburgh edition. Revised and chronologically arranged, with brief prefaces and occasional notes, by A. Cleveland Coxe, D.D. (Buffalo, The Christian literature publishing company, 1885-96. 10 volumes).Grand Rapids Michigan: WM. B. Eerdmans Publishing Company.

Secondary Sources

Baker, J. "Postscript" 1977. In Danielou. J. 1977. *The history of early Christian doctrine before the Council of Nicea. Volume Three, The Origins of Latin Christianity.* Translated by J. Baker, p. 469-477. London: Darton, Logman and Todd.

Barnes, T. (1985). *Tertullian: A historical and Literary study, revised edition,* Oxford: Clarendon.

Danielou, J. 1977. *The history of early Christian doctrine before the Council of Nicea. Volume Three, The Origins of Latin Christianity.* Translated by J. Baker. London: Darton, Logman and Todd.

Dunn, G. 2004. *Tertullian. Adversos Judaeos 68-104. The Early Church Fathers.* New York: Routledge.

Finto, D. 2016. *Your people shall be my people.* Minneapolis, Minnesota: Chosen.

Fulton, J. 2011. Tertullian's *Adversos Judaeos*: A Tale of Two Treatises. A thesis submitted to the Faculty of The Graduate School of Arts and Science in Candidacy for the degree of Master of Arts. The Department of Theology. Providence Collee, Providence, Rode Island.

Gilson, E. 1938. *Reason and revelation in the Middle Ages.* New York: Charles Scribner's Sons.

Kinzer, M.S. 2015. *Searching her own mystery. Nostra Aetate, the Jewish people, and the identity of the Church.* Eugene, Oregon: Cascade Books.

Krewson, W. L. 2017. *Jerome and the Jews: Innovative supersessionism.* Eugene Oregon: Wipf and Stock Publishers.

Lieu, J. 2006. "The Jewish matrix", p. 214-229. In *The Cambridge History of Christianity, Origins to Constantine,* Volume I. Edited by M. Mitchell and f. Young. Cambridge: Cambridge University Press.

Lustiger, Cardinal J.M. 2002. *The Promise.* Grand Rapids, Michigan: William B.E. Eerdmans Publishing Company.

Sedley, D. 1998. "Stoicism." In *The Routledge Encyclopedia of Philosophy,* Volume 9, p. 141-161, Edited by E. Craig. New York: Routledge.

Swenson, D. 2021. *A History of Judaism and Christianity: Towards healing of the Original Would of Division.* Blooming, IN: Westbow Press.

CHAPTER FIVE

Jewish Christian Relationships From the Early Medieval Era to the end of the Early Modern Period: Remembering, Repenting, and Reconciling

Orientation

This chapter is outlined by the author to assist the reader in understanding the relationship between the Christian Church (Western or Roman, Byzantine or Orthodox, and the Protestant extensions) and Judaism. Historians have divided Western history, from the time of Christ, into the following eras: The Apostolic Era (time of Jesus to the end of the first century), The Late Classical Era (100 CE to 475 CE), with the collapse of the Western Roman Empire in 475 CE, the Early Medieval Era (475 CE to 1050 CE), the Central Medieval Era (1050-1300), the Late Medieval period (1300-1500), the Early Modern Period (1500-1775), the Modern Era (1775-1970), and the current, the Post-Modern Era from about 1970 to the present. The first and second chapters covered the Apostolic and the Late Classical eras. This section will focus on the Medieval Era (475 CE to the end of the Early Modern Era (1775). The sixth chapter will be devoted to the Modern and Post-Modern Eras.

Several concepts are useful in this interpretation: the images of *Ecclesia et Synagoga*, secularization, and *Adversos Judaeos*. The latter two were both presented in the previous chapter on the division between Gentile believers in Jesus and Jewish believers in *Yeshua.*. The image of *Ecclesia et Synagoga* emerged in the late period of the Early Medieval Era but became prominent during the Central Medieval Era. This will be discussed when we outline our topic that focuses on that era.

A version of secularization are the terms to describe two kinds of Christian leadership: kenotic and secular. The kenotic type can be described as: being empty of self, not grasping for power, being like a slave or servant, exhibiting humility, waiting on others and washing their feet, not being boisterous, not crushing a broken person, not defensive, being last, meek and gentle. The secular leadership style is having a focus on self, being boastful of accomplishments, being served, grasping for power, defensive, authoritarian, self-interested, using force and valuing oneself above others (see Swenson, 2018). Two subsets of secular leadership are hierocracy and Caesaropapism. Hierocracy designates a political system of priests, virtuosos, or clerics have power and authority over secular authorities and non-sacred social/cultural systems. Caesaropapism indicates the subordination of priestly to secular powers. It is when a civil leader (king, prince, president) acts as a priest and has power over the sacred institutions (Swenson, 2018).

A thesis of this work is the church's adversarial relationship to the Jews is a consequence of secular leadership styles (either hierocratic or Caesaropapist). A subsequent thesis is that secular leadership style is concomitant with Anti-Semitic ideologies, values, actions and elements of *Adversos Judaeos*,

The Early Medieval Era: 475-1050 CE.

This era marks the convergence of Anti-Jewish attitudes of the Church Fathers, Councils, and Legislation that did give some legitimacy to Judaism, some protection, but an inferior status and negative images, exclusion, and discrimination. This is how Bat-Sheva (2008) begins his article on "Christians and Jews" during the period.

Jewish communities were well established throughout the East and the West in Greece, Palestine, North Africa, Egypt, Germany, Spain, Italy, Asia Minor, Syria, France and England. Two images capture this era which one might call: Protected but Inferior and Hostile and Excluded. The Bishop of Rome, Gregory the Great (540-604 CE) encouraged the first image while, the Bishop of Seville, Isidore (560-636 CE), represented the second. Gregory saw the Jews as guardians of the Scripture, they should be loved, not be forcibly converted, be protected, and be allowed to worship freely. A famous document, *Sicut Iudaeis*, was an important document that outlined these elements. This corresponds to the ideal type of the stranger within as presented by Simmel in *The First Wound of Division* is this text.

The second image, instituted by Isidore, closed the Patristic Era of declared hostility towards the Jews and considered them impervious to the call to conversion. He wrote a famous treatise called "On the Catholic Faith against the Jews" and, according to Bat-Sheva, it "stands at the head of Western polemical literature" (2008:170). His theology was a classic replacement kind of theology and is part of the *Adversos Judaeos* that was socially constructed in the first centuries of the Christian church as documented in the previous chapter.

This era was also witness to these two kinds of images. Among the Merovingians and the Carolingians of France, Jews were seen in a positive light. Louis the Pius (king of the Franks from 814–840) gave protection to the people, offered exemption from taxation and military duty and started a process of no persecution among the Emperors of the Holy Roman Empire until 1106. A specific example given by Bat-Sheva was a Bishop of Speyer. In 1084, this bishop gave land and a graveyard to the Jews, allowed them their own provost to arbitrate disputes, were free to engage in commerce and to defend themselves[50].

Towards the end of this era the images of *Ecclesia et Synagoga*, art forms, were socially constructed. One may theorize that *Synogoga* had a positive image because of the Carolingian social environment was conciliatory towards the Jewish minority in the Holy Roman Empire. A second reason is offered by Seiferth (1970). During this period and space, the *Concordia Veteris et Novi Testament* of the Carolingians was published. It was a text that accented the inner harmony of the Old and New Testaments, that the seeds of the Old were planted and

---

[50] Europe as a haven for the Jewish people was not universal and antisemitism was common among the Visigoths of Spain and in Byzantium. The Visigoth kings, supported by the Church, wanted to expel the Jews from the land, counselled forced conversions, enacted legal codes that were merciless to the Jews, and, after a council in 633, headed by Isidore, required children to be taken away from their parents and be raised as Catholics. Jews were not allowed to hold any kind of public office and were blamed for the economic and social crisis of the time. Life for the Jews in Byzantine were not better. The Emperor, Heraclitus (610–641 CE), used the Caesaropapist model of leadership and sought for complete uniformity of religion and demanded forced conversion among the Jewish people. After the Second Council of Nicaea, in 787, the emperors persecuted all and every dissident group, including Jews. Indeed, one can see how the genre, *Adversos Judaeos,* secular style leadership both of the hierocratic and Caesaropapist models, and the Jew as an outsider is illustrated by these historical data.

watered by the New Testament. Events in the history of Israel parallel the Early Church and what was hidden in the old was revealed in the new. There does not appear to be any indication of supersessionism or replacement theology.

An early relief of the *Ecclesia et Synagoga* in Darmstadt, created about 1050, showed *Ecclesia et Synogoga* as two beautiful women, one to the left of the crucified Christ and another to the right. Both were dressed well and majestic. The left woman was not domineering or supercilious towards the woman on the right. Both look up to Christ with erect banners. *Synogoga* was not humiliated nor was she blindfolded. These reliefs were illustrative of positive relationships between the two religions.

However, rapid changes happened in the artistic representation of the two women. More and more, the woman depicting *Ecclesia* became much more domineering and *Synogoga* stood humiliated and subservient to the other woman. Seiferth wrote it well: "The last vestiges of life still dormant in the Concordia had ushered in a new era in the relationship of the two religions. Humiliation, suppression and naked force became justified" (1980:69).

One of the most common art forms that illustrated the two women were the monumental statuaries. But there were many more, such as: in passion plays, ivory tablets, stain-glassed windows, church implements, manuscripts, and miniatures. The large monumental statuaries appear in Bamberg, Strasbourg, Freiburg, Trier, Magdeburg and in many other centers.

The following table, documented by Seiferth, illustrates these contrasts:

Table 5: 1: *Ecclesia et Synogoga* from 1050 to 1500

Approximate year and location	Ecclesia	Synogoga (Common: she is blindfolded)
Image I: 1100	Majestic and proud	Having a spear used to illustrate the killing of Christ

Table 5: 1: *Ecclesia et Synogoga* from 1050 to 1500

Approximate year and location	Ecclesia	Synogoga (Common: she is blindfolded)
Image II: Copenhagen	Ecclesia received the blood	Her spear is broken as she pierces the feet of Jesus
Image III; 1150: St Peter's in Salzburg	Majestic and proud	She wears a pointed hat which was distinctive clothing for Jews of the Medieval eras
Image IV: on a platter	-	These words were written: "Synogoga, since she rejects Christianity, deserves the abyss of hell. God's grace bestows heavenly joys on the toga of ecclesia."
Image V: In the portal of Notre Dame in Paris		Synagoga's head is surrounded by a serpent's coil
Image VI:		On her wrist, she has a money purse illustrative of avarice and usury
Image VII: 1215–1240: Cathedral in Chartes		A devil is depicted as shooting an arrow at her
Image VIII: (not known)		In a crucifixion scene, an angel pushes her away from the cross
Image VIII: in a crucifixion scene	She wears a crown, carries a chalice, has a banner over her head, has a halo, carrying a shield, a helmet and a banner	*Synagoga* leaves the scene, she wears a crown that has fallen, her eyes are blindfolded and she is in shackles
Image IX:	resolute	Weak with dangling arms

Table 5: 1: *Ecclesia et Synogoga* from 1050 to 1500

Approximate year and location	Ecclesia	Synogoga (Common: she is blindfolded)
Several other images:	Having an ascending rhythm	Having a descending rhythm
Several other images:	Older and wiser	Younger without wisdom
	Like the wise virgins of the Gospels	Like the foolish virgins of the Gospels
		Has a broken lance
		Is prepared for exile
		A seducing spirit flirts with her

The artistic representation of the two women went beyond the monumental statuaries to appear in drawings and carvings in Bibles. In these Bibles, *synagoga* appears as an old woman, dressed in black with torn banners and broken flagstaffs. In one drawing, Christ, *Ecclesia* and God are bent over her, scorning and smiting her. In another depiction, she lies on the ground and *Ecclesia* takes away from her the Ten Words Tablets of Moses. Moses and she must die and the Law is now gone. As she lies there, she dies and is lowered into a sarcophagus. This is a classic pictorial image of replacement theology.

Yet, in the midst of this darkness, there was some light. Sugar (1081-1151), an architect and the designer of the Cathedral of St. Denis (in the city of St. Denis in France), emphasized light and not darkness. He saw light as life-giving, creative, and divine. In this spirit, he returned to the original symbol of the two women as it appeared in Concordia. They appeared as figures on the windows of the chancel of the church. Both women were clothed in majestic robes and both crowned as queens. The future was foretold that at the end of times, there would be a mystical union between the two women.

Another major art form during this era was drama—especially

in the passion plays. In one version of the play, men dressed as Jews replaced the Roman soldiers. These plays highlighted the belief that the Jews were the killers of the Christ and that they committed deicide. The impact of the plays is documented by Seiferth who wrote:

> The passion plays reduced *Ecclesia et Synogoga* to figures in the realm of popular entertainment; the intrinsic distance from *Concordia,* the Christian theology that had taken shape in monumental statuary, could hardly have been greater. Religious art lost interest in the two female figures, one of which was already in the process of transformation into Mary the Queen of Heaven and Mother of God, while the other is dragged into the streets of antisemitism and banished to the underworld of demonic beings (1970:145–146).

The beginning of the sixteenth century saw the demise of this art form. It was a major teaching tool to an illiterate society. Its problem, however, was that it became imprinted on the imaginative nature of people which at any time could be sparked into violence. This is exactly what happened in the beginning of the following era that had accented the crusades.

The Central and Late Medieval Era: 1050-1500 CE.

This period during the Middle Ages commences with the emergence of the hierocratic-secular model of leadership. Inaugurated, according to Seiferth (1970), at the hands of Pope Gregory VII (1020-1085). He became a champion of clerical omnipotence and the social construction of Papal Monarchy. His goal was not only to dominate the church but also the state where the church resided. He advocated for a total supremacy of the papacy in both sacred and secular matters. Where did this imagery come from?

False documents. Medieval scholars have documented how two

forgeries, the *Donation of Constantine* and the *Pseudo-Isidore False Decretals,* hand no historical foundation and both were fabricated to augment the papal claim to dominance (Robinson, 2004). These were documents attributed to Popes of the Early Medieval Era but were found to be constructed in about 800 CE. The authors created a strong distinction between the clergy and the laity. The clergy, by virtue of their sacramental ordination, were superior to the laity. They were considered holy, and were of "heaven" while the laity were "of the earth." Flowing from the *Pseudo-Isidorian False Decretals,* the bishops were immune to lay challenges and were typified as: eyes of the Lord, pillars of the Church, chief priests, servants of God, thrones of God, gods, and saints. The canonists of the Church created an image of the Church based on these false Decretals. Laws, policies and teachings went beyond the Decretals to consider disobedience to authority as heresy and subject to excommunication. Because the Papacy and the higher clergy were "all powerful," they could coerce the laity into obedience through the system of "righteous persecution." For example, justification for the persecution of Jews.

Duffy (2009), a historian, fleshes out more of the primary themes of Papal Monarchy. The Bishop of Rome was the 'lord of the world." Many of them were embroiled in internecine and dynastic warfare, and some were violent and debauched. The Pope had so much power that he was able to subdue kings and emperors.

It is this era, the Central Medieval Era, that the crusades occurred[51]. Of all the atrocities inflicted on the Jews, the crusades take on a primary meaning to the Jewish consciousness. Why is this? The following will answer this question and Lloyd (2002) begins our conversation: "One immediate consequence [of the crusades] was the appalling violence unleashed against the Jews of northern France in the Rhineland, the first in a series of pogroms and other forms of antisemitism that would become closely associated with crusading activity in succeeding generations" (2002: 35-36).

---

[51] Officially, with some variation, there were 8 crusades against the Muslims of the Levant: 1096, 1146, 1189, 1198, 1227, 1239, 1249, 1270, and 1271-1272. Of all, the only one which had a military success was the first in 1096. All others failed.

Late in the eleventh century, and during this time of heightened Papal Monarchy, Urban II (1035-1099) launched the first crusade, eventually resulting in an army, against the Muslims in the Levant in the year 1096[52]. Besides this army, a second one was led by Emicho, a minor prince from Germany. Emicho's troops of 12,000, attacked Jews in cities along the Rhine, the Main and Danube rivers.

In 1096, Emicho (1034-1108), a prince in Germany, gathered together a motley number of French and German nobles, townsfolk and peasants, and knights to begin the long journey to Jerusalem. But their journey, according to Runciman (1951/1994 and (Seiferth, 1970), took a horrific turn against the Jews of the cities and towns of the Rhineland and Hungary.

They first came to Spier and twelve Jews were killed who refused to renounce their faith and embrace Christianity. Next, they travelled to Worms and, despite the protection of the bishop, 500 lost their lives. The next city to be targeted was Mainz. Many Jews found refuge in the archbishop's palace, but the mob broke through, burned the palace, and, eventually, 1000 Jews were massacred. Emicho continued to Cologne. The Jewish synagogue was burned, several Jews were slain but further excesses were prevented with the intervention of the local bishop.

He and his army, after much resistance, entered Hungary and continued his nefarious activities. In the Prague, they massacred more Jews. At this juncture, the army was split up. They came to Trier, Neuss, Wevelinghofen, Eller and Xanten. All along the way, more and more Jews lost their lives. Those continued to go through Hungary, met their match and the army was dispersed and many of the crusaders lost their lives. Emicho and his army was finally defeated and he returned to his home. Never did they go to Jerusalem.

Montgomery and O'Dell (2019) count the victims into the thousands. There is an estimate that before this first crusade, there were 20,000 Jews in the Rhineland. After this, it was reduced to

---

[52] The day was the ninth of Av or *Tisha B'Av*.

8000 people. No wonder Jews to this day are so suspect of the cross—at that time a symbol of death and destruction not of life and abundance.

Even more horrific was the siege of Jerusalem that started on the 7th of June and ended on the 15th of July. The siege army was massive: 12,000-foot soldiers and 1200 knights. They scaled the impressive walls and poured into the city. The army rushed through the streets and into the houses of Jews, Christians and Muslims and killed without any sense of mercy. None escaped the massacre (except the Muslim leader, Iftikhar, and his companions). Men, women and children alike were killed. The Jews ran to their main synagogue but lost their lives as the sacred building was burn down.

An eyewitness recalled the evil victory:

> Regardless of age and condition, they laid low, without distinction, every enemy encountered. Everywhere was a frightful carnage, everywhere lay heaps of severed heads, so that soon it was impossible to pass or to go from one place to the other except over the bodies of the slain. Already the leaders had forced their way to various routes almost to the centre of the city and wrought unspeakable slaughter as they advanced. A host of people followed in their train, athirst for the blood of the enemy and wholly intent on destruction (William of Tyre, 1994:93–94).

However, all was not bad news for the Jews in this Central Medieval Age. Lemor (2009) recorded that by the early 13th century, Jews were well integrated in their environments, their communities flourished, and relationships with Christians were by and large neighborly. They tended to live in cities and made a living in commerce and financial ventures. They benefited greatly benefited by the new urban setting. In addition, they were the only group allowed to live in Christian society.

Chazan (2004) adds to this observation. The original presence of the people, before the Central Medieval era, gave them many commercial opportunities. However, this changed as antisemitism provoked restrictions on the Jew to engage in commercial activity which eventually led them to money-lending. They played a significant role in the banking systems of Northern Europe particularly in England and France.

Chazan (2004) added that during the 12th century, in spite of more and more restrictions, a "Jewish renaissance" emerged. There was an enhanced emphasis on *Talmudic* studies that was championed by the erudite rabbinic scholar, Rashi (1040-1105). His commentary on the Babylonian *Talmud* is legendary. Other scholars focused on the highly respected Hebrew Bible. Chazon wrote: "In a variety of ways then, accurate understanding of the biblical legacy was a *sine qua non* for medieval Jewry" (2004:651). Education, so central to the Jewish mind, went beyond its focus on the Bible and the *Talmud* and became passionately interested in the Greek tradition in its Arabic formulations in search for metaphysical truth.

In part, this was due to the actions of Pope Calixtus II (1065-1124) who composed a treatise called *Constitutio pro Iudaeis* in 1120. In it, the Pope gave protection to the Jews and prohibited any abuse against them that violated their rights. They were not to be forcibly converted.

However, polices changed during the reign of Pope Innocent III (1160-1216) who summoned and lead the Fourth Lateran Council of 1215. The council mandated the following:

1. The Jews were restricted in charging interest rates on loans.
2. They were barred from public office.
3. If a Jew became a Christian, he or she was to renounce all things Jewish (such as prayers, following kosher dietary laws, and the celebration of feasts)[53].

---

[53] Thomas Aquinas, who we will meet shortly, considered this to be a mortal sin (1272-1273/1952:302). In the original writing, this referred to *Summa Theologica*, Part I of the Second Part, Questions 98-105.

4. Christians were mandated to have little social contact with Jews.

5. All Jews were required to have a specific dress code (which later became known as the infamous yellow badge).

6. They were required to live in separate quarters or ghettos that were often remote and unhygienic.

To this was added the background of *Adversos Judaeos* which provided the ideological setting of the codes and the many restrictions. Limor estimated that from the second century to the sixteenth century, there were some 240 documents published reflecting this genre (2009:139). Interesting there was an opposite response known as *Sefer Nizzahon Yashan* [54]written composed by some Jewish scholars to challenge the *Adversos Judaeos* documents.

It was mostly the educated clergy who would have access to this literature. However, the genre became known to the Christian populace in homilies, epistles, historical chronicles, artistic paintings and images, poetry, religious drama and, for the educated, commentaries on Scripture. Indeed, Limor acknowledged, that during the 12th century, the genre flourished.

Yet, in spite of the genre being so common, there were some friendly disputations between Christian and Jewish scholars. The central point of intellectual exchange was the meaning of Messiah. The Christians claimed that Jesus of Nazareth was the Messiah while the Jews argued that the Messiah was yet to come. Some literate Christians showed some interest in Hebrew and the Jewish traditions.

It was during this atmosphere that St. Thomas Aquinas (1225-1274 CE) wrote treatises on the Jews in his famous *Summa Theologica*, and his commentaries of Romans, Psalms, John, and Matthew. He did carry and believe in many of the *Adversos Judaeos* themes such as the Jews are prideful, obstinate, malicious, hypocritical, unjust,

---

[54] The (old) Book of Victory" is an anonymous 13th Century Jewish apologetic text originating in Germany.

violators of the Mosaic Law, faithless, ungrateful, avaricious, cruel, hard in heart and selfish (Hood, 1955/1999:60–65).

Aquinas's view of the Jews of his time was prefigured by his perception of them during Old Testament times. Hood enumerates his view: they were proud, obstinate, malicious, hypocritical, and unjust. They failed to assist the poor, their priests misinterpreted the scriptures, promulgated bad statutes and routinely violated the precepts of the Mosaic Law.

The saint-scholar also adhered to replacement theology. In his own words: 'The Jewish people were chosen by God that Christ might be born of them. Consequently, the entire state of that people had to be prophetic and figurative" (1272–1273/1952:305) [55]. What he is saying here is that the only value of the Jewish people before Christ was for Christianity and that they had no value in and of themselves. In other words, the people of Israel are not at all included in the divine plan of salvation. The argument against this has been outlined in the Introduction.

However, like Jerome and Augustine, he had much to admire about the Jews and Judaism. A common theme from the Patristic tradition was that all the Jews killed Jesus. Aquinas disagrees. Using his inherited Aristotelian logic, he categorized the first century Jew into the elite and the people. It was the elite who were hypocritical, filled with pride, and cruel who had Jesus killed. It was the ordinary Jew (including the marginalized) who more than likely to accept the Messianic claim of Jesus. It was not the Jew in general who orchestrated the crucifixion of Jesus but the Jewish elite. Indeed, it was God behind his death for the sake of humanity.

He admired them for it was the Jews alone of all peoples who understood God's true nature and that he was not to share worship of himself with the gods of the nations. In addition, their morality was far superior to the ethics of the ancient tribes because of the Mosaic Law. Knowing the way of life asked of them from *Adonai* enabled them to distinguish between right and wrong.

---

[55] Aquinas quoted Augustine who said the same thing.

From Aquinas' (1272-1273/1952) own hand, we learn more of this admiration. What he calls the "Old Law" of Judaism, he saw this law is good for it forbade all kinds of sin. It was given by the Good God and ministered by the angels to Moses. This Law and was not given to any other people groups but to the Jews. He wrote:" The Old Law was given to the Jewish people that it might be given a prerogative of holiness" (1952:244) and who "alone remained faithful to the worship of one God, while the others turned away to idolatry; hence the latter were unworthy to receive the Law, lest a holy thing should be given to dogs" (1272-1973/1952:242).

Regarding social policy and various violent actions against the Jews, Aquinas supported the "Jewish Cause." The blood libels and desecration of hosts are to be rejected as popular fanaticism, confiscation of Jewish property should be forbidden, and Jewish children in Christian homes are not be coerced into Baptism. Jewish rituals should be encouraged by the Jews themselves and commercial social interactions were allowed (but not personal social interactions). Forced conversions of adults are wrong and should be forbidden.

These two images of Jews by the saint-scholar led ambiguity and tension in his interpretation of the Mosaic Law and of Jews in general. Hood writes of him: "Throughout his *Treatise on the Old Law,* as well as in his analysis of Jewish history, there is an unacknowledged tension between one description of the Jews as holy and beloved of God, and another that depicts them as sinful and degraded" (1955/1995:61).

Hood does ask the question, in the context of Aquinas' support of the Jews, did he contribute to their persecution? Yes, but only indirectly. He reinforced the Church's tradition of mandating usury as evil and that all interest taking in loans was intrinsically unjust. This teaching was in contrast to the Jewish understanding of the legitimacy of usury as a legitimate way of making a living in an atmosphere of Jewish restrictions to many offices and means of livelihood. Limor wrote: "Over time this occupation became the distinguishing mark of the Jews" (2009:145).

Aquinas' teaching was written in the form of a long letter to a noble woman that was later published and widely distributed. Unknowingly, his teaching gave legitimacy to Christians to confiscate Jewish property. Some events were tragic. In 1290, Edward I of England used the pretext of Jewish usury to confiscate their property and to expel them from England. Philp IV of France, in 1306, did the same thing.

Hood wrote of the leaders of Europe:

> They accepted the stereotypes theologians such as Aquinas had helped develop and perpetuate images of Jews as dangerous infidels, as usurers, as Christ-killers and acted on them by seeking to remove the Jews from their midst. In the face of such pressures, the more tolerant teaching that Thomas Aquinas represented was simply irrelevant (1955/1995:111)

Contrasts and boundaries between Christians and Jews grew more and more intense through these eras. The people most responsible for the promulgation of the *Adversos Judaeos* and subsequent exclusion and violence were the mendicant religious orders: the Dominicans and the Franciscans. They became aware of the long traditions of Judaism in the *Talmudic* literature and the monks used them to delegitimize Judaism. They argued that the Jews of their time lived not from the Scriptures but from the *Talmud*. They considered that the *Talmud* was redolent with heresy and blasphemy. They broadcast these teaching that led to the burning of 24 cartloads of the volumes of the *Talmud* in 1242 in France.

It was during this era that antisemitic attitudes, values, codes became increasingly more and more discriminatory. With the rise of an urban culture and the ability of a few to make more and more money, there was an increase in the gap between the rich and the poor. Who was to blame? It was the Jew who was scapegoated. More and the Jew was demonized to be seen as satanic and maliciously evil. Trachtenberg (1943) expanded on the phenomenon.

The Jew was thought to be alien, antisocial (recall the accusation among the Ancient Egyptians, Greeks and Romans), anti-human and, even sub-human. The focus of antisemitism among the Patristics was textual directed to a literate people. The foci during these eras was imagery, carvings, drawings, chronicles, legends, poems, songs and morality plays. These carried with them vile epithets, accusations, curses and the definition of the Jew as evil. It was a common folk belief that "The devil and the Jew joined forces" (Trachtenberg, 1943:21).

Examples of the antichrist legends: the Jew with horns and tails and the Jew as sorcerer. The antichrist legends reversed the Jewish tradition of awaiting the Messiah as sent by *Adonai* to free his people. These legends imaged the Jewish messiah as the antichrist-one who would come and destroy Christianity. This antichrist is redolent with Jewish symbols: he would come from the tribe of Dan, be circumcised in Jerusalem, would rebuild the second temple, establish his throne in Jerusalem and proclaim himself as god. But, according to the Christian eschatological belief, Jesus Christ would send Michael the Archangel to destroy all the Jews. Trachtenberg noted that fear permeated the consciousness of the Medieval Christians for rumors of the antichrist were kept alive by the theologians and higher clergy.

Other images of the Jew consisted him as being horned, having a tail, and riding on a Billy Goat who was created by the devil. Along with this imagery were texts that accused the twelve tribes of Israel of afflicting pain and suffering on Jesus: beating him in the Garden of Olives, striking him on the cross, throwing lots for his clothing, scourging him, crowning him with thorns, slapping his face and offering him vinegar. Compare this to the Gospel accounts where there is no evidence that it was the Jews but, rather, it was the Roman soldiers who inflicted pain on Jesus.

The third major accusation was that the Jew was full of sorcery for he was thought to engage in magical powers, incantations, fortune telling, discovering hidden treasures, able to change the weather, the cursing of animals, astrology, alchemy, attributing magical powers to gems and creating amulets with nefarious powers within them. Behind all this was the devil.

The accusations of sorcery go back to the Patristic era and the Reformation: Chrysostom (357-407), Origin (185-254), and Luther (1483-1546). These accusations were not restricted to the illiterate public but were documented in ecclesial synods. For example, the Synod of Worchester, held in 1240 in England defined the Jew as a magician.

This era came to an end but the imagery of the Jew as a follower of Satan continued through the Early Modern Era alongside attacks against women who also were targeted as sorcerers. According to Morton and Dahms (2006), nearly 50,000 of them lost their lives in this other kind of madness–misogyny.

It was also during this era that accusations of blood libel emerged as a social construction of the masses. This consisted of belief that every year, a Christian child was kidnapped and was used as a blood sacrifice. In 1144 the first libel was promulgated in England. In Bois, France, 40 Jews were burned at the stake with no evidence of the body of the boy ever found.

A second type of libel was termed the Libel of the Host. This happened in Paris in 1290. Jews were accused of stealing consecrated wafers and then abusing them and desecrating them. Limor commented:

> Both libels, that of ritual murder and that of the Host, replicated the original and eternal sin of the Jews—the sin of the crucifixion of Jesus. According to the logic of the libels, the Jews murdered Jesus, even while knowing that he was the messiah, and they repeatedly murder his body (the Host) and his believers (the innocent Christian boys) because their faith commands them to do so (2009:147).

Limor noted that at least 180 blood libels[56] are known which have

---

[56] Montgomery and O'Dell, B. (2019) estimate 107 blood libels from 1144 to 1928 and 34 host desecrations from 1236 to 1836.

been levelled against the Jews and approximately 100 host desecration libels. As a result, many Jews lost their lives.

One is reminded of two myths from the ancient world and the Early Christian church. It was Melito (?-180) whom we met in Chapter Three, was the first to introduce into the *Adversos Judaeos* theme that the Jews killed Jesus and were guilty of deicide. We are also reminded of the Hellenistic myth of the sacrifice of a Gentile youth discussed in Chapter Three. What was the substance of this motif in the *Adversos Judaeos*? Cohen (1983) informs us.

Cohen traces this motif of the Jew being the killer of Jesus (and by implication, the killer of God). His focus was not if the Jews killed Jesus but what was the motive for the murder. He presents this: "While the *Adversos Judaeos* tradition flourished in the Latin West during the early Middle Ages, so did the opinion that the Jews killed Jesus in ignorance of his divinity and messiah-ship" (Cohen, 1983:8).

This is the baseline for changes from the 5th century to the 12th century. He begins by looking at Augustine (354- 430). In an exegesis of John 5:18 ("This answer made the Judeans all the more intent on killing Jesus, for not only was he breaking the Shabbat but also saying that God was his own father, he was claiming equality with God"). Augustine explained the hostility towards Jesus was ignorance. Thus, the killing of Jesus came out of Jewish ignorance but not out of evil intent[57]. This was the common belief until the central Medieval Era that formed the basis of tolerance toward the Jew. His presence was of value to Christianity as he was a "guardian" of the Hebrew Bible or in Christian terms, the Old Testament. Augustine instructed his audience the Christian message must be presented to the Jews in kindness and love even if they refuse to listen. They still have preserved and maintained in good faith the scripture and they must be tolerated but also, not to thrive.

Augustine's position was supported by Bishop Ambrose (340- 397), Gregory the Great (590-604) and Isidore of Seville (556-636).

---

[57] Another text from the New Testament came from the mouth of Jesus on the cross: "Father, forgive them; they do not understand what they are doing" (Luke 23:34) which substantiates this claim.

However, in the eight century, new interpretations, in contrast to the Augustinian one, began to emerge. Bede (672-735), and some Carolingian writers judged the Jewish conscience of evil intent. This opinion became dominant among the friars of the twelfth century.

A common theme emerged from the Biblical interpretation of the New Testament from Anselm of Laon (1050-1117), pseudo-Hugh of St Victor (1096-1141), Peter Lombard (1100-1160), Herveus of Bourg-Dieu (1080-1150), St. Thomas Aquinas (1225- 1274) and many Mendicant masters of Paris. Together they argued: the killing of Christ involved evil intent, being influenced by demons, envy, blindness, willfulness, hatred, and malice. Due to this new interpretation the Jews were to be expelled, excluded from occupations, and endured pogroms and massacres.

Because of these new accusations, the Jewish people were thought to believe more in the *Talmud*, believed to be filled with error and heresy, and not the Biblical text. Cohen commented:

> Heretical vis-a-via his own religious heritage, the medieval Jew merited no benign toleration. He was Christendom's most dangerous enemy, and his excessive evils ought not to be endured...it was not ignorance that induced them to spurn the teachings and ministry of Jesus, but that envy, depravity and guile had resulted in their blasphemy (1983:26).

Limor summed his perception of the radically constrained relationships between Jews and Christians with these words:

> In terms of the Jews, the myriad accusations created impenetrable boundaries between the two religions, and their destructive influence is apparent in the late Middle Ages and into the modern period (2009:148).

Emerging from this new definition flowed more accusations: blaming the Jews for fires, for poisoning wells after the Great Plague of 1348-1349; Jewish physicians poisoning their patients; ritual murders; and desecration of hosts. Frequently these accusations led to pogroms, exiles and killings. Trachtenberg documented that after the Great Plague, fanatical asceticism erupted in the form of the Flagellants. They stirred up anti-Jewish riots as they went from town to town.

Another part of the story of the strained and, sometimes, violent relationship between Jews and Christians was present towards the end of this era, the Renaissance. There is some evidence of a rapprochement. Dimont (1990:252-256) provides us with abundant evidence that during this period, the Jew was a vital part of the social order. He observed that Medieval Christian lived in a stratification prison consisting of clergy, royals, and peasants (First, Second and Third Estates). When the Medieval Christian became a member of one of the strata, he lived in it "from womb to tomb." The Jew, however was not part of these estates and Dimont names him as a Fourth Estate. Some members of the clergy and the royals welcomed the Jews into their orbit of life. Dimont offers us many examples of this welcome. The Italians viewed the Jews as learned people who were recipients of Jewish scholarship in philosophy, science, medicine and mathematics. Dimont wrote:

> The Jews participated in practically every profession, trade, and occupation existing in those centuries except farming. They were doctors, surgeons, scholars, poets, astronomers, druggists, finance ministers, royal ministers, silversmiths, goldsmiths, and scientific-instrumental designers. They were lion tamers, jugglers, mule sellers, soldiers, shoemakers, tailors, sailors, and peddlers. They were fur-cloth-and-silk merchants, pawnbrokers, spice dealers, weavers, importers, and exporters, and they engaged is such manual occupations as blacksmiths, metal workers, day laborers, playwrights, and stage directors, actors, dancers, painters, and sculptors....women, too, rose

to new positions of prominence who became doctors and bankers, went on stage, and worked for careers in singing, dancing, and acting (1990:256).

The most important contribution the Jews gave to Christendom was their accent on education during the whole of the Medieval Eras. All sons, regardless of social status, received education in the Bible, Hebrew, poetry, *Talmud*, philosophy and revelation, the logic of Aristotle, the elements of Euclid, arithmetic and Greek scientific literature. In addition to these contributions, Dimont explained that within this religious tradition were the roots of rational capitalism. Sombart (1911/2001) provided evidence for this.

The Early Modern Era

The year1500 ends with continued tragedies against the Jews in Europe through to the modern era. One of the worst tragedies occurred in the Iberian Peninsula and to the infamous Spanish Inquisition.

Jews had been present in the Hispanic Peninsula since the third century, when the land was a colony of the Roman Empire. In the early fifth century, during the era of the barbarian invasions, the Visigoths conquered Roman Spain. Jews had been active citizens of the Empire, but with the coming of the Visigoths and their conversion to Catholicism, anti-Jewish sentiment grew. Another change happened with the coming of the Muslim Moors in 711 CE, their fortunes turned for the better.

According to Kamen (1998), the primary source of this material, harmonious relationships existed among Christians, Jews, and Muslims for centuries. But beginning in the early part of the thirteenth century, the tide began to turn against the Muslims and the Jews. From this time until 1492, Christian princes led a militant Reconquest and finally won Hispania from Muslim dominance.

With the assent of the combined throne of Ferdinand (1452-1516) from Aragon and Isabella (1451-1504) from Castile, the Caesaropapist paradigm of "one faith, one god, one king, and one society" began to take hold. During their time (1492), the Jews were expelled and, under a later monarch, Phillip III (1578-1621), Muslim Moors suffered the same fate.

During the two previous centuries that many Jews (called *conversos*) and Muslims (*Moriscos*) converted to Christianity[58]. The *conversos* and the *Moriscos* were the primary targets of the Inquisition. In 1480 Jews and Muslims (called *Mudejares*) were separated from Christians into territories, called *aljama*[59], and the Vatican Inquisition was set up to investigate how authentic the conversions of these Jews and Muslims were. Thus, began the infamous Spanish Inquisition[60].

The central question for the officers of the Inquisition was the contrast between "Old Christians" (Christians from birth) and converts from Judaism and Islam. This Ecclesial institution, approved by the Vatican (Pope Sixtus IV [1471-1484] passed a Bull in 1478), is what Kamen calls an institutionalized "big lie," based on the belief that all the converts were secretly Jews or Muslims (1998:43). Sixtus IV had two or three priests appointed as inquisitors, with future appointments or dismissals to be made by the Spanish crown. Thus, began the Inquisition that continued until 1834, when a decree of suppression was given by Isabella II (1830-1904).

From the scholarship of Kamen (1998), the following themes capture the essence of this nefarious institution known throughout Europe as a travesty of human life. The institution itself consisted of priests educated in canon law as well as lay authorities, called *familiars*. It was a system where the institution itself had its own judges, jury, prosecutors and defence. Its most public event was called the *auto de*

---

[58] [51]Most of these conversions were forced indicative of what O'Dea and O'Dea (1983) call the dilemma of power: conversion through choice or coercion.

[59] A term of Arabic origin used in official document in Spain and Portugal to designate self-governing communities of Jews and Moors living under Christian Rule in the Iberian Peninsula (aljama).

[60] Montgomery and O'Dell (2019) numerate eight different inquisitions: Episcopal (under the authority of a local bishop) in 1184; Papal in 1231; Spanish from 1478-1834; Roman from 1542-1860; Goa from 1560-1820; Peruvian form 1570-1820; Mexican from 1571-1820 and the Maltese from 1574-1798.

fe (act of faith). This began in the middle of the sixteenth century and was an elaborate ceremony of shame and death for many accused of heterodoxy and heteropraxy (heresy of moral practice). Some of them consisted of Protestants, witches, bigamists, insincere *conversos* or *Morsicos*. and opponents to the Inquisition. Maximum public participation was organized with a procession of the accused with marks on their backs along with the inquisitors carrying crosses. Mass was celebrated in the morning and then the accused were displayed. Many confessed and were freed; those who did not were burned at a stake[61].

Much of the process was socially constructed. Many friends, neighbours, and family members used the system to avenge a wrongdoing or settle a score. This was predominantly false. For example, in Castile, 1,500 people were burned at the stake based on false testimony. This social construction was parallel with the tribunal itself. The accused was brought to the tribunal and imprisoned without recourse. Properties were confiscated. Witnesses were brought forward to prove the accusations. If the inquisitors found the accused guilty, he/she was given a chance to recant. Then the accused was punished in a variety of ways: wearing a *sanbenito* (clothing with a mark of guilt), condemned to death (about two percent of all found guilty), flogged, banished, or sent back to prison.

The evidence is striking that the secular image (both *Caesaropapist* and *hierocratic*) or ideal type of Christian leadership was most pronounced. We saw that the monarchs and the church officials imposed their power and beliefs on the *conversos*, the *Moriscos*, the Protestants, and illuminists. Even ordinary, middle–class, literate people experienced the imposition of the *Index of Forbidden Books*. Conflict was also used by ordinary people who used the Inquisition to avenge wrongs from friends, neighbours and kin. There is also evidence for sources of conflict within the consciousness of many who exhibited prejudice, xenophobia, fear and racism. Indeed, the Spanish

---

[61] Montgomery and O'Dell (2019) estimate that 113 events occurred in Spain, Portugal and their colonies from 1481-1850 CE.

Inquisition was another one of the darkest eras in Christian history. A question may be asked: what are the effects of the collective memory of the Inquisition upon the lives of the Spaniards in particular and the Christian Church in the world?

The scholar Bodiam (2007) summarizes of the study of the relationship between Christians and Jews in the Early Modern Era from 1500 to 1670. Because of centuries of exile and dispersion of Jews from their homelands, by 1500, only a few were left in the original Christian lands. They were permitted to live in three areas of Europe: in the Italian States, the Holy Roman Empire, and in Poland-Lithuania. Yet, even though they were allowed to live in these regions, their lives were precarious. Daily insecurity was a reality even though they had some basic protection. They continued to endure many restrictions and taxes and they were surrounded by images (like *Ecclesia et Synagogia*) that conveyed hostilities.

However, many changes were on the horizon. Bodiam wrote:

> By the second half of the sixteenth century, opportunities for interaction were opening up elsewhere. The decades between 1500 and 1600 saw a demographic shift that was to be the greatest significance for Christian-Jewish relations (2007:496).

It is to outline the elements of this shift that Bodiam documented the following. She begins with presenting the characteristics of one of the three places of settlement: Poland-Lithuania.

By 1660, this region was home to about 300,000 Jews who came there escaping persecution and exile from the more western parts of Europe. The geographical space housed various Christian traditions: Roman Catholic, Orthodox, Armenian, Lutheran and Calvinist. This indicates that there was not a sacred-political monopoly that did allow for social diversity. These Christians knew nothing of the Blood and Host libels common in the West. In 1624, the bishop of the diocese of Cheln forbade any violence against the Jewish people. The Jews were allowed to engage in a variety of social occupations and were not mandated to wear any kind of distinctive clothes. In this accepting environment, Jewish culture flourished.

Changes were happening in central and Western Europe. Throughout the centuries noted in this paper, gradual processes were occurring. Figure 5:1: depicts these changes and the causes for the changes:

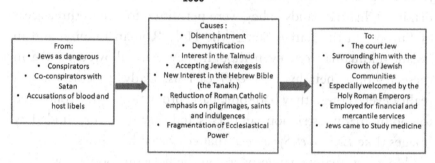

Figure 5: 1:Changes from 1500 to 1660

From:	Causes:	To:
• Jews as dangerous • Conspirators • Co-conspirators with Satan • Accusations of blood and host libels	• Disenchantment • Demystification • Interest in the Talmud • Accepting Jewish exegesis • New Interest in the Hebrew Bible (the Tanakh) • Reduction of Roman Catholic emphasis on pilgrimages, saints and indulgences • Fragmentation of Ecclesiastical Power	• The court Jew • Surrounding him with the Growth of Jewish Communities • Especially welcomed by the Holy Roman Emperors • Employed for financial and mercantile services • Jews came to Study medicine

These changes occurred primarily in the Holy Roman Empire, Venice in Italy and in the Netherlands. In the Holy Roman Empire (especially during the reign of the Hapsburgs), "Court Jew" was introduced who was most welcomed in the courts of the royals. Their primary contribution was to the financial and mercantile segments of Early Modern Europe. Vibrant and flourishing Jewish communities emerged about them. In Venice, they were welcomed and many Christians employed Jews to learn Hebrew, music, and dancing. At the University of Padua, Jews came to study medicine. In this city, although the Jews did live in a ghetto, many esteemed friars, priests and noblemen came to hear rabbis preach and experience the celebrations of the Jewish feasts.

Most significant, though, were the changes in the Low Countries, particularly the Netherlands. *Conversos* from Spain and Portugal were made welcome. A remarkable process happened: many of the *conversos* returned to their original Judaism but were not castigated for their return. The *conversos* merchant elite became involved in the Atlantic colonial trade from Antwerp and benefited greatly. Regulations were created that gave freedom to the Jews to live where they wanted, and to engage in commerce. They were not burdened by extra taxes.

"Throughout western Europe, and to some extent in central Europe as well, the sixteenth and seventeenth centuries saw an erosion of the barriers between Christians and Jews" (Bodiam, 2007:498). This was caused, in part, from three sets of innovations: Christian Hebraists, radical Christians and the descendants of the Iberian *conversos*.

Some Christian scholars became interested in the Hebrew language for it was thought that the Christian Bible could be better understood if the Hebrew Bible could be studied in its original language. Among some circles, it was thought that Hebrew was the original language spoken in the Garden of Eden. Utilizing both Christian and Jewish Kabbalah literature, these scholars sought to discover the common faith both of Judaism and Christianity.

The radical Christians (those outside the orbit of Roman Catholicism, Lutheranism and Calvinism) were keen on interpreting the Bible in its literary form and not the usual allegorical or symbolic sense. To do so, they were attracted to eschatology. The future of Israel had a vital place. There also emerged an interchange between Christian and Jewish scholars.

Beside the contribution of the Iberian exiled *conversos* of the Iberian Peninsula, trade, commerce and mercantilism, many of them engaged in learning more about their Rabbinic heritage. They used this new found knowledge to debate with Christian scholars and in doing so, stringent boundaries between the Christians and *conversos* began to melt. Menasseh ben Israel[62], a Portuguese rabbi was at the center of efforts to make rabbinic texts available to Christian readers. In Venice, another learned rabbi published a text with the aim to soften the Jewish hostility towards Christians. He took a conciliatory view towards the historical Jesus, the Trinity. Jesus could very well have been the messiah.

---

[62] He was a Kabbalist, writer, diplomat, printer and publisher. He also founded the first Hebrew printing press in Amsterdam in 1626 (Menasseh ben Israel).

LAMENTATIONS FOR THE SUFFERING THE FIRST-BORN SON OF GOD, ISRAEL AND PRAISES.

Antisemitism was ubiquitous and was common in Europe, Eastern Europe, Russia and the Americas. Many were the accusations against the Jews such as: being demonic, of the antichrist, sorcery, blood libels, libels of the host and Christ killers. Many synagogues and Jewish authored books were burned. Laws and codes restricted Jewish activity and livelihood were promulgated. Many suffered from the Spanish Inquisition and were frequently expelled from a host country. Children and adults were forced to convert, and many experienced the horror of pogroms. Mongomery and O'Dell (2019), in an extensive list of the persecution of Jews by Christians, documented from 500 CE to 1775 CE, there were approximately 550 cases of antisemitic crimes, expulsions, pogroms, massacres, the passing of restrictive laws, forced conversions, burnings, and exclusions. Much must be repented of.

Clearly, Jerusalem was again being crucified. And, along with her crucifixion, *Yehusa,* Messiah, suffered along with her and beside her. The following texts illustrate this suffering:

Of the Messiah: Who believes our report? To whom is the arm of *Adonai* revealed? For before him he grew up like a young plant, like a root out of dry ground. He was not well-formed or especially handsome; we saw him, but his appearance did not attract us. People despised and avoided him, a man of pains, well acquainted with illness. Like someone from whom people turn their vases, he was despised; we did not value him (Isaiah 53:1-3).

Of Jerusalem: How enveloped in darkness *Adonai,* in his anger, he made the daughter of Zion! He has thrown down from heaven to earth the splendor of

Israel, forgotten his footstool, the sanctuary on the day of his anger.

Without pity *Adonai* swallowed up all the dwelling of Jacob. In his wrath he broke down the strongholds of the daughter of Judea, them down to the ground, thus profaning the kingdom and its rulers.

In his fierce anger he cut off all the power of Israel, withdrew his protecting right hand at the approach of the enemy, and blazed up in Jacob like a flaming fire devouring everything around it.....Her gates have sunk into the ground; he destroyed and broke their bars. Her king and rulers are among the nations, there is no more *Torah*, and her prophets do not receive visions from *Adonai*. The leaders of the daughter of Zion sit on the ground in silence. They throw dust on their heads; they are wearing sackcloth. The unmarried women f Jerusalem lower their heads to the ground. My eyes are worn out from weeping, everything in me is churning; I am empty of emotion because of the wound to my people, because children and infants are fainting away in the streets of the city (Lamentations 2:1-3 and 9-11).

Central to the passage on Jerusalem is the pain, the suffering, the tragedy the writer is experiencing. Can we join Messiah and acclaim: "My eyes are worn out from weeping, everything is in me is churning, I am empty of emotion because of the wounds of my people?" Yes, so very many are the wounds of Israel through the centuries as they endured the many daggers of antisemitism at the hands of Christians.

On the other hand, there did appear signs of rapprochement between the two religious. This is a cause for rejoicing and celebration. Could this have been a seed that *Yeshua* planted and prayed on the eve of his death and is coming to be: "I pray not only for those, but also for those who will trust in me because of your word that they be one" (John 17:20)?

CONCLUSIONS

This review does not do justice to the complexities of Jewish-Christian relationships during the Medieval Eras and the Early Modern period. Several salient issues are prominent.

There were several cycles of receiving the Jew as an insider stranger (a contributor to Christendom) and an outsider stranger (being alien and a perceived threat to Christianity). Always, even in the best of times for these people, the Jewish constituency of Europe was in a precarious position. Tides changed with new political and clerical leaders. The Jew as an outsider was prominent. He was so frequently the victim of secular leadership in the form of hierocracy. His life was one of a life of persecutions, pogroms, expulsions, exiles, and death. Yes, the collective sin of Christianity beckons repentance, soliciting forgiveness from the Jews, and reconciliation. It is hard for an institution to admit wrong doing but it is imperative for this to happen.

The analogy of the lives of two kings of Israel aids us in understanding this mandate: David and Solomon. Both sinned in major ways: David, adultery and murder. David's sin was not only against Bathsheba and her husband, Uriyah but against *Adonai* who called the sin of David, through Nathan the prophet, a great blasphemy (II Samuel 12:14). Solomon's sin was idolatry: he married many foreign wives (forbidden by the Torah) and in doing so, followed their gods and goddesses. The book of Sirach is telling us of Solomon:

> But you laid your loins beside women, and through
> your body you were brought into subjection. You put
> stain upon your honor, and defiled your prosperity, so

that you brought wrath upon your children and they were grieved by your sin (Sirach 47:19-20).

Yet, the end is not this. Even though *Ecclesia* is likened to Solomon, there is still abundant hope and mercy. Sirach wrote again:

> But *Adonai* will never give up his mercy, nor cause any of his works to perish; he will never blot out the descendants of his chosen one, nor destroy the posterity of him who loved him; so he gave a remnant to Jacob, and to David a root of his stock (Sirach 47:22)

REFERENCES: CHAPTER FIVE

Aljama. https://en.wikipedia.org/wiki/Aljama

Aquinas, T. 1272-1273/1952. *Summa Theologica*, Part II. Volume 20, *The Great Books of the Western World*. Chicago: Encyclopedia Britannica, Inc.

Bat-Sheva, A. 2008. "Christians and Jews." In Volume Three, Early Medieval Christianities c. 600-c. 1100, *The Cambridge History of Christianity*, p. 159-177. Edited by T. Noble and J. Smith, Cambridge, UK: Cambridge University Press.

Bodiam, M. 2007. "Christianity and Judaism." In Volume Six, Christianity: Reform and Expansion, 1500-1660, *The Cambridge History of Christianity*, p. 485-503. Edited by R. Po-Chia Hsia. Cambridge, UK: Cambridge University Press.

Bowd, S. 2015. "Tales from Trent: The construction of 'Saint' Simon in manuscript and print, 1475-1517. *In The saint between manuscript and print: Italy 1400-1600*, p. 183-218. Edited by A.K. Frazier. Toronto: Toronto Centre for Reformation and Renaissance Studies.

Chazan, R. 2004. "The Jews in Europe and the Mediterranean basin." In Volume IV, *The new Cambridge Medieval history, c. 1024-c.1198 Part I*, p. 623- 657. Edited by D. Luscombe and Johnathan Riley-Smith, Cambridge, UK: Cambridge University Press.

Cohen, J. 1983. "The Jews as the killers of Christ in the Latin tradition, from Augustine to the Friars." *Traditio*, Volume 39: 1-27.

Gorny, G. and J. Rosikon. 2020. *Vatican Secret Archives: Unknown pages of Church History*. San Francisco, CA. Ignatius Press.

Duffy, E. 2009. *Saints and sinners: A history of the popes*. London: The Folio Society.

Dumont, M. 1990. *Jews, God and history*. Second Edition. New York: Signet Classics, a Division of Penguin Group.

Farmer, D. 2011. *Oxford Dictionary of the Saints.* Oxford, England: Oxford University Press.

Hellig, J. 2003. *The Holocaust and antisemitism.* One World Publications.

Hood, J. Y. B. 1955/1995. *Aquinas and the Jews.* Philadelphia: University of Pennsylvania Press.

Kamen, H. 1998. *The Spanish Inquisition.* London: The Folio Society.

Kohl, J. 2018. "A murder, a mummy, and a bust: The newly discovered portrait of Simon of Trent at the Getty." *Getty Research Journal*: 37-60.

Lazenby, F.D. 2003. "Simon of Trent." In *The new Catholic Encyclopedia. Second Edition,* Volume 13, edited by the Editorial Staff of the Catholic University of America Press, p. 133-134. Washington DC: The Catholic University of America Press.

Limor, O. 2009. "Christians and Jews." In Christianity in Western Europe, c. 1100-1500", *The Cambridge History of Christianity,* Volume Four, p. 135-148. Edited by M. Rubin and W. Simons, Cambridge, UK: Cambridge University Press.

Menasseh ben Israel. https://en.wikipedia.org/wiki/Menasseh_Ben_Israel

Montgomery, R. and B. O'Dell. 2019. *The List: Persecutions of Jews by Christians throughout history.* Israel: Root Source Press.

Morton, P. and V. Dahms 2006. *The trial of Temple Anneke.* Peterborough ON: Broadview Press.

O'Dea, T., and J. O'Dea 1983 (Second edition). *The sociology of religion.* Englewood Cliffs, NJ: Prentice Hall.

Po-Chia Hsia, R. (1992). *Trent 1475. Stories of a ritual trial.* New York: Yale University.

Robinson, I. 2004. "Reform and the Church, 1073-1122," In *The new Cambridge medieval history,* Volume IV, edited by D. Luscombe and J. Riley-Smith, p. 268-305. Cambridge: Cambridge University Press.

Runciman, S. 1951/1994. *A history of the crusades. Volume I: The first crusade and the Foundation of the Kingdom of Jerusalem.* London: The Folio Society.

Schafer, D. 1997. Judeophobia. *Attitudes towards the Jews in the Ancient World.* London: Harvest University Press.

Sefer Nizzahon Yashan https://en.wikipedia.org/wiki/Sefer_Nizzahon_Yashan

Seiferth, W. S. 1970. *Synagogue and Church in the Middle Ages.* Translated by L. Chadeayne and P. Gottwald. New York: Frederick Ungar Publishing Co.

Seth. https://en.wikipedia.org/wiki/Seth

Sombart, W. 1951. *The Jews and Modern Capitalism.* Glencoe, IL: The Free Press.

Trachtenberg, J. 1943. *The devil and the Jews: The Medieval conception of the Jew and its relationship to modern Antisemitism.* New York: Yale University Press.

Swenson, 2018. *A history of Western Christian Leadership. From the Apostolic Era to the Post-modern period.* Beau Bassin: Mauritius: Scholar's Press.

William of Tyre. 1994. "The capture of Jerusalem by the French Crusaders." In N. Cantor, Editor, *The Medieval Reader*, p. 93-94. New York: HarperColllins Publishers, Inc.

CHAPTER SIX

JUDAISM AND CHRISTIANITY IN THE MODERN ERA AND POST-MODERN ERAS EXCLUSIVE OF 1933-1945: REMEMBERING, REPENTING AND RECONCILING TOWARDS HEALING

ORIENTATION

As the reader will discover, antisemitism is not a phenomenon of the past but continues to the present age. The good news, however, is that there is a new hope for reconciliation and healing that has not happened in the nearly four millennia. This reconciliation is unique in the Post-Modern Era and could be a harbinger of a future union of Gentile and Jewish believers in what Paul calls a new humanity: "His (*Adonai*) purpose in this was, by restoring peace between us to create a single New Humanity out of the two of them, and through the cross, to reconcile them both to God in one body" (Ephesians 2:15–16).

The first part of this presentation is a history of Jewish and Christian relationships that covers the last part of the eighteen century until the present in what historians call the modern and post- modern eras. The second section is devoted to the coming of Messianic Judaism followed by a discussion on the healing of the ancient wound as a core reality of the Ecumenical movement of the disciples of Jesus.

JEWISH CHRISTIAN RELATIONS DURING THE MODERN AND POST-MODERN ERAS

This section of history covers the last part of the eighteen century until 1914 in the twentieth century. Dates are not exact but have been established by historians and scholars who have specialized in these eras.

The Modern Era: 1775-1914

One set of major historical events, revolutions throughout Europe, and one specific event, the Dreyfus Affair, capture this era. Using Carroll (2001) as the primary source, I will summarize how these two historical events to capture the continued spirit of antisemitism.

The primary locus of the political revolutions was in France and they occurred between 1789 through to the end of the nineteenth century—in the social construction of the republican system of government. The primary background was the movement away from the *Ancien Régime* [63], rooted in the political hierarchy of both secular and sacred realms. Also, the individual rights of men were ferociously advocated, philosophically, politically and legally.

Carroll traces the establishment of these revolutions and the accent on the rights of individual men to their Enlightenment philosophers of Benedict Spinoza (1632-1677)[64], Voltaire (1694-1778) and Karl Marx (1818-1883). Spinoza, a Jew, and a citizen of Holland offered a radically new concept of the human condition but paid dearly for his views. He was excommunicated by the Amsterdam synagogue, rejected by the Calvinist Synod of North Holland, investigated by the Catholic Inquisition of Spain, and, for a time, banished by the civil authorities of Amsterdam.

Spinoza's key tenet was religious tolerance that was based on the equality of sects. He accented human rights, a constitutional polity, that a society should not be based on a religious ethic but, rather, a secular one. He became known later as the "Father of Modernism," and a philosopher of revolution.

Voltaire, not a Jew, but a former Roman Catholic, devoted himself to justice for all and attacked the Catholic Church for its inhumane actions against the Jews during the Inquisition. His attack went further, to religion itself, which included Judaism. He is pivotal in the new social construction of antisemitism that focused in the "innate character of the Jew" who was, by nature, inferior to others. He was the "father of secular antisemitism" that jettisoned Christian

---

[63] The political and social system of the Kingdom of France from the Late Middle (*circa* 15th century) until 1789, when hereditary monarchy and the feudal system of the French nobility were abolished by the French Revolution. The term is occasionally used to refer to the similar feudal systems of the time elsewhere in Europe (*Ancien Régime*).

[64] Spinoza was the son of a *conversos* from Portugal. Recall from the article on the Early Modern Era, that Holland was a refuge to many Jews who were exiled from Spain and Portugal. There they had relative freedom to practice their Judaism and to live peacefully.

antisemitism (with the focus on Blood libels and deicide) to be replaced "by a new, international, secular, anti-Jewish rhetoric in the name of European culture rather than in religion" (Carroll, 2001:423).

As Spinoza and Voltaire focused on human rights and constitutional polity, Karl Marx accented revolution. He was a son of a long line of righteous rabbis but renounced his Jewishness to the point of being antisemitic. He wrote an essay entitled "On the Jewish Question" in 1843. In this article, he called *Yahweh* as "nothing but the personified selfishness of the Israelite people" and "Money is the jealous god of Israel, beside which no other god may exist" (quoted by Carroll, 2001:429-431). He went further and argued:

- The basis of Judaism is self-interest.
- The god of Israel is money.
- The Jew is antisocial.
- The basis of Capitalism is the Jewish ethic. The figure of the Jew and the figure of the capitalist is identical. He is the archetype of the financier.
- He is an embodiment of materialism.

Marx's response to capitalism and religion (which includes Judaism) is revolution. He became the living embodiment of revolution and even though he renounced his Jewishness, he was known as *the Jew*. By a twist of fate, the Jew now became identified as the revolutionary and an enemy of Europe and the Roman Catholic Church. New secular adjectives of the Jew were established in this century: the Jew as a financier (capitalist), a revolutionary and a Communist. This fueled the already Christian ethic of antisemitism and added a secular dimension to it.

For a short period of time, the Papacy, under the leadership of Pius IX (1792-1878) and Pope from 1846-1878), initiated positive relationships with the Jews. He gave amnesty for political prisoners and ordered the dismantling of the walls in Rome of the Jewish ghetto. But this was short lived. The revolution of 1848 struck across many cities of Europe. Revolutionaries, consisted of workers, the urban poor and the disgruntled. Pius IX, along with Austria, Spain, and France rallied against the revolutionaries and "Revolutionaries were persecuted, Jews thrown back in the Ghetto-violent regulations against the Jews followed" (Carroll, 2001:442). Now a more permanent accusation against the Jew was reinforced-the Jew is a revolutionary!

Following this construction of the walls, a pattern existed throughout the nineteenth century: from liberation to servitude in the Ghetto: 1808 and 1816, 1830 and 1831, 1848 and 1849. In one case, living within the Ghetto, in 1867, was deadly. Just outside the Vatican property, 10,000 Jews lived in poverty, with poor hygiene, and in desperate situations. Cholera hit and half of the population died. Several years later, matters for them changed in 1870 with the creation of the modern state of Italy. This secular model (not Christian) freed the Jew from the Ghetto. He would be a citizen of Italy along with others in this new society and have a home and country of his own—being treated not as a Jew but as a human being with rights.

It was also true in this century of revolutions that some new accusations were created against the Jew not on sacred or secular grounds but on biology, the pseudoscience of biogenics. This came to be at the core of Nazi Socialism. The false belief that the Germans were of the Aryan race and the Jews of an inferior race. Having no basis in reality, the racial identity of the Germans and the Jews turned for the worst. It was the primary category of who a Jew was contingent on ancestry.

The second phenomenon that resulted in a renewal of both sacred and secular antisemitism became known in history as the Dreyfus Affair (l'affaire Dreyfus). It revolved around a gifted Jew, a Captain in the Army of the French Third Republic (1870-1940), Alfred Dreyfus (1859-1935), who was appointed as a Captain in 1892. The story begins with a false accusation, in a one-page document, against him that he spied for Germany. He was arrested and when this was made public, volumes of anti-Jewish literature erupted. He was tried, found guilty and sent to a prison island near French Guiana. Sometime later, one of his supporters uncovered a document matching the original that was written not by Dreyfus but another officer. Dreyfus was denied a retrial. In 1899, a second trial was held but did not acquit him. A superior court, in 1906, did exonerate him and he was freed. However, Jews were not freed of hatred, prejudice and rejection as rounds of antisemitic literature began to be circulated.

In 1898, the Vatican newspaper, *L'Observatore Romano* wrote of the Jews: "Jewry can no longer be excused or rehabilitated; the Jew has the largest share of wealth; he holds the credit of States in his hands; he influences public ministries, the civil service, the armies, the universities and controls the press."

A focus of this literature was in France. Hundreds and maybe thousands of Catholic priests attended antisemitic congresses, gave teachings and enflamed Catholic congregations in many parts of France. Common stereotypes were invoked that harbor back to some of the *Adversos Judaeos* genre of the Medieval Eras: killer of Christ, ritual murderer, traitor and more recently, revolutionary and financier. A book published in 1886 by Drumont (1844-1917) imaged the Jew as: Money-grabbing, greedy, scheming, subtle, by nature a merchant, and does everything to deceive his fellow citizen and a parasite in the middle of civilization" (Carroll 2001:462). The stereotypes had a daily voice in a newspaper called La Croix (the Cross), owned and operated by the Assumptions' Order. Some of the publications accused the Jews of being responsible for the secularization of French society that consisted of curtailing Catholic education, taking down crucifixes in public spaces, and restrictions on clergy. It was during the years of *l'affaire Dreyfus* that this paper was the most widely read Catholic publication and it counted more than twenty-five thousand Catholic clergy among its readers.

Additional stereotypes, prejudices and discriminations occurred among the Frist-Born son, Israel, and known from ancient times to the present as the Jews. Montgomery and O'Dell (2019) provide us with abundant evidence of antisemitism during the nineteenth century. Three major explosions happened during this time: in

Austria (1843), United States (1862 in Tennessee, Mississippi and Kentucky) and Moscow, Russia in 1891-1892). We have already met the blood libel accusations in a previous chapter. During the 100 years of the 19th century, there were 27 such accusations and one host desecration accusation. In 1806, Augustin Barruel (1741-1820), a Jesuit priest, published papers arguing that the Jews were responsible for the French Revolution.

Napoleon (1769-1821) did much to emancipate the Jews in Italy but in 1808, issued a decree that all debts with the Jews were annulled (which nearly caused the Jewish Community to collapse), that they were to be restricted in migration and were required to have their Jewish names changed to French. Many states granted more and more freedoms to the Jews but, in 1819, riots erupted against the pattern in Bavaria, Denmark and Poland. In the Greek war of independence in 1821, the rebels killed 5,000 Jews accused of various infractions.

During this century, there were several publications defending antisemitism. Joseph Comte de Gobineau (1816-1882) wrote an essay and argued that the Aryan race is superior to all other races and that Adam was the ancestor of the white race. One such publication was written by Hermann Goedsche (1815-1878), a classic piece of literature of conspiracy theory. In it he claims that every year a council of Jews meets to plan for world domination through the acquisition of landed property, the transformation of craftsmen into industrial workers, the infiltration into high public offices and to control the press.

Much more vitriolic is a German Lutheran pastor and theologian, Adolf Stoecker (1835-1901) who added much more to the conspiracy theory: "They control the arteries of money banking, and trade; they dominate the press and they are flooding the institutions of higher learning. But this development is ominous we are moving towards the point when public opinion will be completely dominated and labour by the Jews" (quoted in Montgomery and O'Dell, 2019:368). He further argued that the Jews were responsible for all of Germany's problems and called them parasites, leeches, and an alien drop in our (the German) blood. Not only is his language vitriolic but deadly:

"The ancient contradiction between Aryans and the Semites, can only end with the extermination of one of them and it was the responsibility of the Germanentum to settle once and for all with the Semites" (2019:367).

Heinrich von Tretschke (1834-1896), a German historian, political writer, wrote of the Jew having no significant place in the German (Aryan) state, having a disintegrating influence and is of no more use to the world. Eugen Duhring (1833-1921) continued this argument saying that the Jews have not contributed anything to modern life and culture: no mathematics, no natural sciences, no logic, no scientific understanding of political forms and have left nothing but a self-seeking religion.

Antisemitism was also reflected in collective actions. In 1880, leading German anti-Semites wrote a petition that was signed by 265,000 Germans. It was given to the Prussian House of Deputies in 1880 and to Bismarck in 1881 who disregarded it. The petition consisted of four elements: the immigration of alien Jews be at least limited if not prevented; that the Jews should be excluded from all positions of authority and the judiciary; that only Christian doctrine should be taught and that a special census be instituted.

Several actions against the Jews brought the century to a close. A pogrom in Russia in 1884, expulsions from Russia between 1891-1892 involving 14,000 Jewish families, a ritual murder trial in Greece in 1891, and Jews blamed for cholera[65].

I offer a summary of the various stereotypes and accusations against the Jews that were common during this era: the major themes of *Adversos Judaeos* genre; inferior by nature in contrast to the superior Aryan; unsocial, a revolutionary, a capitalist, Jewry can no longer be excused or rehabilitated, the Jew has the largest share of wealth in the world, he holds the credit of nations in his hands, he influences public ministries such as the civil service, the armies, the universities and the press and a financier. All based on misinformation, prejudice,

---

[65] Montgomery and O'Dell (2019) counted a total of 167 expulsions from 139 BCE to 1945 CE.

irrational thinking and deep feelings of hatred. Indeed, the Jew is an outsider stranger who is not welcome, judged and condemned.

LAMENTATIONS FOR THE SUFFERING THE FIRST- BORN SON OF GOD, ISRAEL.

With the coming of the enlightenment also came the modern or secular version of antisemitism. As indicated above, one such "enlightened philosopher", Voltaire believed the Jew, by nature, to be of an inferior race. Historians believe Voltaire to be the "Father of "secular antisemitism." One of his successor enlightenment philosophers, Karl Marx, expanded on this secular version of antisemitism. He argued that the basis of Judaism is self-interest, that the god of Israel was money, and that the Jew is antisocial[66]. In Marx's monumental critique of capitalism, he argued that its basic ethic is Judaism. The Jew now had a new stereotype the archetype capitalist.

Opponents to the new revolutionary spirit added further stereotypes: the Jew as a revolutionary and a Communist. This fueled the religious antisemitism with Papal support of the Jewish ghetto and the authors of official documents of the Vatican claiming the Jew as being wealthy at the expense of others, is the holder of State funds, interferes with public ministries, the civil service, the armies, the press and the universities.

Laws restricting Jewish presence, expulsions, continuations of elements of the Spanish Inquisition, accusations of being responsible for cholera, blood libels, the practice of pogroms and restrictions of immigration from one country to another (Montgomery and O'Dell, 2019).

All of this was deadly to the Jewish people. One is invited can stand for Israel as did Elisha who wept over what the King of Aram was to inflict on Israel: "Because I know the disasters you will bring on the people of Israel. He will set their fortresses on fire, you will kill their young men with the sword, and you will dash their little

---

[66] As shown in Chapter Three, this was the image of the Jew in Ancient times.

ones to pieces and rip their pregnant women apart" (II Kings 8:12). This is likened to the suffering of Israel in this era

> **Of Jerusalem** All our adversaries open their mouths to jeer at us. Panic and pitfall have come upon us, desolation and destruction. My eyes stream with rivers of water over the destruction of the daughter of my people. My eyes sweep ceaselessly there is no respite, until *Adonai* looks down and sees from heaven. My eyes make me so upset at the fate of the women in my city. Those who are my enemies for no reason hunted me down like a bird. They forced me alive into a pit and threw stones on me. Water rose above my head I thought 'I am finished'.

> Even jackals bare their breasts in order to nurse their young, but the daughters of my people have become as cruel as ostriches in the desert. The tongue of the baby at the breast sticks to the mouth roof of its mouth from thirst young children are begging for bread but no one is giving them any people who want to hit only the best are like dying in the streets those who are raised wearing purple are clawing at piles of garbage (Lamentations 3:46-54 and 4:3-5).

And Messiah, *Yeshua,* joins himself in this intense suffering:

> **Of the Messiah:** In fact, it was our diseases he bore, our pains from when he suffered; Yet we regarded him as punished, stricken and afflicted by God. But he was a wounded because of our crimes, crushed because of our sins; the discipline that makes us whole fall on him and by his bruises we are healed. We all, like sheep, went astray; we turned each one of us to his own way; yet *Adonai* laid on him the guilt of all of

us. Though mistreated he was submissive-- he did not open his mouth. Like a lamb led to be slaughtered, like a sheep silent before its shearers, he did not open his mouth. After forcible arrest in sentences he was taken away; and none of his generation protested his being cut off from the land of the living for the crimes of my people, who deserved the punishment themselves he was given a grave among the wicked in his death he was with us rich man (Isaiah 53:4-9).

One may have thought that as Western Civilization moved more and more from Christianity that antisemitism would also be moved away from the social actions of humans. Not so. Christian antisemitism has been fundamentally replaced by secular antisemitism. There is a call on Christians not only to repent of and renounce Christian antisemitism but also to vicariously repent of this sin committed by our fellow citizens.

The Modern and Post-Modern Era between 1945 and 2000.

Langton (2006) has informed us of the relationships between Jews and Christians during the years between 1914 and 2000. Why these years? It is because of two major events that occurred during this time; the attempt to destroy European Jewry via the Nazi Holocaust (*Shoah*) of 1933-1945 and the establishment of the state of Israel in 1948. Both these events had a profound effect on the relationships between the two Abrahamic faiths.

Entering this era, both Christianity and Judaism were divided in many ways. Christianity with its thousands of variations and Judaism with its traditions: Ultra-Orthodoxy, Orthodoxy, Conservative, Reform, Liberal and Progressive. To write of Judaism, Langton argues, is to include all the categories of the faith. Yet, there is a basic commonality to the horrid realities of the *Shoah* and the creation of the State of Israel.

The sources of the *Shoah* were documented in Chapter Seven of this document. It was argued that the factors cannot be simply linked to Christian antisemitism or the genre, *Adversos Judaeos*. They are not sufficient causes but are necessary causes. Thus, all Christians are in some way responsible for the horror of the *Shoah*. Such literary pieces reinforced the racist propaganda and made it possible for professing Christians to partake directly as death camp staff and mobile killing squads along with the many bureaucrats and technocrats involved in the genocide. Ordinary Europeans of peasant stock did not object to the confiscation of Jewish property for they believed that the Jews were being punished for deicide.

It will be presented that in Chapter Six that Church officials were also implicated. The Catholic Church, under the leadership of Pope Pius XII (1876-1958), in a Christian message of 1942, spoke in general terms of many people were being killed but did not mention the Nazis or the Jews by name. The newly formed German Evangelical church as a federation of Lutheran, Reformed, and United territorial churches was host to an antisemitic right winged faction. This faction resurrected the Marcion heresy[67] of the second century arguing that the Old Testament and Paul's letters should be expunged from the canon on the grounds that they were Jewish. This faction also supported the myth of Aryan racial supremacy. Going against the great tide of Nazism, the German pastor, Dietrich Bonhoeffer (1906-1945), protested against the treatment of the Jews and was executed in 1945.

In the aftermath of the *Shoah*, a new hope for the Jewish people was created. Both Jewish and Christian Zionists had been active before WWII. A major political event occurred in 1917 in the form of the British Balfour Declaration. It stated, in part, that the Government of Great Britain supported "the establishment in Palestine of a natural home for the Jewish people" (Langton, 2006:486)[68]. However,

---

[67] See the chapter in this text called "The First Wound of Division-The Separation of Gentile Believers in Jesus from the Jewish Believers in *Yeshua*: Remembering, Repenting and Reconciling."

[68] The declaration took the form of an open letter from Arthur Balfour (1848-1930, a British Statesman and Prime Minister from 1902-1905) to Lord Rothschild,

there were opponents. In 1904, Pope Pius X (1835-1914) informed Theodor Herzel (1860-1904), that the Catholic Church would not support the Jews in the acquisition of the land of Israel considered to be the land of the Christians because of Jesus. Further, the Vatican refused to recognize Israel as a legitimate state and it was not until 1993 that the Vatican did finally approve.

There were also signs of hope for the Jews, the state of Israel and Christianity. During the 1970s, throughout Western Europe and the United States, Jewish institutions were created that would remember the *Shoah*. The twentieth century was witness to official church pronouncements that Langton (2006) saw as a tectonic shift in the history of Jewish-Christian relations. In 1947, and inter-denominational statement was issued in Seelisberg, Switzerland, condemning antisemitism and rejection of the accusation of Jewish deicide. Later Protestant leaders accented the importance of the Jewish roots of the Christian faith, the recognition of Christian co-responsibility for the *Shoah* and Jewish self-definition, Israel's permanent divine election, Israel as a legitimate state, and the rejection of replacement theology and supersessionism.

Although the Catholic Church was slow to accepting Israel as a legitimate state, it removed a derogatory prayer against the Jews the Good Friday liturgy in 1959 and the proclamation of *Nostra aetate* of the Vatican Council II.

It is during this time that Pope John Paul II (1920-2005) made significant contributions to the relationship between the two traditions. According to Lustiger (2007), (a Jew) saw that some of the rapprochement occurred when John Paul II visited the great synagogue of Rome, went to Israel and prayed at the Western Wall (*Ha Kotel*). He counsels Christians to discover the Jewish people by looking at them and not just the Bible and the history of the past two millennia. Lustiger wrote: "For this reflection understands human history in the light of Revelation. It invites us to understand the meaning for all people, of the Election of the Jewish people.

November 2, 1917.

Misunderstanding or renouncing this Election would deprive the history of salvation that founds the Christian faith—perhaps all human history as well—of its meanings" (2007:141).

This period was also witness to a renewed interest in Judaism and the relationships between the New Testament and the Old Testament. Some scholars focused on The Church of the Circumcision, the Nazarenes, and the Messianic Communities of the first century. New links were being discovered as there began dialogues between Christian and Jewish scholars. Langton summarizes this period with the following conclusion:

> In terms of Jewish–Christian relations the twentieth century has seen an attempt by increasing numbers of Christian individuals and institutions to recognize the legitimacy and vitality of post-biblical Judaism and to conform their traditional stereotypes and theological informed prejudices. The unique relationship between the Jewish and Christian faith communities as a result of their shared origins, the resulting prejudices and difficulties in relating theology to one another, and the communities' long memories of the often traumatic history of the interaction of their peoples, means that the relationship between Christianity and the *Jewish other* remains fragile (2006:493).

Lustiger (2007) presented some challenging musings on the future. Israel and the Jewish people are discovering their way while Christians reflect how they can enjoy the rich sap of Israel (Romans 11: 17). He counselled his readers to reflect upon the place of Israel within Christian thought and her special place in her Election which was a permanent. He himself mediated the establishment of steady and trustful relationships between those who represented the Catholic hierarchy and the leaders of the most zealous of Jewish orthodoxy. There is a need to restore mutual confidence in a dialogue that had never taken place in former centuries but is possible now.

One commonality between the two is faith, prayer, Scripture and a common mission toward humanity. Lustiger concluded his book with this:

> The new millennium does open up for the future new and so far, unhoped-for possibilities of "dialogue." This may mean "dispute or contradiction," or "disagreement," depending on the translation of the adjective *antilegomenos* (speak against) in Luke 2:34. But the word has been deprived of its polemical dimension, and rather remains a goal that turns our eyes toward the ultimate horizon of human history, as hope for the Kingdom of God fills our hearts (2007:177).

Two major phenomena happened in regard to reconciliation between Jews and Christians and restoration of the people of Israel during the latter part of the 19th century and throughout the 20th into the 21st century: Zionism and Messianic Judaism. From the scholarship of Kinzer (2018), I will discuss Zionism and Messianic Judaism. To Messianic Judaism, I will refer to several other Messianic Jewish scholars.

ZIONISM

Zionism is to be part of what Kinzer believes to be the whole of the message of the kingdom that necessarily includes Israel, the Jewish people and the land of Israel. Karesh and Hurvitz (2008) define it as: "A Jewish nationalist movement born in the late 19th century, a period of rising nationalistic feelings throughout the world. Its founders believed in a Jewish return to a permanent, independent homeland in Israel" (2008:570-5 71). Kinzer (2018) adds that it is part of the divine plan in the eschatological restoration of Jewish life in the land of Israel as an essential fruit of the resurrection of Israel's messianic king, *Yeshua*.

The Emeritus Rabbi expands this to include:

1. The catalyst to the establishment of the State of Israel was the *Shoah* and the return to the land as a precedent to the restoration of Israel, the creation of a new heaven and new earth and the return of the Messiah.
2. The *Shoah* is to be compared to the passion and death of Messiah *Yeshua* and his identification with *Shoah's* victims.
3. The establishment of the State of Israel is the beginning of or the first signs of a resurrected Jerusalem just as Messiah rose from the dead.

All of this is to be believed as part of a global, universal plan of *Adonai* that is His action in human affairs for the final coming of the kingdom of God on earth with Yeshua reigning as King from Mount Zion.

MESSIANIC JUDAISM

Scholars have debated for some time now how long did Jewish believers in *Yeshua* continue during the first millennium of the Christian Church. One set of authors claim that Messianic Judaism ceased to exist after the first Jewish war against Rome in 70 CE. Others contend that the final demise of the faith happened after the second Jewish war, the revolt of *Bar Kokhba* in 135 CE. These dates have now been disputed due to archeological findings of the Church of the Circumcision that testify to the fact of a continued presence for many centuries.

Mancini (1970) provides us with evidence that the faith continued well into the fifth century. Finegan (1969) commented on an archeological finding in a village in Northern Israel the remains of a house that had a cross surrounded by scrolls which depicted the cosmic ladder and the coming of the millennium. Dates given were between 427 and 614 CE. Finnegan argued that neither 70 nor 135 CE mark the end of the Church of Jewish origin. In regions outside of cities and towns the Church of the Circumcision remained active for more than 200 years.

However, silence continued for many centuries. The first breakthrough of this silence occurred during the movement of renewal called Pietism among Lutherans and Calvinists. According to Rudolph (2013), Count Nikolaus Ludwig von Zinzendorf established a Pietist Brethren Community in Germany in 1735. *Yeshua*-believing Jews were encouraged to live their Jewish life and identity. In the late 19th and early 20th century, Jewish missionary societies emerged out of the United Kingdom churches which encouraged Jews to become Christians and to join with the Protestant churches. Some converts, however, did not want to assimilate but to retain their Jewish history and identity. They called themselves Messianic Jews. In December of 1910, a journal was published called *The Messianic Jew*. It was devoted to a new way of living the life of *Yeshua* by living within the orbit of Judaism and embracing the Torah-observant life.

Earlier, Messianic Judaism also has its origins in South Russia. It began at the hands of Joseph Rabinowitz (1837-1899). In 1882, he journeyed to Palestine (now the land of Israel). He found himself in Jerusalem on the Mount of Olives and *Yeshua* appeared to him as Yeshua of Nazareth, King of the Jews, Messiah of Israel and Son of God. He accepted Him in faith and began to experience him as: Son of Joseph, the prophet (foretold in Deuteronomy 18:15-19), Son of David, Son of Jesse, King, the Lord, mighty God, Prince of Peace, and the man (Kjaer-Hansen 1988:121). She adds: "Yeshua the Nazarene was crucified for our sins; for this Yeshua is not a God who cannot save, for he is mighty to save (p.121).

Rabinowitz created a liturgy that included the readings of the Torah and the Prophets. Both are central to mainstream Judaism. He also added readings from the New Testament. The liturgy was housed in a building called "The Somerville Memorial Hall" that began to be built in 1890. It was constructed to hold 150 members. Monies from the Midway Mission Society were used to construct two plaques in front, a Torah Scroll and the Gospel Book. The text was read in Hebrew and in Russian. Several rituals stand out as central to Rabinowitz: the keeping of Shabbat, the celebration of the Jewish feasts and circumcision. There are two sacraments, baptism, and the Lord's supper. The existence of the Somerville Memorial Hall also fits well with the organization feature of the Israelites of the New Covenant.

The sad part of the congregation and its movement, though, Rabinowitz did not have a successor and the congregation and movement dissolved. What really is impressive is what he established in rural Russia is part of the modern Messianic Movement. His heritage is striking:

- Focus on the Lord Yeshua.
- Yeshua is divine, is the Son of God, the Messiah and will return to Jerusalem in Power and Glory
- Unrelenting love for Israel.
- Circumcision
- Baptism not into a Gentile Church but into the Body of Messiah.
- He and the followers retained their Jewishness.
- Yeshua is the fulfillment of the Torah.
- Continued use of the Feast Days.
- The non-authoritative nature of the Talmud.
- Retention of the Shabbat.
- Retention of the major dietary laws

According to Finto (2001), the movement began to take roots in America in 1967 as part of the Charismatic Renewal Movement. A Jewish couple, Marty and Yohanna Chernoff, dedicated to retain their Jewish heritage as well as their belief in *Yeshua,* reached out to the Jewish youth who embraced Jesus as Messiah. They began to disciple them and to encourage them to combine their Jewish heritage along with their belief in *Yeshua.* In early 1970, Marty received a vision of the term *Messianic Judaism* and shortly after that started a Congregation called *Beth Messiah* in Cincinnati and later, in Philadelphia. By the end of the last decade of 1999, there were 80 congregations in the United States and 81 in Israel. By the turn of the 21st century, there were 350 synagogues with about one million members.

Rudolph defines the movement from a statement of The Union of Messianic Jewish Congregations:

> A movement of Jewish congregations and groups committed to *Yeshua* the Messiah that embrace the covenantal responsibility of Jewish life and identity rooted in the *Torah*, expressed in tradition, and renewed and applied in the context of the New Covenant (2013:33).

The Roman Catholic priest, Fr. Peter Hocken (2013) augmented several elements that characterize the movement: (1), the unique eschatological vision of how they envision the Parousia as being centralized in Israel and Jerusalem, (2) by helping churches to return to their sources in Israel, and, (3) by recalling the churches to the realization that the original unity of the church was the engrafting of Gentiles into the body of Jewish believers.

Rudolph offers to us an important conclusion and perspective of Messianic Judaism:

> Like the miracle of the State of Israel rejoining the community of nations after millennia, the Messianic Jewish community has been restored to the Jewish-Christian world after a hiatus of more than sixteen hundred years. For centuries, the church and synagogue have marginalized Messianic Judaism, treating it as an excluded middle. Today, there are signs of change. The Messianic Jewish Movement is growing in support as New Testament scholars and theologians increasingly demonstrate that Messianic Judaism is consistent with the teachings of the Jewish apostles and the experience of the earliest communities

of *Yeshua*-believing Jews in the land of Israel, Syria and
beyond. The movement is also winning sympathizers
in the Jewish world as Messianic demonstrate that
Messianic Judaism through their actions that *Yeshua*
is good for the Jewish world (2013:35).

Kinzer offers some insights to a spiritual meaning of the
movement. Zionism and Messianic Judaism are linked to God's
providential plan for the healing and the restoration, first of Israel,
and then to all of humanity. A special characteristic of the movement
is its ecumenical dimension that includes Gentile believers in Jesus.
He wrote, in part:

> These historical realities (the *Shoah* and the return
> of Israel to the land) create the possibility of a union
> of Gentile and Jewish believers. This points to the
> unquenchable love that the resurrected Messiah of
> Israel has for his people and his determination to
> make his glory known through them. He dwells in
> his Church, but he also abides in hidden form among
> his own flesh and blood only together do these two
> communities bear witness to the saving purposes of
> God for the world (2018: 270).

TOWARDS HEALING OF THE WOUND

From the second to the 20th century, replacement theology,
supersessionism, and the constant theme or genre, *Adversos Judaeos* has
been part not only of the Roman Catholic Church but of Christianity
in general. According to Krewson, some Reformed Protestants, The
Orthodox Church, and some Evangelicals also adhered to these
antisemitic traditions.

Among Roman Catholics, a major break to this tradition came with
the papacy of Pope St. John XXIII (pope from 1958-1963) and with
some evangelicals who have renounced all the tenets of replacement

theology and the *Adversos Judaeos* theme. One spokesperson for the evangelicals quoted by Krewson, wrote (2017:153)[69]: "The Jews are a special people chosen not by you or me or themselves but God-chosen for a special service in human destiny as God's People, a holy nation set apart."

The strongest opponents to these theologies have been those who have purged all remnants of it from church tradition. There began to be a consensus on this among Roman Catholics and mainline Protestants in the middle of the twentieth century. In 1958, Pope St. John XXIII began this monumental change in church history by deleting a prayer from the Good Friday liturgy which prayed for the "faithless" and "perfidious Jews"[70]. More officially, this theology was radically changed in the Vatican II Council (1963-1965) in the document called *Nostrae Aetate*. (Abbot,1966). The bishops acknowledged the Church's indebtedness to the Jews, the renouncement of accusing them as "Christ-killers," and they were not rejected by God. Other important declarations followed: 1990: antisemitism is a sin and the call for a collective repentance; 2007: God did not revoke His covenant with Israel, that Israel and the Church were equally bound together, that new dialogue is possible and the church rejects any hostility to the Jews; 2015: the celebration of the 50th anniversary of *Nostrae Aetate*, further statements were released: the church does not replace Israel; Israel continues to be the people of God; and the Jews are participants in God's salvation plan[71].

---

[69] 2017:153 and Oden, 2003:110.

[70] This was updated in 2007 by Pope Benedict XVI: "Let us also pray for the Jews: That our God and Lord may illuminate their hearts, that they acknowledge Jesus Christ is the Savior of all men. *(Let us pray. Kneel. Rise.)* Almighty and eternal God, who wants that all men be saved and come to the recognition of the truth, propitiously grant that even as the fullness of the peoples enters Thy Church, all Israel be saved. Through Christ Our Lord. Amen" (https://en.wikipedia.org/wiki/Good_Friday_prayer_for_the_Jews#Changes_by_John_XXIII)

[71] In the same year, there was a gathering in Calgary that reaffirmed the teaching of the Council that was represented by the Bishop of the Calgary Diocese, a Protestant representative, a Rabbi and a member of the Church of Jesus Christ of Latter-day Saints.

These teachings were updated in *The Catechism of the Catholic Church* (United States Catholic Conference, 1994). In various places the Catechism affirms: the call and gifts of God to Israel are irrevocable; Israel is the priestly people of God: the first to hear the word of God and the people of the "elder brother" in the faith of Abraham; that God loves His people, Israel, more than a bridegroom his beloved; God chose the patriarchs, brought Israel out of Egypt, and created and formed her; He revealed His Law (which is holy, spiritual and good) to them; and, many other affirmations, God revealed Himself to His people Israel.

Similar teachings were presented by Presbyterians, Lutherans and Mennonites. Along with the World Council of Churches, they no longer considered it important to share the Gospel of Jesus Christ with the Jews. Along with the rejection of these replacement theology themes, there has also been a rising support for the state of Israel. In the early part of the 20th century, among some evangelicals, an eschatological theology of the coming of the Messiah to Israel as part of the world-wide conversion to faith in *Yeshua*, Messiah, has grown. They are called Christian Zionists.

Further movements of reconciliation occurred at the level of the state. In 1993, full diplomatic relations between the Vatican and Israel were established. Personal and collective repentance over the tragedy of the Holocaust came at the hands of three Popes who visited Israel: Pope St. John Paul II, Pope Emeritus Benedict and Pope Francis. These popes' visits to the Western Wall and the Holocaust Memorial, resulted in the following:

- Papal regrets for Christian antisemitism.
- The affirmation of Israeli rights for a secure future that was free from terrorism.
- The safeguard of the sacred places of Christianity in Jerusalem, Nazareth and Bethlehem.

However, there continues to be controversy as the Roman Catholic Church is reticent to link the Jews with the land of Israel.

Further, several Christian traditions, including the Orthodox, refuse to give support to the State of Israel as being the rightful home of the Jewish people.

I contend that the conduit for reconciliation and the creation of the unity of Gentile Christians and Jews is through Messianic Judaism-the modern version of the Nazarenes who were ecumenical, covenant, and charismatic. This would fulfill, in part, the vision of St. Paul: "His (*Yeshua's*) purpose in this was, by restoring peace, to create a single New Person out of two of them, and through the cross, to reconcile them both to God and in one Body" (Ephesians 2:15).

A Search for her mystery: The Roman Catholic Church's Reproachment with Judaism.

An earlier publication by Kinzer (2015)[72] augments the many dialogues and official publications of the Roman Catholic Church in her relationship to Judaism. His primary thesis is that the Roman Catholic Church had lost her identity in her historical distancing from Judaism, Israel, and the Jewish people world-wide. This publication by Kinzer is his admirable attempt to see how this branch can rediscover the roots of her faith in Judaism, Israel, and the Jewish people. But this is not the whole story. Israel also needs to recognize that her destiny and her identity is discovered within the Christian reality. She has lost much because of centuries of denial of the Messiah of Israel. But this is a new season of grace for her to grow until faith in her own Messiah, *Yeshua* the Nazarene.

Several new terms from Kinzer need to be defined to guide us through the Rabbi's theology. Used throughout the text is the term *Israel-Christology* and *Torah-Christology*. By these terms he means: "According to this perspective, Jesus is the perfect representative and individual embodiment of the Jewish people. He is the Christ-the Messiah, the King of the Jews. He demonstrates that he is such obeying the *Torah* as God always intended it to be obeyed" (2015:13).

---

[72] Christoph Cardinal Schonborn, Archbishop of Vienna, Austria, has written the Forward to the text.

A term that corresponds closely to this term is *Israel-Ecclesiology*. By this Kinzer means (with Cardinal Lustiger,2007) that the ecclesiology of the church necessarily includes Israel as the mature olive tree that the church is grafted into. It also means that the mystery of Israel remains at the center of Christian faith and ecclesiology.

Another term unique to Kinzer is *genealogical-Israel*. He wrote: "I am referring to the Jewish people as a community that traces its descent back to biblical patriarchs and matriarchs. This term is equivalent to Paul's 'Israel according to the flesh or physical descent" (2015: 24). Two terms not unique to Kinzer and refers to the Body of Messiah in the first century CE are *ecclesia ex gentibus* (church from the gentiles) and *ecclesia ex circumcisione* (church from the circumcision).

Kinzer unites all these terms to establish his primary thesis:

> My fundamental theses should now be clear. I am proposing that *Israel- ecclesiology* derives from *Israel-Christology* and the mediation of the *ecclesia ex circumione* and that the church is joined to the mystery of *genealogical-Israel* through the same realities. I am proposing that Christ is as much the inner mystery of the Jewish people as he is the inner mystery of the church (2015:60).

The author continues to develop a new understanding, informed by Israel, of the priesthood, baptism, the Eucharist, and Jewish life as signs or sacraments of the Holy[73].

The key understanding of the priesthood (both lay believers and the clerics of holy orders) of the Christian people is an extension of the meaning of priesthood of *genealogical-Israel*. The genealogical Israel understanding is that the tribe of Levi was to care for the sanctuary, approach and serve *Adonai*, to teach the people the difference between the holy and the profane, to judge fairly, invoke divine blessings on Israel, to honour the feasts and to keep Shabbat (see Ezekiel 44:

---

[73] Kinzer includes other features of his thesis not presented here.

15-31). Translated to our time, believers in *Yeshua* are to care for each other, serve *Adonai*, teach the path of holiness, call down divine blessings on God's people and to honour major feast days. Sacrifices now take the meaning of the sacrifice, *Yeshua*, who has now entered the divine sanctuary, the Holy of Holies and invites us to join him.

Baptism takes on a deeper meaning. *Yeshua* was a Jew, is one now, and will return as a Jew. To be baptized into *Yeshua* is to be baptized into the whole history of genealogical-Israel with all its richness. It indicates a radical solidarity with Israel, a cleansing of fire, and an anticipation of Messiah's return to transform all of creation into His Kingdom here on earth: "Just as the new heavens and the new earth that I am making will continue in my presence" (Isaiah 66:22) and "wait for new heavens and a new earth, in which righteousness will be at home" (II Peter 3:13). Through Baptism we are brought to be: "In union with him (*Yeshua*) the whole building is held together, and it is growing into a holy temple in union with the Lord. Yes, in union with him, you yourselves are being built together into a spiritual dwelling place for God" (Ephesians 2:21-22).

The Eucharist also takes on a new meaning. The new covenant is not really a "new" covenant that is discontinuous with the first covenant established on Mount Sinai (see Exodus 24:4). It is a renewal of this original covenant. Thus, the Eucharist is another link to *genealogical-Israel.* Those who participate in the Eucharist not only share in the body and blood of the Messiah but also in the very body and blood of *genealogical-Israel.* The new covenant is like the earlier one but now more brilliant and radiant. The consecrated bread, which is to be believed in the Catholic tradition as the real presence of Messiah, is not just human flesh but Jewish flesh. So those believers, when they partake of the body and blood of Jesus, partake of him as the Jewish Messiah.

The last element in outlining Kinzer's primary thesis is to consider Jewish life dedicated to holiness. He believes that these signs are really sacraments as they produce the divine action of transferring divine holiness to the genealogical-Israelites but also to Gentile branches. He presented five ways to share in the divine action of "making holy" not only to genealogical Israel but also to *Yeshua's* disciples (see Leviticus 21: 8, 15 and Leviticus 22: 16). They consist of:

- Israel is holy- **sacred people.**
- Shabbat and feasts set apart as holy-**sacred time.**
- Israel and Jerusalem are holy-**sacred spaces.**
- *Torah* is holy-**sacred words.**
- *Mitzvot* or laws are holy-**sacred laws.**

Table 6:1 details these signs or sacraments:

Table 6:1: Judaism's Five Fundamental Signs (Sacraments) of Holiness

Israel as a holy people	Shabbat as set apart to be holy	The land of Israel and Jerusalem are holy	*Torah* as Holy	Mitzvot (ethical rules of life)
Holy nation (Exodus 13:2)	From creation (Genesis 2:1-2)	The sanctifying of place or space	Torah means teachings Key *Ha Shem*	To the heart of the Torah Translated as the Law
Divine presence among the people	Sign of the eternal rest	The land of sacred promise	Elements:	Doing and living holiness daily
Israel goes where Adonai goes	Points to the Tabernacle	Holiness because of Adonai's presence	1 Scroll of the Five books of Moses	Key teaching: *tikkun olam* (the repairing of the world)
Each person is holy and is to be honoured and deeply respected	The sanctifying of time	Has implications for the end of this age	2 Ordering of society	The decalogue
When we judge, criticize, hurt, or use others, we profane that which is holy.	Focus on the end times and return of Messiah	Anticipation of Messiah's return	3 Includes the prophets and the writings	Meaning behind the Shema Israel

Table 6:1: Judaism's Five Fundamental Signs (Sacraments) of Holiness

Israel as a holy people	Shabbat as set apart to be holy	The land of Israel and Jerusalem are holy	Torah as Holy	Mitzvot (ethical rules of life)
	In the Decalogue This rest also includes the major Feast days—all sacred time	Reverence for the land as sacred	4 Given at Shavuot or Pentecost	

For believers in *Yeshua*, these five signs (sacraments) link them more and more to genealogical-Israel. In other words, Gentile believers dwelling in genealogical-Israel and genealogical-Israel dwelling within the Gentile Church. This is what Pope John-Paul called "mutual indwelling" between Christianity and Judaism.

In concluding this section, it is well to know how deep and intimate is Israel, Judaism, and the Jewish people to the Christian Church. It is in this rediscovering an ancient truth that Gentile and Jewish believers were united in one body. A task before us is to prepare our selves to be one bride ready and able to welcome her groom, *Yesuha* of Nazareth, king not only of the Jews but also of Gentile believers.

Towards Jerusalem Council II

One practical way for this to happen is through prayer, repentance, and reconciliation initiative called "Towards Jerusalem Council II." Its history is remarkable as it came through visions and revelations to Messianic Jews and Gentile Christians. The original vision came to Rabbi Marty Waldman of the *Baruch HaShem Messianic Congregation* in Dallas Texas. His vision consisted of: the augmentation of the First Jerusalem Council recorded in Acts 15 when the Jesus-believing Jews invited Jesus-believing Gentiles to join them in faith without them having to convert to Judaism. The Second Council (Toward Jerusalem

Council II. 2010) is to be a gathering of both, fully accepting one another within the Body of *Yeshua* the Messiah. In such a meeting, the Jesus believing Gentiles would recognize the Jesus believing Jews as an integral part of the church while remaining as contiguous members of the Jewish Community.

In discerning the authenticity of the vision, Rabbi Waldman sought counsel from the Union of Messianic Jewish Congregations who responded with a unanimous voice that the vision was of God. Several others, both Jesus believing Jews and Jesus believing Gentiles, received revelations of a similar kind. One came from a Catholic priest Fr. Hocken (now deceased) who wrote a book believing that Christian unity was impossible without the Jewish witness to Jesus. With such confirmation of the original vision, the first meeting was held in 1996 with seven Jesus believing Jews and seven Jesus believing Gentiles meeting. The vision is "towards" as the meeting would be in the future with major leaders of both expressions of the faith where there would be repentance, reconciliation and reconciliation. The vision consists of:

- To make known to church leaders and Christian scholars the restoration of the Jewish segments of the church (the church of the circumcision).
- To foster repentance for the sins of Gentile Christians and the Christian Church against the Jewish people, especially for the suppression of the corporate Jewish witness to *Yeshua,* the Messiah.
- To foster intercession for all the churches of the nations to abandon all forms of replacement teaching concerning the calling and election of Israel and to recognize the place of the Jew in the Body of Messiah.
- To encourage the Messianic Jewish community in and out of Israel to enter into this vision of reconciliation and restoration and thereby fostering unity among the different streams and organizations with the Messianic Jewish Movement.

- The ultimate purpose is unifying the Body and restoring the Jewish believers to their rightful place is the hastening of the coming of the Lord *Yeshua* in glory and the full accomplishment of His work of redemption in the Kingdom of God (Toward Jerusalem Council II. 2010:37-38).

In practical terms, groups of intercessors around the world gather together at least once a month to pray for this to happen. An interesting part of this intercession is for all the Churches to rediscover their Jewish roots.

CELEBRATION OF THE GENESIS OF HEALING

Kinzer wrote of the resurrection of Jerusalem and the Messiah. The genesis of healing among and between the Church of the Circumcision and the Church of the Gentiles is in its early stages in the first decades of the 21st century. This has been documented in the second half of this chapter. Celebration themes both Messiah and Jerusalem brings this chapter to a close.

Of the Messiah: Light appears both in the reading of Isaiah 53 and the Book of Lamentations. These prophets wrote of the resurrected Messiah:

> After this ordeal, he will see satisfaction. By his knowing pain and suffering, my righteous servant makes many righteous; it is for their sins that he suffers. Therefore I will assign him a share with the great, he will divide the spoil with the mighty for having exposed himself to death and being counted among the sinners, while actually bearing the sin of many and interceding for the offenders (Isaiah 53:11-12).

In the New Testament, this resurrection theme is repeated:

> Though he was in the form of God, he did not regard
> equality with God something to be possessed by force.
> On the contrary, he emptied himself, in that he took
> the form of a slave by becoming like human beings
> are. And when he appeared as a human being he
> humbled himself still more by become obedient even
> to death- death on a cross as a criminal! Therefore
> God raised him to the higher place and gave him the
> name above every name; that in honor of the name
> given *Yeshua* every knee will bow- in heaven, on
> earth and under the earth- and every tongue will
> acknowledge that *Yeshua* the Messiah is *Adonai*- to the
> glory of God the Father (Philippians 2: 6-11)

As did *Yeshua* rise from the dead so is Jerusalem rising from the
dead to become the City of the great King (Psalm 48:3) with Messiah
ruling from Zion on the renewed heaven and earth. "On that day his
feet will stand on the Mount of Olives" and "On that Day *Adonai* will
be the only one, and his name will be the only name" (Zechariah 14:
4 and 9). "Jerusalem will be inhabited in her own place, Jerusalem.
Adonai will save the tents of Judah first so that the glory of the
House of David and the glory of those living in Jerusalem will not
appear greater than that of Judea. When that day comes, *Adonai* will
defend those living in Jerusalem" (Zechariah 12: 6-8). The Book of
Lamentations, redolent with sorrow, breaks into hope for Jerusalem:

> **Of Jerusalem**: But in my mind I keep returning to
> something, something that gives me hope that the
> grace of *Adonai* is not exhausted, and his compassion
> has not ended. On the contrary, they are new every
> morning! How great your faithfulness! *Adonai* is all
> I have. I say, therefore I put my hope in him. The
> rejection of *Adonai* does not last forever. He may

cause grief, but he will take pity, and keeping with the greatness of his grace. For he does not arbitrarily torment or punish human beings (Lamentations 3:21–24 and 3:31–33).

The restoration of Jerusalem will be complete at the end of the temporal age. John, the Revelator wrote:

Come! I will show you the bride, the wife of a Lamb. He carried me off in the spirit to the top of a great, high mountain and showed me the holy city, Jerusalem coming down out of heaven from God. It had the *Shekinah* of God so that its brilliance was like that of a priceless jewel, like crystal clear diamond. It had a great high wall with 12 gates at the gates were 12 Angels and inscribed on the gates with the names of the 12 tribes of Israel. Three gates to the East, three gates to the North, three gates to the South and three gates to the West. The wall of the city was built on 12 foundation stones, and on those stones the 12 names of the 12 apostles of the Lamb. The city is laid out in a square, it's length equal to its width with his rod he measured the city at 1500 miles, with length, width and height the same, he measured its wall at 216 feet by human standards of measurement, which the Angel was using. The wall was made of diamond in the city of pure gold resembling pure glass, the foundations of the city were decorated with all kinds of precious stones the first foundation stone was diamond, the second sapphire, the third chalcedony, the fourth emerald, the fifth sardonyx, the sixth carnelian, the seventh, chrysolite, the eight beryl, the ninth topaz, the tenth chrysoprase, the eleventh turquoise, and the twelfth, amethyst. The twelve gates were twelve pearls and each gate made of a single pearl. The city's

> Main Street was pure gold transparent as glass. I saw
> no temple in the city for *Adonai*, God of heavens the
> heaven's armies is its Temple and is that lamp that city
> had no need for the sun or the moon to shine on it,
> because God's Shekinah gives it light and this lamp is
> the Lamb (Revelation 21:9-23).

How so very much joy there will be for the believers in *Adonai*
and His Messiah, *Yeshua*. All tears will be wiped away and there
will be no more death or destruction. All the things of the past that
caused so much offence will be gone forever. These saints will live
forever and forever being in a bubble of eternal life with *Adonai* Our
Father, *Yesuha* His Messiah and the Holy Spirit giving an infinity of
love and joy.

CONCLUSIONS

This chapter has been divided into two sections: an accent on
remembering that invites the reader to a past that is in so many ways
tragic and, a second part, an emphasis on repentance and a gradual
movement towards reconciliation. This chapter will end with an
accent on hope rooted and grounded in God's favor for His elect,
Israel, and His grafted- in election, Gentile Christians.

Four series of events capture the latter part of the 19th and the 20th
centuries: the age of revolutions and the construction of modernity,
the Dreyfus Affair, the *Shoah*, and the creation of Israel. Three
philosophers laid the basis for the age of revolution and modernity-
Spinoza, Voltaire and Marx. Each were responsible for central elements
of our age. Two, however, Voltaire and Marx, are also remembered
for their contribution to a secular variation of antisemitism.

Although the Dreyfus Affair may not have been significant as a
travesty of French jurisdiction, it is remembered for an explosion of
a literature of antisemitism within the Roman Catholic Church in
France. All of this and more led to the most horrific genocide of all

of human history-the *Shoah,* stealing the lives of six million Jews of whom countless Christians were implicated.

After this, however, an amazing resurrection happened! It was like the fulfillment of the dry bones vision of Ezekiel the prophet (37:1-14). He recorded: "Then I will place you in your own land; and you will know that I, *Adonai,* have spoken, and that I have done it, says *Adonai*" (verse 14). This occurred in our time, May 14, 1948 with the creation of the State of Israel. After that, many small steps of repentance with some reconciliation have occurred.

Another resurrection also occurred: the genesis of the Messianic Jewish Movement. It may be seen as a potential bridge between Christianity and Judaism. Within that movement, is an intercessory-repentance movement called Towards Jerusalem Council II. Finally, we are all called to celebrate for the genesis of healing is happening in this generation anticipating living forever in the New Jerusalem coming down from heaven.

References: Chapter Six

Abbot, W 1966. Editor. *Nostra Aetate* (Declaration on the Relationship to non-Christian religions. *The Documents of Vatican II*. New York: Guild Press.

Ancien Régime https://en.wikipedia.org/wiki/Ancien_ R%C3%A9gime.

Carroll, J.2001. *The sword of Constantine: The Church and the Jews. A history*. A Mariner Book. Houghton Mifflin Company. Boston.

Commission for religious relations with the Jews, 2015. *A reflection on theological questions pertaining to the Catholic-Jewish relations on the occasion of the 50th Anniversary of Nostra Aetate*. Rome: The Vatican.

Finegan, J. 1969. *The archeological of the New Testament*. Princeton, NJ: Princeton University Press.

Finto, D. 2001. *Your people will be my people*. Minneapolis: Chosen.

Hocken, P. 2013. *Pentecost and Parousia*. Eugene Oregon: WIPF and Stock and 2016. *Azusa, Rome and Zion: Pentecostal faith, Catholic reform and Jewish roots*. Eugene Oregon: Pickwick Publications.

Karesh, S. and M. Hurvitz 2008. *Encyclopaedia of Judaism*. New York: Checkmark Books.

Kinzer, M. 2015. *Searching her on mystery: Nostrae Aetate, the Jewish People, and the identity of the Church*. Eugene Oregon: Cascade Books.

Kinzer, M. 2018. *Jerusalem Crucified, Jerusalem risen*. Eugene Oregon: Wipf and Stock Publishers.

Kjaer-Hansen,K. 1988. *Joseph Rabinowitz and the Messianic Movement..* Grand Rapids, Michigan: Wm. B. Eerdmans Publishing Co.

Krewson, W. L. 2017:2-3. *Jerome and the Jews: Innovative supersessionism*. Eugene Oregon: Wipf and Stock Publishers.

Langton, D. 2007. "Relations between Christians and Jews, 1914–2000." In Volume Nine, World Christianities c. 1914-2000,

The Cambridge History of Christianity, p. 483-493. Edited by H. McLeod. Cambridge, UK: Cambridge University Press.

Lustiger, Cardinal Jean-Marie. 2007. *The Promise.* William B.E. Eerdmans Publishing Company. Grand Rapids, Michigan.

Mancini, I. OFM. 1970. *Archeological discoveries relative to the Judeo-Christians.* Franciscan Printing Press. Jerusalem.

Montgomery, R. and B. O'Dell. 2019. *The List: Persecutions of Jews by Christians throughout history.* Israel: Root Source Press.

Oden, T. 2003:110. *The rebirth of orthodoxy: Signs of new life in Christianity.* San Francisco: HarperCollins

Pixner, B. 1990. "Church of the Apostles found on Mt Zion". *Biblical Archeology Review.* May/June.

Rudolph, D. 2013. "Messianic Judaism in Antiquity and in the Modern Era." In *Introduction to Messianic Judaism,* edited by D. Rudolph and J. Willitts, p. 21-36. Zondervan. Grand Rapids, Michigan.

Toward Jerusalem Council II. 2010. *Toward Jerusalem Council II: Vision, Origin, and Documents.* Dallas: *Baruch HaShem* Messianic Congregation: Dallas.

United States Catholic Conference. 1994. *The Catechism of the Catholic Church.* New York: Image Books.

CHAPTER SEVEN

THE TRAGIC INTERLUDE: THE *SHOAH* 1933-1945: REMEMBERING, REPENTING AND RECONCILING

Outline

The thesis of this chapter is to present a picture from historical sociology and the contrasts between distal and proximate causes. Distal factors refer to the far past while proximate indicate the close factors surrounding an historical event. Historical sociology is unique in that it not only posits events in history but also factors or causes of these events. This will be the methodological tool used to gain understanding of how the Holocaust came to be. As presented in the Introduction, sample scholars include Sckopol (1984) and Bloch (1961). Sckopol argues that historical sociology can be considered as a science wherein one can look at causes and effects and subsume them in theory. Both she and Bloch focus on causal regularities that will be the pattern used in this text.

Figures 7:1 and 7:2 illustrate the historical background to the Shoah, the contrasts between distal-proximate factors.

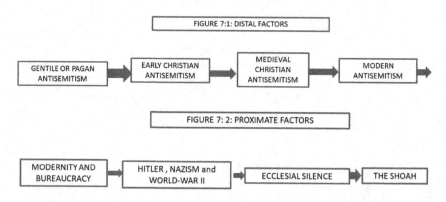

FIGURE 7:1: DISTAL FACTORS

GENTILE OR PAGAN ANTISEMITISM → EARLY CHRISTIAN ANTISEMITISM → MEDIEVAL CHRISTIAN ANTISEMITISM → MODERN ANTISEMITISM

FIGURE 7: 2: PROXIMATE FACTORS

MODERNITY AND BUREAUCRACY → HITLER, NAZISM and WORLD-WAR II → ECCLESIAL SILENCE → THE SHOAH

An Overview

Langton (2006) has informed us of the relationships between Jews and Christians during the years between 1914 and 2000. Why these years? It is because of two major events that occurred during this time; the attempt to destroy European Jewry via the Nazi Holocaust (*Shoah*) of 1933-1945 and the establishment of the state of Israel in 1948. Both these events had a profound effect on the relationships between the two Abrahamic faiths.

Fichtenbauer (2019) tells of a woman named Marthe Robin (1902-1981), a famous French mystic, who spent much of her life paralyzed and had to be confined to bed. Many Catholic leaders and laity sought her counsel. While she was young, she had a vision in which she saw a man whom she later identified as Adolf Hitler. This man stood before the Dragon, Satan, and asked him how he would gain importance and influence and have dominion over the earth. In response, the dragon said "If you hand over to me all the Jews on the earth, I will give you dominion over the whole world"[74]. Martha understood from this vision:

1. Satan had found the ultimate way to block God's plans for the salvation of all humanity.
2. The key to doing so would involve eliminating the Jews from the world stage and history.
3. One day, a young German would sell his soul to become the instrument of extermination of the Jewish people.

A fundament truth of the Christian faith so much referred to in this document is that from God's perspective, Israel is in the centre of everything of importance! All spiritual developments of global perspective are related to Israel. The God whom we serve will always be the "God of Israel" (Fichtenbauer 2019:3).

---

[74] Remember, in the temptation of *Yeshua*, the devil said "I will give you all this power and glory. It has been handed over to me, and I can give it to whomever I choose" (Luke 4:5-6).

Entering this era, both Christianity and Judaism were divided in many ways. Christianity with its thousands of variations and Judaism with its traditions: Ultra-Orthodoxy, Orthodoxy, Conservative, Reform, Liberal and Progressive. To write of Judaism, Langton argues, is to include all the categories of the faith. Yet, there is a basic commonality to the horrid realities of the *Shoah* and the creation of the State of Israel.

What were the sources of the *Shoah?* All factors cannot be simply linked to Christian antisemitism or the genre, *Adversos Judaeos,* They are not sufficient causes but are necessary causes. Thus, all Christians are in some way responsible for the horrid tragedy of the *Shoah*. Such literary pieces reinforced the racist propaganda and made it possible for professing Christians to partake directly as death camp staff and mobile killing squads along with the many bureaucrats and technocrats involved in the genocide. Ordinary Europeans of peasant stock did not object to the confiscation of Jewish property for they believed that the Jews were being punished for deicide.

Church officials were also implicated. The Catholic Church, under the leadership of Pope Pius XII (1876-1958), in a Christian message of 1942, spoke in general terms of many people were being killed but did not mention the Nazis or the Jews by name. The newly formed German Evangelical church as a federation of Lutheran, Reformed, and United territorial churches was host to an antisemitic right winged faction. This faction resurrected the Marcion heresy[75] of the second century arguing that the Old Testament and Paul's letters should be expunged from the canon on the grounds that they were Jewish. This faction also supported the myth of Aryan racial supremacy. Going against the great tide of Nazism, the German pastor, Dietrich Bonhoeffer (1906-1945), protested against the treatment of the Jews and was executed in 1945.

The chapter will be divided into nine sections:

---

[75] See Chapter Three of the document called "The First Wound of Division-The Separation of Gentile Believers in Jesus from the Jewish Believers in *Yeshua: Remembering, Repenting and Reconciling.*"

DISTAL FACTOR ONE: GENTILE OR PAGAN ANTISEMITISM

From the genesis of Judaism and the Jewish people until the present, antisemitism has been a constant phenomenon. This people have endured millennial of years under the shadow of this prejudice, stereotype, discrimination, exile, deportation, ostracization, and death. It begins in the ancient civilization of Egypt. The Jewish Bible records: ... "the Egyptians came to dread the people of Israel and worked them relentlessly, making their lives bitter with hard labor" (Exodus 1:13). But this did not satisfy the "dread" for the Pharaoh for he commanded: "Every boy that is born, throw in the river" (Exodus 1:22).

Chapter Three was an extended study of the antisemitism of the ancient world that consisted of Egypt, Greece and Rome. Sevenster (1975), Feldman (1993), and Schafer (1997) are the scholars who researched in-depth. Prejudices, stereotypes, and discriminatory action common throughout history against the Jews have their origins in these ancient societies. They were accused of being hateful of humanity and intent on controlling all societies (the conspiracy theory). Many stereotypes were attributed to them such as being lazy (because they did not work on the Shabbat)[76], degenerate, crude,

---

[76] The Egyptians accused the Hebrews of being lazy and the Pharaoh demanded that they gather straw for the building of bricks (see Exodus 5:8 and 17). Pharaoh

lustful, abominable, base, misanthropists, and strangers or misfits to society.

Circumcision of the males was considered to be mutilating the human body, shameful, disgraceful, ugly, crude and barbaric. One of the most horrific of accessions was the belief that every year, a Gentile youth was captured to be fattened up, sacrificed, and eaten. In addition to these prejudices and stereotypes, there was violence. The most infamous of them happened in Alexandria-a pogrom.

In the year 38 CE, mobs (made not only of Alexandrian but also naturally born Egyptians) perpetrated violence against the Jews. Synagogues were destroyed, the Jews were thought to be aliens and foreigners. The first pogrom was created when all the Jews were forced to live in one section of the city. Schafer (1997:140) writes: "It was the first known ghetto of the world." Not only that, homes, shops and businesses were pillaged. Worse than that, if they left the ghetto, they were stoned, beaten, slain and burnt. Degradation went further when the mobs dragged the bodies of the slain and mutilated them in the streets of the city.

As we journey through this history, it will become clear that similar prejudices, stereotypes, discriminations have been present in Western societies from this ancient beginning until the present.

DISTAL FACTOR TWO: EARLY CHRISTIAN ANTISEMITISM

Chapter Three of this manuscript goes into depth of the phenomenon of antisemitism with terms such as "replacement theology," "supersessionism," and "*Adversos Judaeaos.*" Replacement theology and supersessionism are similar in meaning.

Krewson (2017:2-3) provides us with a definition as applied to Judaism and Christianity:

---

said: "Lazy! You're just lazy! That why you say, 'Let us go to sacrifice to *Adonai* (verse 17).

Christian supersessionism is the belief that the Jewish people and religion have been entirely replaced by the Christian people and religion, and that divine favor rests only with those (both Jew and Gentile) who follow Jesus as God's Messiah. Jews therefore can find religious legitimacy only as members of the Christian church.

The meaning of *Adversos Judaeos is* taken from Chapter Three. The term refers to a series of homilies preached at various times and places in the Late-Classical Era. These texts, which go back to the second century, are directed against the Jews, Judaism and "Judaizing" Christians, i.e., members of the Christian communities who espoused Jewish beliefs or participated in elements of their religious practice. The contents, which were initially presented as polemics and later settled into convention formed a repertoire for anti-Jewish and later Anti-Semitic ideas (Rainer, 2011-2017).

This genre was taught by many of the Church Fathers. Ignatius of Antioch (355-107 CE), accused the Nazarenes of heresy because they celebrated the Shabbat. Marcion (85-166 CE) argued the deletion of the Old Testament because it taught that God was an angry God. Justin Martyr (100-165 CE) advocated supersessionism while Melito (died in 180 CE) introduced the phrase "Christ-killers" or those guilty of deicide. This would become one of the most horrific appellations leveled against the Jews down through modern times that had deadly effects, especially in the blood-libels to be discussed in the next section.

Tertullian (150-225 CE) adds that because the Jews forsook God, his grace has been taken from them and they are now a "posterior people." Hippolytus (170-235 CE) taught that when Jesus said to the people: "Father forgive them," this was not meant for the Jews but for the Gentiles. Hippolytus went so far as to curse them.

Bishop Ambrose (337-397 CE) called the Jews liars and that it was just to burn their synagogues. The Eastern Church Father, Chrysostom (347-407 CE) called the synagogue a whorehouse, a den of thieves where debauchery reigned. They were to be excluded from public office. The last of the Fathers, Augustine (354-436) taught that God casted off the Jews, that they were killers of Christ and that they practiced magic. Yet, he argued that they should survive but not thrive.

One might ask what were the sources of this antisemitism that the Church Fathers drew on? I have argued in Chapter Three that a possible source was the education that these men received. They went to Greek and Roman academies where they were exposed to Hellenistic and Roman law, philosophy, and world views. One could make a case that they adapted their Christian faith to these teachings. We do know, for example, that Melito was steeped in Hellenistic ways of thinking and world views. Could it be argued that the other Church Fathers were also exposed to these teachings?

These teachings form the basis of antisemitism within the Catholic Church that was not renounced until the Vatican II council in 1965. Still to come is the renunciation of the teaching of *adversos judaeos* of these church fathers. One might argue that this may have been some of the straw that lead to the fire of the holocaust.

DISTAL FACTOR THREE: MEDIEVAL CHRISTIAN ANTISEMITISM

Towards the end of the era of the Church Fathers (around the 6th Century CE), two images of the Jews were depicted: the first one, represented by Pope Gregory the Great (540-604 CE) presented an inspiring and positive image of the Jew. The second image, reflected in the writings of Isidore of Seville (560-636 CE), accented the *adversos judaeos* tradition (there circulated about 230 documents that reflected this genre). He saw the declared hostility towards the Jews and considered them impervious to the call to conversion. He also was a champion of supersessionism.

As noted in Chapter Five, many believers during the Medieval Era were illiterate and relied on images, statutes, stained glass windows to learn of the faith. Two prominent figures were *Ecclesia et Synagogia*.

The large statue, *Ecclesia* is depicted as majestic and proud, wearing a crown, has a halo around her neck and is the wise woman like the wise virgins of the Gospel narrative. *Synagogia* stands in stark contrast to her. She is blindfolded, is ready for the abyss of hell as she rejected Christianity, is seduced by a demon and carries a broken lance.

Negative stereotypes emerged during the Medieval Era. The Jew was thought to be alien, antisocial (recall the accusation among the Ancient Egyptians, Greeks and Romans), anti-human and, even sub-human. The focus of antisemitism among the Patristics were textual—directed to a literate people. The foci during these eras was imagery, carvings, drawings, chronicles, legends, poems, songs and morality plays. These carried with them vile epithets, accusations, curses and the definition of the Jew as evil. It was a common folk belief that "The devil and the Jew joined forces" (Trachtenberg, 1943:21).

It was also during this era that accusations of blood libel emerged as a social construction of the masses even though Pope Innocent IV (Pope from 1243-1254) proclaimed they were false. This consisted of belief that every year, a Christian child was kidnapped and was used as a blood sacrifice[77]. According to Hellig (2003), the first one recorded was in 1146 in Norwich, England. The libel continued even into the twentieth century in Kiev, Ukraine in 1912 and in Poland in 1946. Hellig commented: "The blood libel became the most colorful and dangerous fiction of all time, providing a rationale for a protracted cycle of slaughter" (2003:213).

One of the infamous blood libels was directed at the Jews in Trent in 1475. A child went missing and was discovered dead in a sewage channel. Po-Chia Hsia, R. (1992) used a trial record (*The Yeshiva Manuscript*) to document in detail the legal proceedings against three Jewish families of Trent. After 15 men had been arrested, the local

---

[77] The great irony was that the Jew was forbidden to consume blood (Deuteronomy 15:23).

bishop, Hinderbach, approved of them being tortured until they confessed to the ritual murder of Simon. All were hung and whipped in a most horrific manner. Of the fifteen, nine were convicted of the ritual murder. They, under torture, fabricated the story of the ritual murder of Simon. There was never solid evidence of the ritual and the bishop and magistrates felt justified in their eventual execution of the Jewish men. This was the second most horrific episode that Po-Chia called "The theater of death." Their deaths consisted of their body parts torn apart and then burned alive on a stake.

Towards the cessation of the Medieval Era, a national campaign against the Jews was conducted for many centuries in Spain and Portugal called the "Spanish Inquisition." The central question for the officers of the Inquisition was the contrast between "Old Christians" (Christians from birth) and converts from Judaism and Islam. This ecclesial institution was approved by the Vatican. Pope Sixtus IV (1471-1484) passed a Bull in 1478 that gave legitimacy to the inquisition. Kamen calls it an institutionalized "big lie," based on the belief that all the converts were secretly Jews or Muslims (1998:43). Sixtus IV had two or three priests appointed as inquisitors, with future appointments or dismissals to be made by the Spanish crown. Thus, began the Inquisition that continued until 1834, when a decree of suppression was given by Isabella II (1830-1904).

From the scholarship of Kamen (1998), the following themes capture the essence of this nefarious institution known throughout Europe as a travesty of human life. Maximum public participation was organized with a procession of the accused with marks on their backs along with the inquisitors carrying crosses. Mass was celebrated in the morning and then the accused were displayed. Many confessed and were freed; those who did not were burned at a stake.

Much of the process was socially constructed. Many friends, neighbours, and family members used the system to avenge a wrongdoing or settle a score. Much of this was false. For example, in Castile, many Jews were burned at the stake based on false testimony. This social construction was parallel with the tribunal itself. The accused was brought to the tribunal and imprisoned without recourse.

Properties were confiscated. Witnesses were brought forward to prove the accusations. If the inquisitors found the accused guilty, he/ she was given a chance to recant. Then the accused was punished in a variety of ways: wearing a *sanbenito* (clothing with a mark of guilt), condemned to death (about two percent of all found guilty), flogged, banished, or sent back to prison.

Clearly, antisemitism was significantly prominent during this era. By the end of the early modern era, this became embedded into the very culture of Europe. This culture was common among intellectuals, clergy, and laity. One can argue that this was part of the straw that was sparked during the Nazi era of the twentieth century.

Distal Factor Four: Modern Antisemitism

During what one may call the genesis of the modern era (1775-1914), Europe underwent radical changes. One most dominant new reality was secularism or the dismantling of the sacred as understood in Christianity. Because antisemitism had been linked to Christianity from the first centuries, one would think that it would cease. Not so. A new form was socially constructed: secular antisemitism. Two of the most prominent figures were Voltaire (1694-1778) and Karl Marx (1818-1883).

It was argued in Chapter Five the fundamental secular social construction of anti-Semitism was created by Voltaire and Marx. In summary form, they presented a negative stereotype in which the Jew was, by nature, inferior to the rest of humanity, selfish, whose god was money, antisocial, revolutionary, and a destroyer of society.

This period of history was also the time of the creation of large numbers of Jewish ghettos. In one case, living within the Ghetto, in 1867, was deadly. Just outside the Vatican property, 10,000 Jews lived in poverty, with poor hygiene, and in desperate situations. Cholera hit and half of the population died. Several years later, in 1870, matters changed for them with the creation of the modern state of Italy. In Italy, there was good news for the Jew, for the secular model (not Christian) freed the Jew from the Ghetto. He would be a citizen of Italy along with others in this new society and have a home and country of his own—being treated not as a Jew but as a human being with rights.

Another form of modernity was the social construction of eugenics which gave rise to racial theory- - the false belief that the Germans were of the Aryan race and the Jews of an inferior race. Having no empirical basis, the racial identity of the Jews turned for the worst. The primary category of who a Jew was contingent on ancestry.

Another form of modernity was the social construction of eugenics which gave rise to racial theory. The false belief that the Germans were of the Aryan race and the Jews of an inferior race. Having no basis in reality, the racial identity of the Germans and the Jews turned for the worst. It was the primary category of who a Jew was contingent on ancestry.

During this period of Europe, The Roman Catholic Church entered another period of anti-Semitism. In 1898, the Vatican newspaper, *L'Observatore Romano* wrote of the Jews: "Jewry can no longer be excused or rehabilitated; the Jew has the largest share of wealth; he holds the credit of States in his hands; he influences public ministries, the civil service, the armies, the universities and controls the press."

A focus of this literature was in France. Hundreds and maybe thousands of Catholic priests attended antisemitic congresses, gave teachings and enflamed Catholic congregations in many parts of France. Common stereotypes were invoked that harbor back to some of the *Adversos Judaeos* genre of the Medieval Eras: killer of Christ, ritual murderer, traitor and more recently, revolutionary and financier. A book published in 1886 by Drumont imaged the Jew as: Money-grabbing, greedy, scheming, subtle, by nature a merchant, and does everything to deceive his fellow citizen and a parasite in the middle of civilization" (Carroll 2001:462). The stereotypes had a daily voice in a newspaper called La Croix (the Cross), owned and operated by the Assumptionist Order. Some of the publications accused the Jews of being responsible for the secularization of French society that consisted of curtailing Catholic education, taking down crucifixes in public spaces, and restrictions on clergy.

One of the most striking of things a person may observe is that during this era, the common prejudices, serotypes, and discriminatory actions were consistent with the past. Not much had changed except there was a movement away from a religious antisemitism to a secular one. None the less, it was still against the Jew.

PROXIMATE FACTOR ONE: MODERNITY AND BUREAUCRACY

This is the first of a series of proximate factors to the Holocaust. Before we begin the discussion on this topic as it relates to the Holocaust, several terms need to be defined that come from the work of Weber (1864-1920). He is known as one of the major founders of sociology. Two terms are important to our understanding of this factor: social action and bureaucracy (Weber 1978 and 1962).

Weber (1978:24-25) offers four kinds of social action (our relations with one another): value-rationality, affectual and traditional. Instrumental rationality is when the end, the means, and the secondary results are all rationally taken into account. This is seen as a pragmatic kind of social action when values of social action are not taken into account. Value-rationality is in contrast to this. It means an actor bases his or her decision on values such as goodness, beauty, justice, or ultimate values. Traditional social action is when the actor adheres to action that is established by tradition and affectual action has to do with emotion and feeling.

Bureaucracy is a basic feature of modern society that focuses on the rule of law. It consists of: official business is conducted on a continuous basis; it is conducted in accordance with stipulated rules in an administrative agency; every official's responsibility and authority are part of a hierarchy of authority; officials are responsible to the resources they are given for a specific task; the incumbents of an office do not own the office and official business is conducted on the basis of written documents (Weber, 1962:424).

Bauman (1989) builds on the meaning of instrumental rationality and bureaucracy, as a fundamental part of the modern world and as a basis to understand the Holocaust. He wrote: "I purpose to treat the Holocaust as a rare, yet significant and reliable, test of the hidden possibilities of the modern society" (1989:12). German elites and people built their actions against the Jewish people by accenting instrumental rationality that was void of values and used bureaucratic means to attempt to annihilate the Jewish population of Europe. Scores of people (including all levels of German society that also included the Christian Church) took "moral sleeping pills' (1989:26) silenced any sense of morality. Thus, the kind of social action was exclusively instrumental rationality and the use of bureaucracy to achieve the stated goal: the deletion of the Jews in Europe.

Part of the means to achieve this was to create an ideal type of the Jew called the "conceptual Jew." This emerged as an effect of the Nazis to force all Jews away from their homes and livelihood and to put them into ghettos. This removed them from intimate contact with other Germans who may have had a personal relationship to them. In effect, it produced an attitude of "out of sight–out of mind."

The conceptual Jew was slimy who defied the order of things and was accused of boundary breaking (living a life different and in contrast to the Christian majority). He was a prototype of all nonconformity, heterodoxy, anomaly and aberration.

This image varied from European state to others. In Poland, the Jew was blamed for social inequality rather than the elite. They were accused of being Communist or revolutionary. On the other hand, which seems illogical, they were judged and condemned for being capitalist,

As referred to in the previous section, the Jew was considered to be of another race who was inferior to the Aryan race who were dominant. This appellation would have been impossible without modern science which was never true. Bauman expands on its meaning:

> Racism stands apart by a practice of which it is a part and which it rationalizes: a practice that combines strategies of architecture and gardening with that of medicine—in the service of the construction of an official social order, through cutting out the elements of the present reality that neither fit the visualized perfect reality, nor can be changed to that they do (1989:65).

Jews are now defined as having a permanent nature that cannot be changed. Evidence for this is that those Jews who became Christians were still targeted to be killed. Continued prejudices and serotypes include the Jews distort the natural order of the universe and are a cancer to society. Hitler built on this 'science" in speaking of the Jew as a disease, as an infestation, an infection, a pestilence, a vermin and as decomposing worms. Bauman uses a garden to illustrate a modern society. A garden needs a gardener, tools, and order. A fruitful garden (as envisioned by Hitler) was harmony, conflict free, docile to rulers, orderly and controlled. Weeds (the Jews) are to be "pulled out."

The Holocaust is unique in history because it brings together some ordinary factors of modernity normally kept apart. These factors consist of a very powerful state power, an antisemitic ideology, a centralization of power, a major military presence, a sophisticated bureaucracy and the acquiesce of the German people. It was also made possible by a racist and antisemitic Nazi power, covered over by an international war and a policing of all members of society.

By nature, a modern bureaucracy is indifferent to the incumbents of an office. In some way, one may consider them to be de-humanized with no image of personhood. This was especially accentuated during the Nazi era. A part of this dehumanizing effect was the biomedical scientists who played an active role in the initiation, administration and execution of human subjects.

Bauman concludes his study by showing the Holocaust to be a paradigm of the modern bureaucratic rationality. This paradigm activates maximum results with minimum of costs. All is done to deploy the skills and resources of everyone involved. Any outside influence to subvert the goal are neutralized.

Karesh and Hurvitz (2008) summarize well what Bauman's primary thesis was: "The uniqueness of the Holocaust is found in its systematic, assembly line method and the unflinching goal of complete annihilation" (2008:217).

PROXIMATE FACTOR TWO: HITLER, NAZISM AND WORLD WAR II.

These factors are at the gates of the Holocaust. Previous factors converge with this to create this attempt to exterminate the Jewish people of Europe. Although these people have suffered horribly for over three millennial, this is the second time there was an attempt of extermination The first was a decree to destroy them in 474 BCE at the hand of Haman, a chief administrator of King Achashverosh (also known as Xerxes, 486-465 BCE) of Persia. Through the intervention of Esther and her uncle, Mordekhai, the people of Israel were saved. The similar story structures the Holocaust that although tragedy struck six million Jews, the Jews continue to the present day.

A very similar person to Haman is Adolf Hitler (1889-1945). According to Karesh and Hurvitz (2008) he is central to the initiation of World War II and the Holocaust. He was born in Braunau, Austria in 1889 being a son of an Austrian customs official. Many failures challenged his youth by begin rejected to the Academy of Fine Arts in Vienna, failed to escape conscription into the Austrian army and then failed a physical exam barring from that army. He became interested in the power of politics and developed skills of propaganda while absorbing antisemitic literature and joined the Nazi party— soon to become its head. Right from the beginning, he initiated campaigns against the Jews especially by socially marginalizing them through the Nuremberg Laws.

The chancellor's world view was fundamentally antisemitic. He adhered to a social Darwinist ideology (societal survival of the fittest) and built his platform on post-WW I resentments and blamed the Jews for Germany's defeat. Rees (2017) recognized him as an angry man intending to blame others for failures and mistakes. The primary target was the Jew.

Another source that both Hitler and the Nazi's built their ideologies on was called the *volkisch movement*. The concept of *volk* would become of immense importance to Hitler and the Nazis. The term accented a link to the soil and to the forest. Germans were to find their identity in the soil, in nature. It was a spiritual movement that accented exclusivity based on a mystical relation to the land in contrast to industry and commerce. It is from this movement that the swastika became the symbol of the Nazis. The four F's indicate "fresh," "pious," "happy," and "free." All this excluded the Jew who was in antithesis of the *volkisch* ideal-the Jews were not a people who came from the forest (Rees, 2017).

From various ultra-right movements which were fundamentally antisemitic rose the German Workers Party that became, in 1923, the National Socialist German Worker's Party or the Nazis. Its basis was being a member of the nation that excluded the Jewish membership. The official policy of the organization was to strip the Jews of their citizenship. The Nazi party was not alone in denying citizenship to the Jew. Rees accounts that up to seventy other groups in 1921 all believed in taking away citizenship status to all Jews of Germany.

The Nazis gained a majority of the seats in the government in the early 1930s. In spite of some setbacks in the electoral process in a reduction of their percentage of the government, an event that moved Germany away from being a democratic to being totalitarian. In 1932, a former chancellor, Franz von Papen, convinced Hindeburg (the president of the nation) to name Hitler the new chancellor. This happened in 1933. Bergen wrote "Hitler did not need to seize power. It was given to him (2016:67).

Bergen accented to major concepts that captured Hitler and the Nazis: race and space. The importance of race has already been covered. Space was also central to the Chancellor and the Nazis. The expansion motif took six years in the making: 1933-1939. The plan was to have more space for the Aryan Race and to displace any others who were living in the space that the Nazis conquered.

Beginning in 1933, Hitler targeted the mentally and physically disabled (killing them in mass that numbered to about 14,751 in six euthanasia centers with lethal injections and gassings), the Communists, Jehovah Witnesses, Germans of African descent, homosexuals, the homeless, incurable criminals, the Sini and Roma, the Free Masons, and, most importantly, the Jews.

The murder of the disabled was done, in one case in Brandenburg, There, in a mental hospital, was reconfigured to be a killing facility where "patients" were taken to a room to be gassed to death and their bodies burned outside of the facility.

Much of this was a prelude to the expansion of space-first to Austria, then to Czechoslovakia Poland and beyond. World War II officially began in 1939 with the invasion of Poland. In the western part of Europe, the Nazis conquered Belgium, Norway, Holland, and France. Subsequent to this, back to the East (after a failed attempt against Great Britain) Greece and Yugoslavia. The largest assault was against the Soviet Union in 1941.

War casualties were massive. Three million Russians killed in action, three million as prisoners of war, eight million in occupied Russia, three million in unoccupied Russia three- and one-half Germans, and one million in occupied territories (Crystal, 2004). In total, nearly seventy-five million people died including the war with Japan.

Although there were earlier causalities before the war began, the Holocaust needs to contextualized in this War. Could it be that Hitler began the war not only to gain space for his Aryans but also to cover-up his nefarious plans to destroy the Jewish people?

Proximate Factor Three: Ecclesial Silence

In its very essence is Christianity to be prophetic—of calling nations, societies, and individuals to justice and love as did the ancient prophets of Judaism. Integrated into the very fabric of Israel is this presence of God coming to speak to Israel and to humanity through the human voice of prophets. For this, Martin Buber (1949) has called Israel and Judaism the prophetic faith as presented in Chapter One of this text.

Sadly, throughout the history of the people of German from 1917 to 1945, the Christian churches, both Catholic and Protestant, were silent. They had abdicated their prophetic role and went hand in hand with the Nazis and Hitler to the radical detriment of the European Jew who stood alone in front of a vicious and deadly political movement that had no respect for human life and broke over and over again the fifth word of the Decalogue: "Do not murder." And when the Nazis committed this crime over and over, the Christian voice was silent.

The pivotal event was the infamous Reich Concordat of 1933. Figure 7:3 illustrates this process:

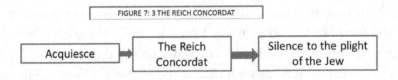

FIGURE 7: 3 THE REICH CONCORDAT

Acquiesce → The Reich Concordat → Silence to the plight of the Jew

To a monumental event like this, the two protagonists are Hitler and Pacelli (1876-1958), the future pope known as Pius XII (pope from 1939-1958. He had close ties to Germany, Hitler and the Nazis. From 1920 to 1930, he served as papal nuncio to Germany. His intent was to provide protection and legitimacy to the Catholic Church in Germany. During the 1930s, there were about 23 million Roman Catholics, amounting to nearly forty percent of the population.

Leading up to the mutual signing of the document was a series of submission to and acquiesce of the whole church (including the Protestant institutions) to Hitler and his regime. But before a long series of acquiesces occurred, Cornwell (2008) posited that the Catholic Church had a significant presence. Catholics hosted a web of social and political associations, trade unions, newspapers, youth groups, publishing houses, women's groups, colleges and schools. All this was to change as all levels of German society (the elite, the middle class, the working class, academics, professionals, Catholic and Protestants bowed down and agreed to the articles of the Concordia.

What were the articles? They could be summarized into two statements:

1. The Reich would support and give legitimacy to Catholic education.
2. The Vatican agrees to separate religious Catholicism and political Catholicism. This meant, in effect that all levels of Catholics from the laity, to the priesthood and to the hierarchy of the bishops, there would be no dissent to the Nazi regime and no disobedience and insubordination. Thus, any Catholic organization that was political in nature was to be disbanded and none could be created.

At first, there was a significant negative response to the Concordia by the German bishops. Bishop Konrad von Preysing distributed a memorandum to the bishop's conference telling them that the Nazis were completely at odds with that of the Catholic Church. His was a minor voice and the bishops, as a whole agreed to the Concordat. A pastoral letter, promulgated on behalf of the bishops, announced the end of the hierarchy's opposition to the Nazi regime. Shortly after this, the Protestant churches across Germany accepted Hitler and his regime.

An extended quote from Corwall is appropriate here:

> A mighty Church with its dedicated pastors and a
> host of lay social and political organizations was in a
> state of self-imposed inertia, looking to the Vatican
> for the next move, the next idea, the next move.

In the meantime, Hitler was taking full advantage of that inaction to outlaw and destroy every vestige of social and political Catholic capacity and identity (2008:147).

As a consequence, the Catholic Centre Party (one of only a few opposed to the Nazi Party) was disbanded and a reign of terror followed of any Catholic that had any affixations with political Catholicism. Catholic and Protestant clergy came on board to give to the regime church records in the attempt of the Nazis to identify Jewish heritage.

The effects of the concordat (Christian silence) had horrific effects on the Jews of Europe during the Holocaust, our next topic.

THE HOLOCAUST OR THE *SHOAH*

It is good to start with several definitions of the Holocaust:

Called *Shoah* in Hebrew, refers to the period from January 30, 1933, when Adolf Hitler became chancellor of Germany, until May 8, 1945, when Germany surrendered to the allies (Karesh and Hurvitz (2008).

and

The brutal and systematic murder of two-thirds of Europe's Jews during the second world war (Hellig, (2003).

Holocaust comes from the Greek word "holokaustor" meaning "fully burnt" while the Hebrew term, *Shoah* refers to "catastrophe." (Hellig, 2003).

Scholars of the tragedy have noted that there never had been a systematic destruction of a people on the basis of their birth. It is new both in Jewish and world history and has a uniqueness about it that conjures up how diabolical and inhumane human beings can be. What is unique, according to Hellig, is Hitler and the Nazis. Both were contemptuous of Christianity, saw the Jew as a demon, selectively used Christian traditions and pseudo-science, used messianic language, called the Jews "Christ-killers," and envisioned the Jew as a pollutant to society and had to be removed to "save" the social order. Hitler's world view is held together, according to Hellig, by antisemitism.

There is a debate among scholars when the Holocaust begin. Karesh and Hurvitz have argued that it began in 1933 with the confirmation of Hitler becoming the chancellor. I would argue that it began in earnest (mass killings) in 1942 with the invasion of the Soviet Union what I would call phase one when the policy of the Einsatzgruppen: A special mobile killing unit of the German army who followed the main army into the Soviet Union as well as other countries such as the Ukraine and Poland. Their sole purpose was to murder Jews. They would force their captives to dig mass graves in fields and forests and then shoot them all. In all, about 1.5 million Jews suffered death between 1941 and 1944.

Phase two, I would argue, happened in the same year in the deportation of Jews from ghettos to killing centers. This latter is what Bergen calls the flashover. She explains. The fire material was like straw that was present from the long history of antisemitism, both Christian and secular. The straw began to burn with Hitler and the Nazis. It reached a fire flashover[78] in 1942 with the Einsatzgruppen and the deportment of Jews from the ghettos of Poland and the other occupied states.

After the Wannsee Conference in 1942, five "killing centers" were constructed in Poland with the sole purpose the mass murders as soon as possible. One, Chemno, was already established. The four new ones consisted of Belzec, Sobibor, Treblinka, and Auschwitz-Birkenau.

---

[78] Bergen's image is from a house fire. It starts very small and when it reaches a certain stage, it explodes to consume the whole house. The latter is called the "flashover."

Even though the administration planned quick assembly line death marches, the camps were sites of torture, rape and corruption. Both Bergen (2009) and Rees (2017) presented images of each.

Chemno was a small village on a railway branch line. Trains brought the Jews and were asked to strip to prepare for a shower. They, ninety, were then taken into a van. The vans drove slowly into the forest and the passengers died with gas and then their bodies were dumped into the fields and the forests. From 1941 to 1942, one-hundred and forty-five thousand Jews died at this camp.

Belzec had a fixed installation for gassing that used diesel engines to generate carbon monoxide. Its opening brought fifteen thousand Jews from Lvov, Poland, to be killed. By the time the camp was dismantled, over four-hundred thousand died along with an unknown number of Roam and Poles. One brave Nazi was horrified at what he saw. He endeavored to sabotage the operation and then went to Berlin. There he told his story to the Papal Nuncio but was meet with silence.

The camp of **Sobibor** was constructed solely for the purpose of killing Jews. The Nazis murdered two hundred and fifty thousand Jews from eastern Poland, the occupied Soviet Union, and Holland.

Once a labor camp, **Treblinka** became a killing center in 1942. From all over Europe, trains transported Jews as well as Roma to this center. An estimated nine hundred thousand Jews and two thousand Roma lost their live there.

Auschwitz-Birkenau was the most infamous of all the camps and most central to the Holocaust. The uniqueness of this place was when doctors did medical "experiments" on the prisoners. They engaged in sterilization processes, used radiation, had the victims stand in icy water and recorded results. Officers engaged in sadistic practices like having men stand naked in a square and beat them. Killing went hand in hand with plunder. Clothes, money, jewelry, shoes and luxury goods were stolen from the prisoners.

Most Jews arrived at the camp by train and were immediately divided into two lines. The elderly, weak and children were gassed while a second group formed work parties in appalling conditions until they died or became too weak to work. They entered the gas chambers to their deaths.

Death tolls were staggering. An estimated 1.5 million Jews, non-Jewish Poles, and Roma lost their lives at this center. After the Germans lost the war, one would think there would be an end to the violence. Not so. Beginning in the fall of 1944, the Germans had lost control of much of their territory. Orders were given to empty the camps of prisoners. They were forced to march under the watchful eye of the soldiers. With no food and proper clothing, many died on route. Bergin wrote:

> In some respects all of the episodes (the death marches) are similar: hungry, sick men and women forced to walk or ride in open trains and trucks, the weakest and least cooperatives of them shot or abandoned to die: brutal, confused guards, many of them hastily recruited from among local police, reserve officers, and soldiers, driving their charges at a murderous pace away from the rapidly advancing fronts, although the swirling chaos of those final fourth month of the war perilously impaired the information they received and their judgement; the stunned, scared inhabitants of the areas through which the prisoners and their guards zigzagged, hunkered down to await the worst and lashing out in panic at the prisoners who embodied their worst fears (2009:291-292).

Bergen estimated that there were two hundred and fifty thousand to three hundred and seventy-five thousand people perished in these marches. Untold suffering and tragedy continued right to the end of the war when Germany surrendered on May 8, 1945.

Where was the ecclesial institution in all of this? Where was the Pope? Catholics and Protestants in Germany were silent. But the silence that had many wonderings was the silence of Pius XII.

Corwell records many delegations and letters were sent to Pacelli. Several of them stand out:

- Through 1942, there continued to be a flow of reliable information to the Vatican.
- A delegate from the United States came to persuade Pacelli to speak out.
- In 1942, the news of the camps and the attacks against the Jews were well known.
- In Holland, the Catholics bishops made a plea to the Pope to speak out.
- Vatican diplomats from France, Poland, Brazil, the United States, and Great Britain acted jointly or individually to encourage for Pacelli to speak out.
- A delegation of Protestants came to talk to the Pope.
- In 1943, Jews from the ghetto in Rome were rounded up and sent to the camps in Poland.

In all cases, the Pope did not speak out of the tragedy. He came close to it. In his Christmas speech of 1942, he spoke against totalitarianism and injustices but did not mention Hitler, the Nazis or the Jewish people. There were never any liturgical functions where one would pray for the victims in the Holocaust. However, when Hitler died by suicide, the Pope offered a solemn mass for r him.

THEOLOGICAL REFLECTIONS.

One distal and proximate factor that has not been discussed is faith based and theological in nature. All the factors mentioned above, except the prejudices and stereotypes embedded in antisemitism, have been external to the individual person. Jews and Christians realize that there is a major motivation to evil that is embedded in the human heart: the tendency to sin. Many scriptures refer to this.

The book of Deuteronomy cautions the people of Israel, as they enter into their promised land that: ..."be careful not to let yourselves be seduced, so that you turn aside, serving other gods and worshipping them" (Deuteronomy 11:32). Jeremiah exclaims: "The heart is more wicked that anything else and mortally sick, who can fathom it?" (17:9). David, in his prayer of repentance, prays: "True, I was born guilty, was a sinner from the moment my mother conceived me" (Psalm 51:7).

Rabbi Jonah of Gerona (2016:1751) wrote of the "evil inclination" within the human person: "One who commits a transgression has been seized by lust and incited thereto, by the evil inclination."

Many are the references in the New Testament to the reality of sin lurking in the heart of humans. *Yeshua* said: "Don't you see that nothing going into a person from outside can make him unclean? ... It is what comes out of a person that makes him unclean. For it is within, out of a person's heart, come forth wicked thoughts, sexual immorality, theft, murder, adultery, greed, malice, deceit, indecency, envy, slander, arrogance, foolishness. All these wicked things come from within, and they make a person unclean (Mark 7:21-23). In the sermon on the mount, Messiah exclaimed: "I tell you that a man who even looks at a woman with the purpose of lusting after her has already committed adultery with her is his heart" (Matthew 5:28).

Saint Paul and James continued a similar theme. "It is perfectly evident what the old nature does. It expresses itself in sexual immorality, impurity, and indecency; involvement with the occult and with drugs; in feuding, fighting, becoming jealous and getting angry; in selfish ambition, factionalism, intrigue and envy; in drunkenness, orgies and things like these (Galatians 5:19-21). James adds to this. He asks "What is causing all the quarrels and fights among you? Isn't it your desires battling inside of you?" James then says of the wisdom of this world: "This wisdom is not the kind that comes down from above; on the contrary, it is worldly, unspiritual and demonic. For where there are jealously and selfish ambition, there will be disharmony and every foul practice" (James 4:1 and 3:15-16).

I would contend that these internal evils captured millions of Christians, both Protestant and Catholic, during the Nazi era. This would include the people of the pew, the pastors and priests, the hierarchy, and, yes, the Vatican.

Yet, there is another factor that is faith-based: the global effort of the Dragon, Satan and all his angels who have a hatred for the Jews. This is depicted in the Book of Revelation Chapter Twelve. We read: "When the dragon saw that he had been hurled down to the earth, he went in pursuit of the woman who had given birth to the male child...the woman escaped by the hand of God and "The dragon was infuriated over the woman and went to fight the rest of her children, those who obey God's commands and bear witness to *Yeshua*" (Revelation 12:17). Now, he carries on attempts to crush Israel and we, the disciples of *Yeshua*. However, his end in immanent when he and his demons will be destroyed forever in the lake of fire (Revelation 20:14-15).

We must be aware that the battle we are engaged in is a cosmic battle. On one side is Israel and those of us who have been grafted into her and on the other side, minions of demons, under the power of the Dragon. They are waging war.

We can be on the winning side if we repent profoundly not only for our sins but our sins that we and our ancestors have committed against the people of Israel. David acknowledges our sin: "Together with our ancestors, we have sinned, done wrong, acted wickedly" (Psalm 106:6). Azariah in the furnace adds to this: "Yes, we have sinned and committed a crime by deserting you, yes, we have greatly sinned; we have not listened to your commandments" ... "But may the contrite soul, the humbled spirit, be acceptable to you" (Daniel 3:29 and 39).

LAMENTATIONS FOR THE SUFFERING THE FIRST- BORN SON OF GOD, ISRAEL.

Sorrow and lamentations have been the major response to the sin against Israel. How grave this sin is given by the prophet Jeremiah: "Israel is set aside for *Adonai,* the first fruits of his harvest; all who devour him will incur guilt; evil will befall them, says *Adonai* (2:3). Many evils have fallen upon the Church. The most blatant is division and the broken body of *Yeshua*. The sufferings of the Messiah, joining with the victims of the *Shoah,* reflect this pain:

Of the Messiah: Though mistreated, he was submissive-he did not open his mouth. Like a lamb led to be slaughtered, like a sheep silent before its shearers, he did not open his mouth. After forcible arrest and sentencing, he was taken away; and none of his generation protested his being cut off from the land of the living. For the crimes of my people, who deserved the punishment themselves. He was given a grave among the wicked; in his death he was with a rich man. Although he had done no violence and had said nothing deceptive, yet it pleased *Adonai* to crush him with illness, to see if he would present himself as a guilt offering. If he does, he will see his offspring; and he will prolong his days; and at his hand *Adonai's* desire will be accomplished (Isaiah 53:7-10).

Of Jerusalem: Because of these things, I weep my eyes, my eye stream with tears for anyone who could comfort me and revive my courage is far away. My children are in a state of shock because the enemy has prevailed. Zion spreads out her hands, but no one is there to console her. Concerning Jacob, *Adonai* ordered that those around him to be his foes. Jerusalem has become for them an unclean filthy thing. Her gates have sunk into the ground he destroyed and broke their bars. Her king and rulers or among the nations, there is no more *Torah,* and her prophets do not receive visions from *Adonai.* My eyes are worn out from weeping, everything in me is churning I am empty of emotion because of the wounds of my people because children and infants are fading away in the streets of the city what can be said of you what can be compared with you, daughter of Jerusalem what example can I give to comfort you, Virgin daughter of Zion for your downfall is as vast as the sea who can heal you. All our adversaries open their mouths to jeer us. They grind their teeth they say we have swallowed her up this is a day we were waiting for, and now we have lived to see it their hearts cried. Daughter of Sion let your tears stream down like torrents day and night give yourself no respite, give your eyes no rest. use an old man or lying on the ground in the streets my unmarried women and young men have fallen by the sword you killed them on the day of your anger you slaughtered them without pity remember my other misery the warm world and the gall there always on my mind This is why I am so depressed on our adversaries open their mouth to jeer. Panic and pitfall have come upon us desolation and destruction. My eyes stream with rivers of water over the destruction of the daughter of my people. How the gold is lost its luster! How the fine gold has changed! How the stones of the sanctuary are scattered in every street corner. The precious sons of Zion are precious fine gold to think that they are now worth no more than the clay jars made by a potter! Remember *Adonai*, what is happened to us look and see our disgrace The land we possessed has been passed on to strangers our homes to foreigners, We have become fatherless orphans, our mothers know now are widows. We have to pay to drink our own water; we have to buy our own wood. The yoke is our necks and we are persecuted; we toil and exhaustion but are given no rest joy has vanished from our hearts are dancing has turned into mourning the Crown has fallen from our heads woe to us for we have sinned. This is why our heart is sick This is why our eyes grow dim it is because of Mount Zion, so wasted that the jackals have overthrown it. *Adonai*, turn us back to you and we will come back renew our days as they were in the past- unless you have total rejected us in the fury that knows no limit (Selections from Lamentations1-5).

CONCLUSIONS

Can anyone of us imagine the great pain and tragedy of over six million Jews who suffered so horribly under the arm of the Nazi's which was under the tutelage of Satan? As the author of Lamentations did so often, to cry, and to cry some more. This calls for some of the most radical kinds of repentance. A repentance like no other repentance in human history which involves individuals, families, communities, states, nations and the whole of humanity. The Good News is that Satan's plan to eliminate the Jews did not happen. The First-Born Son of *Adonai* is very much alive and will be present more and more as the epicenter of history, place (Israel) and of the human race. His role is "being light to the nations" (Luke 1:78-79 and a "blessing to the nations" (Genesis 12:3).

References: Chapter Seven

Bauman, Z. 1989. *Modernity and the Holocaust*. New York: Cornell University Press.

Bergen, D. 2016. *War and genocide. A concise history of the Holocaust*. New York: Rowmand and Littlefield.

Bloch, M. 1961. *Feudal society*. Volume I. Translated by L.A, Manyon. Chicago: The University of Chicago Press.

Buber, M. 1949. *The Prophetic Faith*. New York: Harper and Row, Publishers.

Carroll, J.2001. *The sword of Constantine: The Church and the Jews. A history*. A Mariner Book. Houghton Mifflin Company. Boston.

Cornwall, J. 2008. *Hitler's Pope: The secret history of Pius XII*. New York: Penguin Books.

Crystall, D. (Editor). 2004. *The Penguin Encyclopedia*. London, England: Penguin Books.

Feldman, L. 1993. *Jew and Gentile in the ancient world: Attitudes and interactions from Alexander to Justinian*. Princeton, NJ: Princeton University Press.

Fichtenbauer, J. (Archdeacon). 2019. *The Mystery of the Olive Tree: Uniting Jews and Gentiles for Christ's Return*. Luton, Bedfordshire: New Life Publishing.

Hellig, J. 2003. *The Holocaust and antisemitism*. One World Publications:

Kamen, H. 1998. *The Spanish Inquisition*. London: The Folio Society.

Karesh, S. and M. Hurvitz 2008. *Encyclopaedia of Judaism*. New York: Checkmark Books.

Krewson, W. L. 2017. *Jerome and the Jews: Innovative supersessionism*. Eugene Oregon: Wipf and Stock Publishers.

Langton, D. 2007. "Relations between Christians and Jews, 1914-2000." In Volume Nine, World Christianities c. 1914-2000,

The Cambridge History of Christianity, p. 483-493. Edited by H. McLeod. Cambridge, UK: Cambridge University Press.

Po-Chia Hsia, R. (1992). *Trent 1475. Stories of a ritual trial.* New York: Yale University.

Rabbi Jonah of Gerona (2016). In D. Stern, *The complete Jewish Study Bible.* Peabody, Massachusetts: Hendrickson Publishers.

Rainer, K.(2011-2017) Berlin, "Adversos Judaeos Homilies", in: *Encyclopedia of Jewish History and Culture Online*, Original German Language Edition: Enzyklopädie Jüdischer Geschichte und Kultur. Im Auftrag der Sächsischen Akademie der Wissenschaften zu Leipzig herausgegeben von Dan Diner. © J.B. Metzler, Stuttgart/ Springer-Verlag GmbH Deutschland 2011–2017.. Consulted online on 17 January 2018 http://dx.doi.org/10.1163/2468-8894_ejhc_COM_0003

Rees, L. 2017. *The Holocaust: A new history.* New York: Public Affairs.

Sevenster, J. N. 1975. *The roots of pagan Anti-Semitism in the Ancient World.* Leiden: E. Brill.

Schafer, D. 1997. *Judeophobia. Attitudes towards the Jews in the Ancient World.* London: Harvest University Press.

Skocpol, T. 1984. "Sociology's historical imagination." In *Vision and method in historical sociology*, edited by T. Skocpol, p. 1-22. Cambridge: Cambridge University Press.

Trachtenberg, J. 1943. *The devil and the Jews: The Medieval conception of the Jew and its relationship to modern Antisemitism.* New York: Yale University Press.

Weber, M. 1962. *Max Weber: an intellectual portrait.* Edited by R. Bendix. Garden City, New York: Anchor Books, Double Day & Company.

Weber, M. 1978. *Economy and Society. Berkeley:* University of California Press.

CHAPTER EIGHT

Eschatology and the Return of the Messiah Remembering, Repenting and Reconciling

OVERVIEW

This chapter is devoted to the unveiling of the Jewish-Christian understanding of eschatology. Its focus will be on the theology of Rabbinic Judaism followed by the Jewish believers of *Yeshua* in ancient times. Subsequent to these will be an interpretation of eschatology in the post-modern era through the lens of Messianic Judaism. The fourth part will be Catholic reflections on Christian Eschatology. These insights revolve about the theme of all these elements: remembering, repenting, and reconciling. It is to remember the divergence of Christianity from the original meaning of eschatology, repent of errors and sin, and to move forward in the reconciliation between modern Gentile believers in Jesus and Jewish believers in *Yeshua*. The ultimate goal is reconciliation and the creation of the new humanity (Ephesians 2:15), union between the two to be finalized in the Parousia, the end of *olam hazel*(this world, this age), through the transition, *acharit-hayamim* (the last days) to the genesis of *"olam haba* (the world to come), and the return of Messiah who is "Faithful and True, the Word of God, the King of Kings and the Lord of lords" (Revelation 19:11, 13 and 16).

RABBINIC JEWISH[79] TEACHING OF ESCHATOLOGY

Rich is the tradition of eschatology in the records of Rabbinic Judaism. Its source are the many commentaries of the *Tanakh* known as the *Talmud*, which is the written work in which the "Oral Law was committed to writing, consisting of the *Mishna*, compiled around 220 CE and the *Gemara*. The *Jerusalem Talmud's Gemara* was completed around 400 CE, the larger and more authoritative *Babylonian Talmud*

---

[79] *Yahadut Rabbanit*, also called Rubenism, has been the mainstream form of Judaism since the 6th century CE, after the codification of the Babylonian *Talmud*. Growing out of Pharisaic Judaism. Rabbinic Judaism, is based on the belief that at Mount Sinai, Moses received from God the Written *Torah* in addition to an oral explanation, known as the" Oral *Torah*," that Moses transmitted to the people (Rabbinic Judaism).

a century later" (Stern, 2015:917). The *Mishna* was a commentary of the *Tanakh* while the *Gemara*, a commentary on the *Mishna*. For a further understanding.

The *Talmud* used here was a short summary of the major features of the Talmud compiled by Cohen (1949). This work covers major features of Judaism and, especially, eschatology, our topic here. Under the heading of eschatology, Cohen summarizes the teachings of the Messiah, the resurrection of the dead, the world to come, the last judgment, Gehinnom, and Gan Eden.

Jews have been and always will be a people of life, not destruction, a forward-looking people, a people of the future (*'olam haba*) and awaiting the coming of the Messiah. It is believed that the *'olam haba* was always in the mind of the Creator before creation. This *'olam haba* consisted of the *Torah*, repentance, Gan Eden, Gehinnom, the Throne of Glory, the Temple, but, especially, the Messiah a descendent of David and son of Jacob.

The Messiah.

Before his return, there will be troubles such as children revolting against their parents and elders, meeting places becoming brothels, scribal learning decreasing, a bitter warfare will ensue, and the earth will be destroyed for the days of Gog and Magog will have arrived. After these great troubles, the Messiah will come but as to the timing of his coming, it is not known. His coming will be so very impressive. There will be light, water will flow from Jerusalem, trees will bear abundant fruit, and the City will be rebuilt with sapphires.

Peace will reign that includes all animals enjoying a covenant of peace, weeping will cease, there will be no more death, the blind will see and the lame will walk, and all will understand each other as they will speak a pure, common language. Israel will be restored, the lowly will inherit the earth, there will be no curses and many Gentiles will come to faith. All the tribes of Israel, scattered throughout the earth, will be united and come to Jerusalem. This Holy City will be restored and the Temple will be re-established.

The Resurrection of the Dead.

This teaching enjoyed prominence among the first millennium Rabbis. Several graphic images about the resurrection are given: it is like a woman giving birth from conception, gestation and birthing. It will also be like the formation of the world as presented in Genesis 1-2 and the formation of a new resurrected people, Israel, as recorded in Ezekiel 37:8-14. The protagonist of this process will be Elijah the Prophet: "The resurrection of the dead will come through Elijah" (Cohen, 1949:363) that will have an endless duration.

The World to Come or 'Olam Haba.

There are two Rabbinic versions of the *'olam haba*. One is similar to the millennium era of early Christianity that is a transient one, and the other, is the existing order that will be followed by a new world order. The *'olam haba* is also an important feature of Rabbinic Judaism. It was said that the Holy One gave three major gifts to Israel, the *Torah*, the land of Israel, and the *'olam haba*. The Rabbis contrasted the *olam hazel* (of this age or of this time) and the *'olam haba*. Table 8:1, The *'olam hazel* and *'olam haba*, shows this contrast:

Table 8: 1: The *Olam Hazel* and the *'Olam haba*

Characteristics	Olam Hazel	'Olam Haba
	Those of high rank are at the top of the hierarchy	Those of low rank will be at the top of the hierarchy
	Eating and Drinking	No Eating and Drinking
	Sex and procreation	No sex and procreation
	Business and trade	No business and trade
	Envy and Hatred	No envy and hatred
	Curses on wounds	No curses on wounds
	Not living in the light of Shekinah	Living in the light of Shekinah
	Change fullness	Changelessness
	Temporary Happiness	Happiness

Who are those who pass from one to the other? Those who live the *Torah* and who do good works. Further, "He who is meek and humble, walks about with a lowly demeanor, studies the *Torah* consistently, and takes no credit to himself" (Cohen, 1949:368). In contrast, who will not passover? They who shame their brother in public, deny the doctrine of the resurrection that can be deduced from the *Torah,* are epicureans, who read non-canonical books and who utter spells over a wound.

The Last Judgement.

There are two versions of the last judgment: at the end of individual life and at *acharit-hayamim*. Prominent is the *acharit-hayamim*, when all will be judged-is that of the Gentiles (including Christians) who have been so cruel to Israel. Other sins that the Gentiles, and some Israelites, have will be judged are: creating institutional market place as a resort of harlots; the erection of bath houses; using silver and gold that belongs to the Holy One; conquering of others so they do labor; and for those who destroy the Temple. Here is a quote which calls all to account:

> They that are born are destined to die; and the dead
> to be brought to life again; and the living to be
> judged, to know, to make known, and to be made
> conscious that He is God, He is the Maker, He is the
> Creator, He is the discerner, He is the judge, He is
> the witness, He is the complainant; He it is that will
> be the Hereafter judge, blessed be He, with Whom
> there is no unrighteousness, nor forgetfulness, nor
> respect of persons, nor taking of bribes. Know also
> that everything is according to the reckoning. And
> let not your imagination give you hope that the grave
> will be a place of refuge for you; for perforce you live,
> and perforce you die, and perforce your will in the
> Hereafter have to give account and reckoning before

the supreme King of Israel the Holy One, blessed be
He (Cohen, 1949:373).

There is also a teaching that at the resurrection, there will be a
reunion of body and soul. After judgment, there will be a temporary
punishment to most but those who have intercourse with another
man's wife, who shame another in public, and who call others
opprobrious names will experience eternal punishment.

The Rabbis consider three classes of people: (1), the perfectly
righteous will enter eternal life, (2), those who are completely wicked
will be sealed in *Gehinnom*, and (3), those who go to *Gehinnom* will
suffer for some time and are refined in fire. If they call on the name
of *Adonai*, He will release them.

Gehinnom

This "place" was created before the physical world was created. It
goes by seven different names: *Adaddon* (in Greek, Apollyon) or
Destruction, corruption, horrible pit, shadow of death, neither world,
deep valley, and *Topheth* (led astray). There are three entrances: the
wilderness, the sea and Jerusalem. The sinner enters seven different
levels: *Sheol, Adaddon*, shadow of death, the nether world, the land of
forgetfulness, *Gehinnom*, or silence. What is the nature of this place
of judgment and suffering? It is described as abnormal fire, brimstone
and darkness.

Gan Eden

This is heaven in the language of Christianity. It is an expansion of
the Garden of Eden which also has seven degrees: being in the divine
presence and experiencing Shekinah; entering into the court of the
King; coming into the house of the King; being before the tabernacle
of the King, climbing the Holy Hill of the King, walking towards
the hill of the King-Lord and entering the Holy Place of the King.

It will be a place of marvelous joy where one will be invited to a wonderful banquet, drinking fine wine and eating fine food. The most important characteristic, though, will be "The chief of joy, for they will experience being in the actual presence of God" (Cohen, 1949:385).

Gan Eden has many other characteristics: there will be two gates of ruby; sixty myriads of angels; when one enters, his/her grave clothes are exchanged for eight robes of glory and upon the head, two crowns; eight myrtles will be in his or her hand and the chamber one goes to will have sixty angels attending to one's needs; and, lastly, there will be eighty myriad of trees. In the center or *Gan Eden* will be the Tree of Life that will have 500,000 varieties of fruit.

There are several houses or classes of the righteous: the martyrs, those drowned at sea, those who study *Torah,* those who are covered with divine glory, those who are penitents, virgins, and poor workers who keep the *Torah.*

Finally, the righteous have the honor of sitting at the feet of the Master: "The Holy One, blessed be He, sits in their midst and expounds the *Torah* to them" (Cohen, 1949:389).

Conclusions

I believe it is remarkable that Rabbinic Judaism's image of eschatology is close to the Christian teachings. The prediction of the Coming Messiah is so very similar to the Christian understanding of the return of the Messiah, *Yeshua.* Both traditions acknowledge the resurrection of the righteous and dead, the world to come, the reversal of the values of the world and the values of heaven, the personal and final judgement, and the belief in hell (and a kind of purgatory) and heaven. These insights would have emerged from the many years of studying the *Tanakh* and not from reading Christian literature.

JEWISH BELIEVERS IN *YESHUA* AND ESCHATOLOGY.

A major source of this "unveiling" is the Jesuit Cardinal and scholar, Danielou (1964)[80]. In the conclusion to this work, Danielou accents three features of these Jewish believers in *Yeshua*: cosmos, apocalypse and gnosis. Cosmos refers to the whole universe created by God with humanity centerfold. Apocalypse is indicative of the unveiling of the mystery of creation, of God's relationship to humans who are created in God's image, the central place of Israel and the incarnation-death-resurrection-ascension-return of *Yeshua* the Messiah. Gnosis is not knowledge in the Greek understanding but a saving knowledge or faith.

Our subject matter in this chapter is to be contextualized in the whole drama of divine creation, redemption, restoration and reconciliation. One may consider the primary space or place is Israel as an *Axis Mundi* and the time, as an *Axis Temporis*. All of creation, the whole cosmos revolves around Israel, in place and time, and the Messiah, *Yeshua*, the Messiah of Israel and of the whole human race.

Israel, from the time of Abraham, through to the Messiah, and to the present, is seen as an essential aspect of this cosmic history. It is vitally important to consider the Christian Church as a branch grafted into Israel, the original people of *Adonai*. This was true during the time of Paul as it is today. This profound mystery, being unveiled, is eschatological in nature as Jewish believers in *Yeshua* and Gentile believers in Jesus are being unified (by divine power, action and grace) into one new humanity. Stern, a Messianic Biblical scholar, wrote:

---

[80] The church historian, Oskar Skarsaune, wrote of Danielou: "In his fascinating study, *The theology of Jewish Christianity,* Jean Danielou has tried to create a synthesis of what he considers to be Jewish Christian tradition in the Apostolic Fathers and other Christian writings from the second century. It is a book of immense richness in material, with a brilliant detailed analysis of concepts and ideas of Jewish origin in early Christian literature (2002: 222).

It is difficult for many believers in *Yeshua* to appreciate the impact of this mystery, even though it is fundamental to the Gentiles' inclusion in Messiah. However, revelation is directed to the Jew first, and such is true of the entire biblical record: *Torah*, Prophets, Writings, Gospels, and Epistles. Gentiles are included, but they do not replace Israel or the Jews as the people of God. …. The Bible is written to followers of the God of Israel and his Messiah *Yeshua*—both Jews and Gentiles, bound together in Messiah--in anticipation of the restoration of the kingdom to Israel, which includes the blessings of all nations. (2016:1682).

It is in the future event of the restoration of the kingdom to Israel and abundant blessings to the Gentiles that is the key to understanding the return of the Messiah. The cosmic nature of *Yeshua's* return is fascinating and is to be seen in the context of the many other mysteries situated in Jewish Christianity. These mysteries were covered in the previous chapter entitled "The Mother of all Churches." They included angelology, the Son of God, *Torah*, the cosmic ladder, demons, heavenly books, the incarnation, the redemption, the mystery of the cross, the church, baptism, Eucharist, descent into hell, and personal holiness. All these mysteries can be envisioned in a *hyper cosmic imagery*.

Danielou uses the term millenarianism as an omnibus term to describe the Parousia or the return of Jesus. He then divides it into four subcategories: Jewish Christian eschatology, the first resurrection, the thousand years, and the seventh millennium. His sources are three: The Scriptures (from the Hebrew Bible or the *Tanakh* and the New Testament, Jewish and Jewish Christian apocrypha, and some early Patristic Fathers and other writers. From the Scriptures, the most commonly used texts include: Ezekiel, parts of Isaiah, Daniel, Amos, The Book of Revelation, the Thessalonians, the Corinthians, the Epistles of Peter, and excepts from the synoptic gospels where

Yeshua spoke of the end-times (Matthew 24: 1-51, Mark 13:1-37 and Luke 21:5-36). There are many apocrypha writings which have eschatological themes including: I and II Enoch, Esdras, II Baruch, the Ascension of Isaiah, the Clementine Recognitions, The Book of Jubilees, the Epistle of Barnabas, the Sibylline Oracles, and *Didascalia* of the Apostles.

Danielou referred to a good number of Patristic Fathers as well as other early Christian writers—many of whom were of Gentile origins--who paint an amazing picture of Jewish-Christian eschatology. He referenced Papias (60-130 CE), a disciple of John the Evangelist, Methodius (?-311 CE), Irenaeus (130-165 CE), the Elders, Melito of Sardis (?-180 CE), Justin Martyr (130-165 CE), Tertullian (155-240 CE), St. Jerome (347-420 CE), Lactanius (250-325 CE), Theophilus of Antioch (?-185 CE), and Hippolytus (17-235 CE).

By way of contrast, the Cardinal cited Cerinthus (50-100 CE) who gave a gnostic[81] view of eschatology. It is under gnostic influence that the Jewish-Christian worldview received such a negative impression on the Latin and the Greek churches. The attempt here is to present the actual teaching of the Jewish believers in *Yeshua*, minus the gnostic intrusions, through the scholarship of Cardinal Danielou. He initiates his study by saying: "Millenarianism, the belief that there will be an earthly reign of the Messiah before the end of time, is a Jewish Christian doctrine" (1964:377). It covers the last days of earth (*'olam hazeh*) which includes the return of Messiah, the resurrection of the saints, the general judgement and the inauguration of the New Creation.

---

[81] A variety of beliefs that originated in a Jewish-Christian context in the first and second century AD. Adherents believed that the material world is created by an emanation or 'works' of a lower god or demiurge trapping a divine spark in the human body. This spark could be lit by a spiritual knowledge or gnosis. Some of the belief statements were: matter is bad and spirit is good, the creator of the material universe is not the supreme god and that there is no sin but only ignorance (Gnosticism).

Jewish Christian Eschatology.

There are many end-times images in this literature. It is predicted there will be victory over the Anti-Christ (indicated in Revelation 19:19) and the casting of *Beliar* into the Lake of Fire. All the saints, exemplars of the Beatitudes, will be transformed and will reign with the Messiah. Under the authority of these saints, all animals will live in peaceful harmony with each other (Isaiah 11:6–9):

> The wolf will live with the lamb; the leopard lies down with the kid; calf, young lion and fattened lamb together, with a child to lead. The cow and bear will feed together, their young will lie down together, and the lion will eat straw like an ox......They will not hurt or destroy anywhere on my holy mountain, for the earth will be as full of the knowledge of *Adonai* as water covering the sea.

There will be extraordinary fecundity (Amos 9:13), an increased splendor of the sun and the moon (Isaiah 30:26), the permanent planting of Israel on their own soil from where they will never be uprooted (Amos 9:15), a restoration of Jerusalem and a renewal of the Temple worship. All of this together constitutes what Danielou calls "Asiatic Millennialism" that was most prominent during the years between 50 and 70 CE and especially prevalent in Asia.

The First Resurrection.

It was Irenaeus who believed that there would be a resurrection of the saints that preceded the final judgement. It is for these saints that Irenaeus attributes further features of the millennium: marvelous abundance without toil, no more infant mortality, incorruptibility, lives blessed by *Adonai*, living in close intimacy with their Lord, and longevity. The basic text of Asiatic millenarianism is from Isaiah:

> No more will babies die in infancy, nor more will an old man die short of his days...they will build houses and live in them, they will plant vineyards and eat their fruit...they will not toil in vain or raise children to be destroyed, for they are a seed blessed by *Adonai*; and their offspring with them. Before they call, I will answer; while they are still speaking, I will hear... they will not hurt or destroy anywhere on my holy mountain (Isaiah 65:20-25).

Irenaeus makes an explicit distinction between the earthly rebuilding of Jerusalem during the millennial reign and the descent of the heavenly Jerusalem. In contrast to the Gnostics, Irenaeus did not spiritualize and make it into some ethereal identity but remained true to the fundamental teaching, both of Jewish and Gentile believers, of the incarnation-the eternal Word made flesh.

The Thousand Years.

In this part of Jewish-Christian eschatology, there is a strong link between creation and the Garden of Eden or paradise. The restored land of the return and the reign of the Messiah is similar to the elements of the Garden of Eden. It is here that the phrase "one thousand years" takes root. According to Irenaeus, and his interpretation of relevant passages from Genesis and the Book of Jubilees, the original divine plan was that Adam would live one thousand years. With Adam's disobedience, he experienced early death, and he lived shy of 1000 years, 930 years old (Genesis 5:5). The millennium is one thousand to reflect God's plan of longevity for his son s and daughters to live many years.

This interpretation is similar to Justin Martyr who used texts from the Book of Jubilees. He wrote (quoted by Danielou): "I, and all other entirely orthodox Christians, know that there will be a resurrection of the flesh for a period of a thousand years in a Jerusalem rebuilt, adorned and enlarged, as the prophets Ezekiel and

Isaiah and others affirm" (1964:392). To flesh out this quote of Justin, Danielou presented a more extensive image, again, from Justin:

> Now we are of opinion...that by these words: 'For, according to the days of a tree shall be the days of my people (from Isaiah 65:22) ...he signifies a thousand years in a mystery. For in accordance with that which was said to Adam, that on the day in which he should eat of the tree, in that day he should die (Genesis 2:17), we know that he did not fill up a thousand years. We understand also that the saying 'A day of the Lord is as a thousand years', accords with this. And, further a man among us named John, one of the Apostles of Christ, prophesied in the Revelation that they who have believed on our Christ will spend a thousand years in Jerusalem, after which will come to pass the universal, and, in a word, eternal resurrection of all at once, followed by the judgment. And this to our Lord said, they shall neither marry, nor be given in marriage, but shall be as the angels, being children of the God of the resurrection (1965:393).

The last theme of Jewish-Christian eschatology is a discussion on the "Seventh Millennium." Danielou discussed this theme as a contrasting view of eschatology thus far presented and contrary to the Asiatic view of the millennium.

The Seventh Millennium.

The idea of the seventh millennium was born in Hellenistic Judaism likely from Alexandria where there was a thriving Jewish community and later, a significant number of Christians. This teaching forms no part of Asiatic millenarianism. In fact, it denies the teaching of the millennium. The basic tenet of the Seventh Millennium is no millennium at all but a period after death and the cessation of the world order or *'olam hazeh'*. The eighth millennium is figurative in nature and refers to eternal life. The first seven millennium constitutes the sum of history (*'olam hazeh*) and the period after, the *'olam haba*, or eternity. The belief in a period of time when Messiah would dwell on earth and reign with his saints and they would experience much abundance, longevity, the restoration of the land of Israel and the rebuilding of Jerusalem is gone. The view became part of early Christian theology and worldview exhibited by the author of the Epistle of Barnabas, Hilary of Poitiers (310-367 CE), Gregory of Elvira (?-392 CE), Hippolytus (170-235 CE), and Augustine (354-430 CE).

What was the responsibility of the first Jewish believers in *Yeshua* and the Gentile believers in Jesus from the time of their enlightenment until the return of the Messiah? *The Didache, the Way of Life* offered some the following counsels:

- Be vigilant for your life—do not let your lamps be snuffed out, and do not let your loins be ungirded—but be ready, for you do not know the hour in which our Lord is coming.
- For in the end of days, false prophets and those who cause corruption will increase in number, and the sheep will be changed into wolves, and love will be changed to hate.
- The deceiver of the world will appear as a son of God, and he will perform signs and wonders, and the earth will be delivered into his power, and he will commit disgusting acts such as have never taken place since the beginning of time.
- Then the entire human race will enter the trial by fire, and many will be caused to stumble and will perish, but those who endure in the faithfulness will be saved by the very one who curses.
- And then the signs of the truth will appear: the first sign, an expansion in the heavens; next the sign of the trumpet; and the third sign, the resurrection of the dead.

- However, not the resurrection of everyone but rather as it is said: "The Lord will come, and all the righteous along with him."
- Then the world will behold the Lord coming upon the clouds of heaven (2017/50: Chapter 16).

Conclusions

There is much evidence among Jewish believers of *Yeshua* that there is a millennial era where Messiah will be king, and his saints will enjoy an abundant life on earth before the final judgement and the genesis of a new heaven and a new earth. However, as we will witness later in this presentation, the literal meaning of the millennium so vibrant in Jewish Christianity has essentially been lost. I estimate that this was one of the causalities of the "Great Divorce" between Jewish believers in *Yeshua* (Messiah) and Gentile believers in Jesus (Christ). There is evidence in Danielou that the author of the Epistle of Barnabas and Hippolytus adapted the scriptural texts on eschatology to a Hellenized interpretation or, in sociological language, a secular worldview. Another way to view this is that these authors and later Gentile believers used a figurative or allegorical hermeneutic rather than a literal and historic one.

MESSIANIC JEWS AND ESCHATOLOGY.

For us to appreciate the vital role of Messianic Judaism in eschatology, it is well to know some of the history of various interpretations of the future return of the Messiah. The division between *Ecclesia et Synogogia* has been documented in the previous chapters. Along with this increased division, an augmented dichotomy occurred in Western history in two different interpretations of eschatology.

Hocken (2016) was a Catholic priest and scholar of the Charismatic movement, informs us of this distance and distancing between these two interpretations. The differences are rooted in replacement theology with its assumption that the church has replaced Israel:

"the promises made to Israel were re-interpreted in a spiritualizing sense so that the promised land (a real land) becomes heaven, the earthly Jerusalem is replaced by the heavenly, and the rule of Messiah becomes the glorified Christ's rule from heaven" (2016:149). The Jews and the Old Testament are looked at as carnal and the Christians and the New Testament as spiritual. The only role the Old Testament has for the Christian is that it is a type of the Christ.

Effects of this interpretation is that the covenants of Israel and its religious rites (circumcision, the *Torah*, the celebration of the feast days, and the honoring of the Shabbat) have no more value. In addition, the prophecies of the coming Messiah have totally been fulfilled with the first coming of Christ. Hocken elaborated:

> So the church developed an eschatology that is markedly different from the hope of Israel. In general, the church has looked to a heavenly fulfillment, and Israel to an earthly deliverance and fulfillment. The church sees the fulfillment as outside and above human history, whereas for the Jewish people the fulfillment is within this creation and is the climax to human history. This is one of the most serious results of the separation of church and synagogue (*Ecclesia et Synagogia*) (2016:151).

This priest-scholar is remarkably sensitive to the Messianic Jewish insights into the return of Messiah. He noted that Christians need to rediscover *Yeshua* as Messiah, not only as Savior and Lord but also as Son of David who will reign over the Kingdom of God that is rooted in the land of Israel, centered in Jerusalem and opened up for all Gentiles. None of the promises given to Israel are to be disregarded. He accused Christian believers of jettisoning the teaching of the millennial era and: "to reconsider the concept of the millennium, of a millennial reign of Jesus on earth following the Parousia. The millennium is a Jewish concept, reflecting Israel's convictions concerning time, history and fulfillment" (2016:158).

Although Hocken was not a Jew, but a Roman Catholic Monseigneur, he argued that the Messianic Jews almost universally believe that *Yeshua* is coming back to reign as king from David's throne in Jerusalem. One such Messianic Jew is David Stern (2015) in his commentary on the New Testament. The primary text that outlines the millennium is Revelation 20.

In Chapter 19, verses 1-21, a slice of the future is foreseen with the coming of the Messiah, sitting on a white horse who is called "Faithful and True." He is also known as The Word of God, the King of Kings and the Lord of Lords who comes as victor where he judges and throws into a lake of fire those who have worshipped a false god. It is after this that the millennium happens.

A synopsis of the chapter looks like this: An angel appears and seizes the dragon, Satan, and chains him up for a thousand years. Then those who had not worshiped a false god (named The Beast) and those who were martyred came to life and ruled with Messiah, as priests, for the thousand years. After the thousand years were over, the Dragon is released and he set out to deceive the nations and to gather together a huge army and to come against Jerusalem, the city *Adonai* loves, to attack it. However, a fire came down from heaven and consumed them all and then all were thrown into the lake of fire. It was after this that the dead whose names were not written in the Book of Life rose—this was called the second resurrection. They also were thrown into the same lake of fire.

Stern acknowledges that Revelation 20 is only one of two Scriptural records in the New Testament referring to the millennium. The second one reads: "the Messiah is the first fruits; then those who belong to the Messiah, at the time of his coming; then the culmination, when he hands over the Kingdom to God his Father, after having put to an end to every rulership, yes, to every authority and power" (I Corinthians 15:23-24).

An Interpretation of the Book of Revelation

Several authors provide the basis for an interpretation of the Book of Revelation: Lancaster (2017), Juster (2015), and Thomas and Richardson (2020-2021).Lancaster (2017) initiated his presentation on the Book of Revelation by presenting two generic elements on the interpretation of the work: (1), the meaning of apocalypse and, (2), the various ways the text has been interpreted.

Apocalypse is a literary genre that comes from the Greek word, *apokalupsis,* which means an unveiling, uncovering, or the revealing of something previously concealed. There are eleven such documents of Judaism with common elements such as ascension, translation, vision, dream, angelic tour guides and tours of heaven. The Book of Revelation fits well into this genre.

Seers and scholars have established five ways to interpret the text:

- Futurist: all about the future end times.
- Preterist: all about what happened in the first century of Common Era.
- Historicist: It is all about the whole sweep of history from the first century to the end times.
- Idealist: It is all spiritual symbolism which can be reassigned in different eras
- Eclectic: All of the above. (Lancaster, 2017:5)

Thomas and Richardson (2020-2021) elucidate several themes that provide a base for a better understanding of the sacred text. Although the text is apocalyptic in nature, it has more to do with pastoral concerns and teachings. The heart of this sacred book is *Yeshua,* Messiah. The reader (who is addressed seven times: "Those who have ears, let them hear what the Spirit is saying to the churches"[82]), is to absorb and take into his or her heart a deep mystery of who *Yeshua* is. In Chapters 1-6, He is given the following titles: First Born, Ruler of the earth's kings, coming with the clouds, Son of

---

[82] 2:7, 2:11, 2:17, 2:29, 3:6, 3:13 and 3:22.

man, Alpha and Omega, Living One, Son of God, Holy One, True One, Amen, Faithful, True, Ruler of God's creation, Lion of the Tribe of Juda, Root of David, Lamb of God, and Sovereign Ruler. The reader is to have a loving, intimate relationship with Messiah just as *Yochanan* (John) had with *Yeshua*. In Revelation One, *Yeshua* appears to *Yochanan* in such an awesome glory that all he can do is fall into profound adoration.

The sacred author, in chapter 4, invites the reader into the very throne room of Adonai. The imagery striking on a throne is One who gleams like diamonds and rubies who is surrounded by a rainbow shining like emerald. Elders and four living creatures (like a lion, an ox, a human and an eagle) adore *Adonai* with words of "Holy, holy, holy is Adonai, God of heaven's armies, the One who was, who is and who is coming" (Rev. 4:8). The image of God is an image of absolute separation between Him and all of creation. It is day and night for all eternity that this adoration and worship continues.

According to Thomas and Richardson, chapter 5 is a transitional chapter that is pivotal in human history. Up until the events of chapter 5, *Adonai* and Messiah have been creating a new humanity through the people of Israel and the cross of Messiah that accents infinite mercy and forgiveness of sin. This chapter begins the final judgement of all humanity. Humans have heard this word for centuries and many have not listened. Reckoning now begins. A deep mystery is unfolding here. The Great Judge, Adonai, has in his hand a scroll that is sealed with seven seals. An angel shouts: "Who is worthy to open the scroll and break its seals? But no one in heaven, on earth or under the earth was able to open the scroll or look inside" (5:2-2). *Yochanan* weeps in deep agony.

But then, a great hope emerges: "One of the elders said to me: 'Do not cry. Look, the Lion of the tribe of Judah, the Root of David, has won the right to open the scroll and the seven seals'" (5:5). The Lamb, who was slaughtered, came and took the scroll. Then exuberant shouts of joy, sang and the elders and the four living creatures sang a new song:

> You are worthy to take the scroll and to break it seals
> because you were slaughtered at the cost of blood you
> were you ransomed for God persons from every tribe,
> language, people, and nation. You made them into a
> Kingdom of God to rule, priests to serve Him; and
> they will rue the earth. (5:9-10).

This sets in motion the final move from the kingdom of this world (*Olam hazeh*) to the kingdom of God (*Olam haba*). Most of the rest of the book details judgments on earth for those who did not believe. Chapter 20 outlines the Millennium while chapters 21–22 describe the coming down of the heavenly Jerusalem, the new heavens, the new earth with God and the Lamb when be king, ruling form Jerusalem throughout the whole earth.

Daniel Juster (2015), a Messianic Jewish scholar, approached an interpretation of the work using the Passover-Exodus event and theme of the people of Israel as they left Egypt. They had gained their freedom to be able to receive the *Torah* and to enter the Land of Promise as recorded in the *Tanakh* texts of Exodus, Leviticus, Numbers, Deuteronomy, and Joshua.

His interpretation is both historic and futuristic. Historic: events that have already happened and those of the future. The events of the Passover-Exodus are used to structure his interpretation of the text.

Juster's beginning text is Revelation 12, which parallels events of the Passover-Exodus historical event. The chapter outlines the image of a woman, clothed with the sun (symbolic of light and the Shekinah Glory of God), standing on the moon (indicative of dominion), and having a crown of stars (illustrative of her regal authority and the twelve tribes of Israel). The woman is Israel[83] who is with labor and about to give birth. There is another ominous sign which is that of a "great red dragon" who is a symbol of Satan who attempts to kill the child as soon as he is born but "who was snatched up to God and

---

[83] The Catholic position is that the woman is a symbol of Miriam, the mother of *Yeshua*.

his throne and she fled to the desert... to be taken care of by God"
(Revelation 12:5-6).

Prelude-Chapters 1-4.

The book begins with an awesome experience of *Yeshua* the Messiah.
John is witness to His head and hair white as wool, His face shining like
the sun, His eyes two blazing torches, out of his mouth a two-edged
sword (the word of God), a voice like the roar of the ocean, holding
in his right hand seven stars and his feet like burnished brass refined
in a furnace. Angels are delegated to speak to the seven churches/
Messianic communities of Asia. They are given commandments to
prepare themselves (and us) so we may endure and be protected for
the judgments and tribulations that are to come: repentance, fervent
love, fearlessness, meditating on the divine promises, the need to
discipline those who disrupt ecclesial life, renouncing any control,
listening to strange teaching, not to be sexually immoral (as so many
church leaders have been), being faithful under persecution, and to
offer our whole life to the kingdom of God.

Paul, in his epistle to the Romans counselled them and us:

> Don't let love be a mere outward show. Recoil from
> what is evil, and cling to what is good. Love each
> other devotedly and with brotherly love; and set
> examples for each other in showing respect. Don't
> be lazy when hard work is needed but serve the Lord
> with spiritual fervor. Rejoice In your hope, be patient
> in your troubles, and continue steadfastly in prayer.
> Share what you have with God's people, and practice
> hospitality. Bless those who persecute you---bless
> them, don't curse them (12:9-14)

Chapter Four presents us with an amazing vision of God. A special
image are four living creatures that represent four divine attributes:
the lion (of rule and majesty), a man (of ultimate knowledge and

intelligence), an eagle (indicative of speed), and a calf (showing steadfastness). In Chapter Five, there is the One sitting on the throne with a scroll that has seven seals. The seals are the seven judgements about to be given to the Lamb (The Messiah) who broke the seals, and He sent judgments forth.

Divine Protection and Judgments-Chapters 5-9.

Chapters five through nine expose the various judgments on the unbelieving world as well as the protection of the followers of Messiah. Chapter seven outlines the divine protection and depicts the seals on the believers from the tribes of Israel (7:4-8) as well as the Gentile believers from "every nation, tribe, people and language" (7:9)[84]. All were standing in front of the "throne and in front of the Lamb, dressed in white robes and holding palm branches in their hands" (7:9). Together, they all shouted, "Praise and glory, wisdom and thanks, honor and powers and strength belong to our God forever and ever" (7:12).

Chapter eight through to chapter nine outlines the judgements of *Adonai* upon the unbelieving earth. Seven angels with seven shofars are blown which reminds us of the first fall feast of Israel called *Rosh Hashanah* recorded in Leviticus 23:23-25. It refers to a re-gathering, an offering of repentance and the coming of a king. Isaiah said it well: "On that day, *Adonai* will beat out the grain… you will be gathered, one by one, people of Israel! On that day, a great shofar will sound …. And they will worship *Adonai* on the holy mountain of Jerusalem (Isaiah 27:12-13)[85].

Some of these judgements were similar to those imposed on unbelieving Egypt. Table 8: 2 illustrates these parallels.

---

[84] The seal is the Hebrew letter *tav* which was placed on the men who were lamenting over the sin and abominations committed in Jerusalem before the exile to Babylon in 587 BCE as recorded in Ezekiel 9:4. Those with this sign would be spared from disasters to come. The sign was also the sign of the Father's name (Rev. 14:1).
[85] This interpretation is from Stern (2015:1429).

Table 8:2 Parallel Judgements from the Passover and
the Future Judgements on the Unbelieving world

This future is depicted many times in the Scriptures. One
such one is given by Paul the Apostle: "In the past, God
overlooked such ignorance; but now He has set a Day when
He will judge the inhabited world, and do it justly, by
means of a man whom He as designated (Acts 17:31)

Set One of the Judgments: The breaking of
the seals of the scroll by the Messiah
(6 and 8:1)

Of the Hebrews in Egypt	Of all non-believing people of the World
The instrument of divine judgement: Moses	The instrument of divine judgement: Jesus, the Messiah, breaks the seals
First seal: Pharaoh and Egypt are conquered	First Seal: War is declared over the earth from a rider who is given the right to conquer
Second seal: peace is taken away in Egypt because of the many judgements	Second Seal: the second horseman (on a fiery red horse) takes away peace and people kill one another.
Third Seal: The plagues destroyed crops and livestock causing economic scarcity	Third Seal: Worldwide economic collapse and severe scarcity
Fourth Seal: The Death of the First born in Egypt	Fourth Seal: A pale horse called Death is given authority of the earth to kill with the sword, with hunger, and with disease.
Fifth Seal: no parallel	Fifth seal: Martyrs are revealed who are to wait for justice to be given to them
Sixth Seal: Darkness covered the whole of Egypt and people could not see each other	Sixth Seal: More dramatic than among the Hebrews for the sun turned black and the moon became blood-red; stars fell from heaven and destroyed much of the earth

Table 8:2 Parallel Judgements from the Passover and
the Future Judgements on the Unbelieving world

Seventh Seal: no parallel	Seventh seal: This seal reveals the seven angels with seven shofars which are further judgments

Set Two of the Judgments: Seven Angels with
seven shofars (8:1-9:21 and 11:15)

First shofar: Hail fell like thunder over all Egypt and destroyed vegetation	First Shofar: Hail and fire that burned up one third of the trees. These also destroyed much of the earth's vegetation
Second Shofar: Rivers and waters of the land were spoiled by blood	Second Shofar: a burning mountain was thrown on the Earth and a third of the seas were spoiled by blood, leaving many fish dead
Third Shofar: no parallel	Third Shofar: a great star fell from heaven that produced bitter waters
Fourth Shofar: darkness fell on Egypt	Fourth Shofar: one third of the light of the moon, the stars and the sun was taken away.
Fifth Shofar: Locusts were released to devastate the fields	Fifth Shofar: locusts that looked like horses set out to destroy. They were led by their king, the angel of the abyss known as *Abaddon* or destroyer (9: 11)
Sixth Shofar: no parallel	Sixth Shofar: Four angels are released to kill one third of humankind
Seventh Shofar: singing the song of Moses and Miriam (Exodus 15:1-20)	Seventh Shofar: Loud voices saying: "The kingdom of the world has become the Kingdom of our Lord and his Messiah and he will rule forever and ever"

Juster made an interesting observation with a quote from
Revelation 9:20-21 that those who lived through these judgements
did not change and did not repent of their ways even though, from

Jewish tradition and the meaning of *Rosh HaShanah*, they were given an opportunity to repent. They continued to worship demons, murder their fellow humans, practice witchcraft, engage in the use of drugs, steal and act out sexually prohibited behaviors.

Another table will illustrate the three sets of divine judgment in chapters six through to sixteen. Table 8:3 is the three sets of divine judgments:

Table 8:3 Three sets of Divine Judgments

Yeshua breaking the seven seals Revelation 6:1-8:1	Angels blowing their shofars Revelation 8:7-11:18	Pouring forth of the Bowls of Judgment Revelation 16:1-16:21
Seal 1: White horse and conquest (6:1-2)	Shofar Blowing 1: hail and fire with 1/3 of the earth being scorched (8:7)	Poured by angels. Bowl 1: Disgusting and painful sores poured out on those who had the mark of the beast (number 666 from a beast: 13: 16-18) (16:2)
Seal 2: Red horse and the power to take peace away (6:3)	Shofar Blowing 2: a blazing mountain thrown down on the oceans and 1/3 of the sea turning to blood with the destruction of many animals and ships	Bowl 2: blood poured out on the sea and all living died (1:3)
Seal 3: Black horse and economic collapse (6:5-6)	Shofar Blowing 3: A great star fell from the sky and water was turned bitter (8:10-11)	Bowl 3: bowl poured out onto rivers and springs of water and became blood (16:4-6)
Seal 4: Pallid, sickly horse: authority to kill ¼ of the world's population by war, famine, and plagues (6:7-8)	Shofar Blowing 4: a 1/3 of the sun, the moon and the stars were struck	Bowl 4: Poured on the sun and people were burned (16:8)

Table 8:3 Three sets of Divine Judgments

Yeshua breaking the seven seals Revelation 6:1–8:1	Angels blowing their shofars Revelation 8:7–11:18	Pouring forth of the Bowls of Judgment Revelation 16:1–16:21
Seal 5: Saints who have followed the Lamb and their intercession (6:9–11)	Shofar Blowing 5: the fall of a star fell onto the earth, and an angel was given a key to open the Abyss, and out came locusts who had tails like scorpions who inflicted pain on people. Their leaders were Abaddon or Destroyer (9:1–11)	Bowl 5: poured on the throne of the beast and his kingdom grew dark (16:10
Seal 6: cosmic challenges: earthquakes, darkening of the sun and the moon turning blood	Shofar Blowing 6: Angels released to kill 1/3 of humankind. 9:13–16)	Bowl 6: Poured over the river Euphrates and its water dried up. Out of the mouths of the Dragon, the beast and of the false prophet came unclean spirits who called forth all the kings of the earth to assemble for the War of the Great Day of Adonai-Tzva'ot at Har Megiddo (16:12–16)
Seal 7: The giving of the 7 shofars to the 7 angels and a bowl of incense being thrown down on the earth (8:1–5)	Shofar Blowing 7: Loud voices saying: "The Kingdom of the world has become the Kingdom of our Lord and his Messiah (11:15)	Bowl 7: Poured out to cause lightning, peals of thunder, a massive earthquake and the Great City (Babylon) was broken and the cites of the nations fell. Hail stones fell on people (16:17–21)

The Persecutions of the Messianic Believers-The Anti-Christ: Chapters 13, 17, 18, 10 and 11.

Juster informs us that one does not read the Book as a sequence of sacred history from chapter one to chapter twenty-two. Between the judgements of the seals in chapters five through to nine, the author places the future images of the persecutions of the faithful-both Jew and Gentle as they follow the lamb. The figures represent different dimensions of evil as it tries to destroy God's image in man who has been remade in the image of *Yeshua*, the Messiah. The Anti-Christ is pictured as a grotesque beast (13:1-2)[86]; the dragon is Satan, the Devil or the Adversary (13:2); the false prophet in contrast to the two godly prophets (11: 1-7); the woman, or the harlot, depicts false religion (17-18), also known as Babylon (the ungodly kingdom of this world). Behind them all, is Satan, the destroyer (12:12-13).

The people worship the beast who blasphemes, speaks in boastful terms, is like the many tyrants who have great political power on earth who fight against God and persecute the Messianic People. Throughout history, this Anti-Christ could be, for example, represented by the Greek Antiochus V Eupator (of a noble father)[87] (172-161 BCE), Stalin (1878-1953) or Hitler (1889-1945). However, it may also refer to someone near for we are warned by John that "the spirit of the Anti-Christ is here now, in the world already" (I John 4:3). At this "end of the Ages" or *acharit-hayamim*, this Anti-Christ will engage in violent oppression of the Bride of the Messiah, but she will grow into a fuller maturity and be united more and more in love.

Subsequent to the coming of the Anti-Christ, another beast, the false prophet[88], will arise exercising authority over the first beast who forces all the people of the earth to worship him. It performs great

---

[86] This interpretation is the same as that of Jeremiah (2014) in his book on the agents of the apocalypse.
[87] A ruler of the Greek Seleucid Empire who reigned 163–161 BCE. He was appointed as King by the Romans with his protector Lysias as regent. (Antiochus).
[88] This interpretation, as was the meaning of the beast from the sea, is the same as that of Jeremiah (2014).

miracles and by doing so, deceives the people living on the earth. This creature demands that an image is built of the first beast which comes alive by the breath of the second beast. It forces everyone to receive a mark on their arm or forehead preventing anyone who did not have this mark from buying or selling. The mark was 666 which in Hebrew numerology is the number of a man who is apart from God, creating his own kingdom and claiming power and authority.

In chapters seventeen and eighteen, a scarlet woman sitting on a beast is presented. Named Babylon, she has recently killed many believers and is the representative of the religious, economic and political worlds united to create one ungodly and demonic world system. She is also described as a harlot for she is the zenith of all spiritual adultery (idolatry) or all unfaithfulness to God the Father. Together with the beasts, they illustrate the whole evil system. Yet, in spite of all this power, there is a massive dissension from the beasts: "they will hate the harlot, bring her to ruin, leave her naked, eat her flesh and consume her with fire" (Revelation 17:16). Chapter eighteen sums up her final destruction when an angel, coming with great authority and splendor, picked up a boulder, the illustration of the harlot, and hurled it into the sea.

John, the author, under the inspiration of the Holy Spirit, goes back to his writing in Revelation 10 and 11. In chapter ten, a mighty angel appears who is covered with a cloud corresponds to the cloud of the divine Shekinah that guided the people of Israel from Egypt to the land of promise, Israel. Juster accents verse 10:7: ... "when the seventh angel sounds the shofar, the hidden plan of God will be brought to completion, the Good News as He proclaimed it to his servants the prophets." He interprets this as the Bride of the Messiah who will be completely one, both of Gentile and Jewish origins and "Then *Adonai* will be king over the whole world. On that day *Adonai* will be the only one and His name will be the only name" (Zechariah 14:9).

The city of Jerusalem is central to the return of *Yeshua* and the glorification of the Bride of Messiah. In Chapter eleven, two witnesses, prophets, appear who have great authority who can, as

Moses and Aaron did in Egypt, call down judgments. Yet, battles continue and the Beast from the Abyss (Rev.13:11) conquers the prophets and for a short time, has dominion. But they are raised from the dead and are taken away to heaven in a cloud, similarly, went up Messiah in his ascension. Juster sees in these two prophets the return of the gift of prophecy to the Body of Messiah to specifically lead her to her destiny. As the prophets in this text were killed, so many disciples of *Yeshua* will also be killed. Until the final destiny is reached, the disciples of *Yeshua* are to have holy hearts, be humble, burn with love for God and be rooted in the word of God so that they would be strengthened to resist the evil empire that will be coming.

The Continued Protection of the Body of the Messiah: Chapters 11-18.

Many of the judgments have already happened (Judgements from the seven seals of scroll that Messiah broke) in chapters six through to eight. Additional judgments happened came from the seven angels blowing seven shofars (Revelation 8:6-9:13). The seventh angel and the sounding of the shofar announces the reign of *Adonai* and His Messiah:

> The kingdom of the world has become the Kingdom
> of our Lord and His Messiah, and He will rule forever
> and ever! (Rev.: 11:15).

Chapter fourteen commences with another protection of the saints. First, in 14:1-4, John saw the Lamb standing on Mount Zion (or Jerusalem) with multitudes of Jews who were following the Messiah. Then, there was a gathering of the Gentiles from every nation, tribe, language and people[89]. In a further part of the vision: "I saw what looked like a sea of glass mixed with fire. Those defeating

---

[89] This may be the final reconciliation and unity that Paul referred to as the new humanity-the unity of Jewish and Gentile believers in *Yeshua* (Ephesians 2:13 – 16). It also may refer to the maturity both of the Olive Tree (Israel) and the branch grafted into the tree (Romans 11:16-17).

the beast, its image and the number of its name were standing by the sea of glass, holding harps which God had given them" (Rev. 15:2). Two songs were sung: of Moses and the Lamb indicating the intricate unity between Israel and the ultimate consummation of the Body of the Messiah being composed both of Jews and Gentiles.

The setting is now in place for the third set of divine judgements. Chapter sixteen commences with a loud voice telling seven angels to pour out seven bowls of God's fury. Like the judgements from the breaking of the seals of the scroll, there is a significant correlation between the plagues of the Egypt as outlined in Table 8:4.

Table 8:4: The Parallel Judgements from the Passover and the Seven Bowls of God's Wrath on Unbelieving world

Bowls of wrath: To the seven angels, the command was "Go, and pour out on the earth the seven bowls of God's fury" (Rev. 16:1)

(16 and 17)

Of the Hebrews in Egypt	Of those with the seal of the mark of the beast:666
The instruments of divine judgement: Moses and Aaron	The instruments of divine judgement: The seven angels
The First Bowl-The of dust in the air that caused sores on the Egyptians (Exodus 9:8-11)-	First Bowl: Painful sores (Rev 16:2)
The Second Bowl: River turned to blood (Exodus 7:19-21)	Second bowl: sea becomes blood and living creatures die (Rev. 16:3)
Third Bowl-River turned to blood (Exodus 7:19-21)	Third Bowl: All the rivers of the earth turned to blood (Rev. 16:4).
No contrast	Fourth Bowl: This bowl was poured out on the sun and people were burned with such heat (Rev. 8-9)
Fifth Bowl: The plague of darkness was sent over all of Egypt at the hand of Moses. "People couldn't see each other" (Exodus 10:21-22)	Fifth Bowl: Upon the throne of the beast was poured darkness on his kingdom (Rev. 16: 10)

**Table 8:4: The Parallel Judgements from the Passover and
the Seven Bowls of God's Wrath on Unbelieving world**

Bowls of wrath: To the seven angels, the command was "Go, and
pour out on the earth the seven bowls of God's fury" (Rev. 16:1)
(16 and 17)

Of the Hebrews in Egypt	Of those with the seal of the mark of the beast:666
Sixth Bowl: Frogs were sent to all of the land and invaded every home (Exodus 8:1-3)	Sixth Bowl: "three unclean spirits that looked like frogs; they came from the mouth of the dragon, from the mouth of the beast and from the mouth of the false prophet... they went out to the kings of the whole world to assemble them for War of the Great Day of *Adonai* of hosts. They gathered in the place which in Hebrew is called *Har Megiddo* (Rev. 16:13-16)
Seventh Bowl: A hailstorm falls upon Egypt so that anyone, people and animals, would die (Exodus 9:17-19)	Seventh Bowl: This is the last of all the pouring forth of divine judgement. Earthquakes occurred that cities of the nation's fell. Even Jerusalem was not immune to these judgments. "And huge seventy-pound hailstones fell on people from the sky" (Rev 16:17-21)

A common theme of this chapter is that people did not repent.
In Rev 16:9, 16:10, and 16:21, people who experienced such pain,
suffering, darkness did not repent but, rather, "they cursed the name
of God, who had authority over these plagues, instead of turning
from their sins to give him glory" and "the people cursed God for
the plague of hail, that it was such a terrible plague" (Rev 16:21). It is
implied, however, that just as the people of Israel did not experience
the plagues in the land of Egypt, so also those Jewish and Gentile
believers, who were marked with "the Lamb's and his Father's name
written on their foreheads" (Rev. 14:1), did not suffer from these
judgments.

Both Juster and the authors from The First Fruits of Zion (2017) link the blowing of the Shofars to the New Year Jewish feast day, *Rosh Hashanah* or the Feast of Trumpets. Both authors believe that according to Jewish tradition, the feast announces God's judgements. Juster wrote:

> In Jewish tradition Rosh Hashanah announces God's judgments. The days between Rosh Hashanah and Yom Kippur, the Day of Atonement, is a period known as the Days of Awe. These days are days of judgment and even vengeance for the unrepentant. They continue until Yom Kippur when the repentant may be forgiven and have their names written in the Book of Life (2015:84).

Initial signs of Victory: Chapters19-20:1-3.

Victory to *Yeshua* and His people is close at hand. Chapter Nineteen commences with the roar of a huge crowd in heaven shouting "Victory, glory, and power to God!" Then the ultimate of weddings happens: The Wedding of the Lamb and the Bride, the Body of Messiah. Those of the Body are clothed in fine linen that are bright and clean (Rev. 19:7-8).

Yeshua, from heaven, rides on a white horse, called Faithful and True, The Word of God and "King of Kings and Lord of Lords", to do battle. The beast, the false prophet, along with those who have the mark of the beast, engage in battle against Him. But the second beast, the false prophet is thrown alive into the lake of fire. The followers of the beast and the false prophet are killed with a sword from the mouth of the Messiah. One last enemy remains: the dragon or Satan. An angel descends from heaven and chains him up for one-thousand years so that he cannot deceive the nations anymore.

The Millennium

Daniel Juster's interpretation of the Millennium is very similar to the image already outlined among the initial Jewish believers in *Yeshua*. It is an age of peace, prosperity in which all the nations (including, especially Israel) live together in harmony. It is like ancient Israel entering into the land of promise where there is abundance and prosperity. Juster asks a question that he responds to:

Why transitional?

It is during this time that the effects of the Fall are reversed and a restoration process continues.

1. During the Pre-Flood Era, men and women lived up to 900 years. In the millennium they will live even longer.
2. Satan is now bound. Men and women will be able to live out the *Torah* in its fullness here on earth.

All those who have died for the sake of Messiah will be brought to life. This is known as the first Resurrection. They will be priests of God and they will rule with Messiah for one-thousand years. When this era is over, Satan will be free from prison and will, again, deceive the nations and will gather together a countless number to do battle against Messiah and his people. They will cover the land of Israel and surround Jerusalem but fire will come from heaven to consume them all. Satan will be captured and will be thrown into the lake of fire where the beast and the false prophet are.

A second resurrection will now occur. Books of judgment are opened and the dead were judged according to their deeds. "Then Death and *Sheol* were hurled into the lake of fire...anyone whose name was not found written in the Book of Life was hurled into the lake of fire" (Rev. 20: 14-15).

New Heavens and a New Earth; Chapters 20-22.

An amazing vision of this, the final and eternal age, *'olam haba,* is portrayed. *Yeshua,* the *Alef* (beginning) and the *Tavi* (the end) sits on the throne and invites all to come to drink life-giving waters. The Shekinah Glory will shine. New Jerusalem (measuring 1,380 miles square) will descend from heaven. Its structure will be of precious metal and diamonds. Its twelve gates are named after the tribes of Israel and the foundation stones named after the apostles. Flowing from the Throne of God will be a major river that flows for the healing of the nations (Ezekiel 47:1-14). There is no temple as *Adonai* and the Lamb are the temple. There will be no need for the sun because "God's Shekinah gives its light, and its light is the Lamb" (Rev. 21:23).

Juster offers to us an amazing image of our future:

> How amazing and wonderful! The Bible begins with paradise lost, but it ends with a greater paradise restored that can never again be lost. The Promised Land of the new heaven and earth is ours after all of the foreshadowing Exodus event and land of promise are past. We have seen the Exodus from Egypt and into the Promised Land of ancient Israel...We will see the exodus of God's people into the glory cloud... into the new heaven and new earth with its New Jerusalem where God will dwell with His people forever! (2017:103-104).

A second Messianic Jewish interpretation of the Messiah's Return.

Dalton Thomas (2020) looked closely at the sequence of events at the end of the age through an in-depth analysis of Chapters 24 and 25 of the Gospel according to Matthew. *Yeshua's* disciples asked their master about the end of the age. They asked three questions: when is *Yeshua's* return? Signs of his return? And when the current age will end? Chapter 24 is a teaching of *Yeshua* that sequences the events while Chapter 25, he offers seven parables to help us to understand his return and the divine judgements.

Thomas (2020) focuses on the return of the Messiah and the coming tribulation using Chapters 24 and 25 of the Book of Matthew. The sequence follows:

1. Birth pangs: Such as false messiahs, rumors of war, conflict between peoples, plagues, famines, and earthquakes (24:4-8).
2. Social Pressure: Believers will be tested not to believe with persecutions and even death (24:9-12).
3. Apostasy: Many believers will leave the faith and believe in that not of Judaism and Christianity. (II Thessalonians 2:3).
4. An abomination set up in a throne in the Temple (Matthew 24:15, II. Thessalonians 2:3-4 and Daniel 11:36).
5. Tribulations: Such as Wars against the believers, betrayals, economic collapses and the like (Matthew 24:17-22),
6. Cosmic troubles: Sun darkening, stars falling to the earth. (Matthew 24:29 and Joel 3: 3-4).
7. *Yeshua's* Return in power and majesty (Revelation 19:112 and Matthew 24:30)
8. Gathering of all the peoples and Judgment. Some to eternal life and some to eternal death (Matthew 13: 36-43).

Thomas then continues to offer meaning to nine parables all to do with this return. Believers are called to be alert, ready, anticipating Messiah's coming and not to fear, care for *Yeshua's'* little ones, the Jews being the disciples of him..

There is a remarkable parallel with the book of Revelation discussed above. The tribulations that *Yeshua* referred to in his last speech to his disciples are outlined in sequence in the Book of Revelation:

1. The opening up of the seals for judgment (Rev. 6:1-8:1)
2. The blowing of seven shofars (Reve 8:7-13 and 11:15).

3. The dragon trying to destroy God's people (Rev. 12:17).
4. The beasts (symbols of political entities) trying to destroy *Adonai's* people (Rev. 13:1-18)
5. The Harlot: against God's people (Rev 17).

The end of the Book of Revelation is so promising when all of God's and the disciples' enemies are destroyed (Rev. 18 and 19: 20–21) and the saints will live forever in the New Jerusalem recorded in Rev. 21-22.

The Book of Daniel

Thomas and Richardson (2020) present a dissection of parts of the Book of Daniel pertaining to eschatology. Daniel's prophecies (with a focus on Chapters 10-12) pertained to the times of Nebuchadnezzar (605-562 BCE), of Belshazzar (?-539 BCE), Darius (522-486 BCE), and Cyrus (600-530 BCE). Two years after Cyrus came to power, Daniel had a vision (as in Daniel 10). In this vision, he saw: a great war was coming and a second vision of what was to happen to the people of Israel in the *acharit-hayamim* (the end of days). The historical context is during the period of Cyrus until the Roman era in 60 (BCE), empires fight with one another to achieve ascendency. Of especial note is a prototype of the Anti-Christ, Antiochus IV Epiphanes (215-164 BCE) who in his quest for dominance and power did very much evil to Israel.

The Anti-Christ figure is central to Daniel's prophetic messages. He is called the son of destruction who is seen to be an incarnation of Satan who is opposite to *Yesuah,* the incarnation of God. The Anti-Christ figure calls himself god and sits in the Temple of God as the abomination that causes desolation. (Matthew 24:15-16). But his end is foretold. He is to be destroyed by the breath of Messiah as recorded in II Thessalonians 1:8 and Isaiah 11:4. This is the great hope and is a great encouragement to believers who are to endure suffering to be purified but will eventually be triumphant. In Daniel

12, it is written that there would be no more tribulation, Israel will be delivered, and the dead will rise.

A Catholic Interpretation of Eschatology.

There two sources that I will use to present the Catholic Church's teachings on the question of eschatology. The first one is an official teaching on the subject from The Holy See (1995) and the second is a theological reflection on eschatology by Pohle (1917).

Official Teaching.

The section on eschatology in the *Catechism of the Catholic Church* (Holy See, 1995) is housed in the part of *The Profession of Faith*, under the seventh, eleventh and twelfth articles. Several teachings are rooted in the *Tanakh* and the New Testament. After the ascension, *Yeshua* is seated at the right hand of the Father which is a signal of the inauguration of the Messiah's kingdom which fulfills Daniel's vision of the Son of man: "To Him was given rulership, glory, and a kingdom, so that all peoples, nations and languages should serve him. His rulership is an eternal rulership that will not pass away; and his kingdom is one that will never be destroyed" (7:14). Yet, this is not complete, and the kingdom will not be realized until the Messiah comes again to establish his final kingdom as prophesied by Daniel. He will not return until Israel, as a nation, comes to faith in *Yeshua* as Messiah and the Son of God.

However, before his return, the People of God must endure much suffering and testing and reject the Anti-Messiah or the Anti-Christ. Final victory will take place after the Last Judgement, the judge of the living (those of faith in Messiah) and the dead (those who have rejected the Messiah) and a final cosmic upheaval of the passing world or the *'olam hazeh*.

One teaching of the Catholic Church on eschatology, the denial of the millennium, is not shared by the early Church and a number of early Patristic authors as well as adherents to Messianic Judaism.

The Catechism noted: "The Church has rejected even modified forms of this falsification the kingdom to come under the name of millenarianism" (Holy See, article 676). This is further reinforced by an official document by Denzinger (1908). It reads: "the system of mitigated Millenarianism, which teaches, for example, that Christ the Lord before the final judgment, whether or not preceded by the resurrection of the many just, will come visibly to rule over this world. The answer is: The system of mitigated Millenarianism cannot be taught safely" Denzinger (1908)[90].

Theological Teaching.

Pohle (1927) is the informant on the theology of eschatology of the Catholic Church. He first provides us with a definition of the term and then he divided his text into two major parts: humans as individuals and humans as a race. The latter will be the focus here. His definition consists of:

> Eschatology is the crown and capstone of dogmatic theology. It may be defined as the 'doctrine of the last things,' and tells how the creatures called into being and raised to the supernatural state of God, find their last end in Him, of whom, and by whom, an in whom, as Holy Scripture says, 'are all things' (Romans 11:36 and Pohle, 1927:1)

The elements that follow are what theologians have considered to be relevant to the study: the Gospel needed to be preached to all the world; that all of Israel would be saved; that Enoch and Elijah would return to herald the return of Messiah; there would be a great apostasy and an Anti-Christ would appear to lead many astray; extraordinary upheavals of nature would occur; the coming of a universal conflagration would destroy the earth; the resurrection

---

[90] The distinction between two forms of millenarianism will be discussed with Pohle.

both of the living and the dead and, lastly, the judgment both of the resurrected, some to eternal life and others to eternal death.

As part of the eschatology is the teaching of the millennium or Millenarianism, (Ford, 1992), offers a definition: "Millenarianism is a variant of Jewish and Christian eschatology...it usually follows the destruction of evil and precedes the creation of a new heaven and a new earth and the enjoyment of eternal bliss...the Messiah and the faithful reign in this earthly kingdom" (1992: Volume IV:832). Kirsch (1911), presents these elements: "The early return of Christ in all His power and glory, the establishment of an earthly kingdom with the just, the resuscitation of the deceased saints and their participation in the glorious reign, the destruction of the powers hostile to God, and, at the end of the kingdom, the universal resurrection with the final judgment, after which the just will enter heaven, while the wicked will be consigned to the eternal fire of hell"(Kirsch, 1911).

Pohle challenges the teaching of Millenarianism. During the first century of the believers in *Yeshua,* there were two forms: the sensual indulgent type (chiliastic[91]) and the mitigated form. The first form envisioned the Messiah to come and bring unbridled sensual pleasures. The second type, called the mitigated form, was depicted as time of the reign of Messiah who, together with all his people, would rule the world in peace and justice for 1000 years because Satan was bound up and unable to deceive the nations.

Ford (1992) updates Pohle by indicating that many of the early fathers and authors of the first century adhered to this teaching: Papias, Justin Martyr, Irenaeus, Tertullian, Nepos, Victorinus of Pettau, and St. Hippolytus. Both authors also mention several authors who were closely aligned to the chiliastic version such as Lactantius, Cerinthuis Nepos of Arsine, and Appollinaris of Laodicea. A common text was used from Revelation: "Next I saw an angel coming down from heaven, who had the key to the Abyss and a great chain in his hand. He seized the dragon, that ancient serpent, who is the Devil

---

[91] A variant of millennialism with an accent of 1000 years were the just would enjoy all the sensual pleasures of life-abundant food, longevity, and eroticism.

and Satan (the Adversary) and chained him up for a thousand years. He threw him into the Abyss, locked it and sealed it over him; so that he could not deceive the nations any more until the thousand years were over. After that, he has to be set free for a little while" (Rev. 20:1-3).

In spite of these writers and the text from scripture, Pohle denies its reality and conjectures that the images of Revelation are not to be taken literally but only symbolically. This, according to Ford (1992), was Augustine's position. After starting off with a millennialist perspective, he later spiritualized the thousand-year teaching by saying the millennial began with the birth of Messiah and will end at the return of Jesus.

My theory is that as early Christian scholars adapted the new faith to a Hellenistic world view (which accented the symbolic and the spiritual rather than the material and the historic), the more likely they were to believe not in the literal meaning of the sacred text but its allegorical and symbolic meaning. The official teaching of the Catholic Church is that it does not give official teachings on what the Book of Revelation is about but does adhere to the Augustinian view that the millennium will not occur as outlined by the author of Revelation, but that the text must be taken in an allegorical perspective of interpretation.

CONCLUSIONS

It is vitally important for us to understand that we Gentile Christians owe a huge debt to our Jewish fathers and mothers. It is vital to realize that Christians are a branch that has been grafted into Israel and that she is the root and Christian denominations are the branches (Romans 11:17). There is an urgent call to remember the rich heritage not only of Biblical Judaism but also of Rabbinic Judaism over the last two thousand years.

After remembering, we are to repent for nearly 2000 years of Antisemitism that has been a central teaching and action of the

Gentile Church. Christians have considered themselves to be the root, but it is Israel that is the root. Christians have not followed the direction of Paul the Apostle who cautioned them not to boast and take pride in faith over Judaism. Christians have not obeyed what *Yeshua* taught us: "Do not think that I have come to abolish the *Torah* or the prophets. I have come not to abolish but to complete. Yes indeed! I tell you that until heaven and earth pass away, not so much as a *yud* or a stroke will pass from the Torah—not until everything that must happen has happened" (Matthew 5:17-18).

From the genesis of the Christian faith, many Gentile believers in Jesus have adapted a Hellenistic-Roman world view and have fundamentally jettisoned some of the Hebrew tradition and the Hebrew truth. It is imperative, for the sake of the kingdom, to rediscover the beauty, the riches, and the wonder of Judaism not only in the Old Testament but its legacy, Rabbinic Judaism, for the last two thousand years. I consider before us is to begin with remembering to be repenting and then to reconciling with Judaism, Messianic Judaism and Gentile Christianity.

REFERENCES-CHAPTER EIGHT

Antiochus: https://en.wikipedia.org/wiki/ Antiochus V Eupator

Cohen, A. 1949. *Everyman's Talmud: the major teachings of the Rabbinic Sages.* New York: Schocken Books.

Danielou. J. 1964. *The theology of Jewish Christianity. Volume one of A history of early Christian doctrine before the Council of Nicea.* Translated by J. Baker. London: Darton, Logman and Todd.

Denzinger, H. J. Dominicus. 1908. *Enchiridion symbolorum, definitionum et declarationum de rebus fidei et morum.* (Handbook of Creeds and Definitions). Freiburg, Germany.

Didache 2017/50 CE. *The way of life: The rediscovered teachings of the twelve Jewish Apostles to the Gentiles.* Translated and commented on by T. Janicki. Marshfield, Missouri: Vine of David.

Ford, J. 1992. "Millennium". In *The Anchor Bible Dictionary,* edited by D. Freedman, G. Herion, and, D. Pleains, Vol.4: p. 832–835. New York: Doubleday.

Fruits of Zion. 2017. *Hayesod: The Sabbath Student Workbook.* Marshfield, Missouri: First Fruits of Zion.

Gnosticism. https://en.wikipedia.org/wiki/Gnosticism.

Hocken, P. 2016. *Azusa, Rome, and Zion: Pentecostal faith, Catholic reform, and Jewish roots.* Eugene OR: Pickwick Publications.

Holy See.1995. *Catechism of the Catholic Church.* English translation by The United States Catholic Conference, Inc. Image Books, Doubleday: New York.

https://en.wikipedia.org/wiki/Talmud.

Jeremiah, D. 2014. *Agents of the Apocalypse.* Carol Stream Illinois: Tyndale House Publishers.

Juster, D. 2015. *Passover: The key that unlocks the Book of Revelation.* Clarksville, MD: Lederer Books.

Kirsch, J.P. 1911. "Millennium and Millenarianism". In *The Catholic Encyclopedia.* New York: Robert Appleton Company. Retrieved June 7, 2019 from New Advent: http://www.newadvent.org/cathen/10307a.htm

Lancaster, D. 2017. *The Book of Revelation.* Calgary, Alberta: Council of Messianic Jewish Congregations of Alberta.

Pohle, J. 1927. *Eschatology-The Catholic Doctrine of the last things, a dogmatic treatise.* Adapted and edited by A. Preuss. B. Herder Book Company: St. Louis, MO.

Rabbinic Judaism. https://en.wikipedia.org/wiki/Rabbinic_Judaism

Skarsuane, O. 2002. *In the shadow of the Temple. Jewish influences on early Christianity.* IVP Academic. An imprint of Intervarsity Press: Downers Grove, Illinois.

Stern, D. 2015. *Jewish New Testament Commentary.* Clarksville, Md. Jewish New Testament Publications.

Stern, D. 2016. Translator of *The Compete Jewish Study Bible: Insights for Jews and Christians.* Peabody, Massachusetts: Hendrickson Publishers Marketing, LLC.

CHAPTER NINE
CONCLUSIONS REMEMBERING, REPENTING AND RECONCILING

This manuscript has been an attempt to understand the Jewish roots of the Christian faith. Many books have been published on this topic. Here, I have attempted to frame this using sociological concepts and theories, history and Jewish and Christian theology. The ultimate goal is remembering, repenting and reconciling.

The introduction was an attempt to outline some of the mysteries of the Kingdom. It is important for gentile Christians to realize that they are a branch from a wild olive tree that has been grafted into the true olive tree which is Israel. Kinzer reminded us that the full gospel necessarily includes the restoration of Jerusalem as both *axis mundi* and *axis temporis*. It is from this restored city, known from Psalm 48: 1-2 as the city of God and the city of great king, that the Messiah is to rule the renewed heaven and earth- in all its cosmic dimensions. We also owe to him the teaching how *Yeshua* has been suffering with his first-born son who has endured centuries of suffering and heartache.

Kinzer has also informed us of the vital role of Judaism from the fall of the Second Temple in 70 CE to the present. Those who are observant believers have for centuries longed for the Messiah and have hastened, in Christian terms, the return of the Messiah, *Yeshua*. The original revelation known as the *Tanakh* has been honoured in synagogues from 70 CE to the present. Further, they have accented the *Shekinah* presence with the various dimensions of the Temple: in heaven, the cosmos, the eschaton and the people of Israel.

The gems of what the Old Testament (also called *Tanakh*) has are amazing and full of abundant riches. Chapter one covered such topics as the relationship between *Adonai* and Israel, the God of the Fathers, the Holy Event, the Great tensions, the turning toward the future, and the God of the sufferers.

The mother of all churches, the Jerusalem Church or the Church of the Circumcision, was the focus of Chapter two. The Jewish expression discussed were the Essenes who form a foundation to the teachings of John the Baptist, Jesus, and the Jerusalem Church. Its key elements consisted of angelology, the *Torah*, the cosmic ladder, the books of heaven, the incarnation, the redemption, the cross, the meaning of the church, Baptism and the Eucharist, and personal holiness. The chapter concluded with a look at the Nazarenes, the Jewish believers in *Yeshua* after the first Jewish war of 70 CE.

Chapter three was complex. It also documented a major tragedy in the Body of the Messiah, the division between Jewish believers in *Yeshua* and the Gentile believers in Christ. Several sociological terms were introduced to help us understand this first wound of the Body of the Messiah: ideal types, the sect, the stranger, a movement of renewal and a new religious movement. The sociological theory called secularization was also presented.

The background to this division has an ancient past. As you have read this chapter, you will have discovered that antisemitism was at the very heart of the cultures of Egypt, Greece and Rome. The elements of this antisemitism were misanthropy, human sacrifice, monotheism, dietary laws, the Shabbat, and circumcision. Around these elements grew prejudices, negative stereotypes, discrimination, exile and violence.

In the third part of the chapter, the reader was introduced to Christian anti-Semitic themes consisting of the genre *Adversos Judaeos*, replacement theology and supersessionism. The secularization theory presented a case that the Patristic Fathers constructed these concepts from being immersed in the Greco-Roman educational system and that they absorbed these stereotypes, discriminatory actions and, sometime, exile and violence. The chapter concluded with theories of the division between the two segments of the Body of the Messiah.

The fourth chapter was devoted to Tertullian who laid the basis for anti-Semitism in the Western church. He has been called the "Father of Latin Christianity" by Cardinal Danielou. Thus, his influence on the transition from the Classical era of Christianity to the Medieval era was profound. That is one of the reasons why anti-Semitism had such influence and power during these many years of the Christian faith.

The fifth chapter traced the long history of Christian antisemitism from the Early Medieval Era to the Early Modern Period. Two new ideal types were introduced: *Ecclesia* and *Synogogia*. Two accents of the relationship between the Christian Church and the Jews:

one positive (reflective of the 'stranger within') and one, negative (reflective of the 'stranger without'). The latter predominated. This long period of Western history was witness to the crusades, to the Spanish Inquisition, to countless exiles, massacres, pogroms, and homicides. Horrific false images were perpetrated against these people like they were killers of Jesus, sorcerers, and in league with the devil.

Chapter six had two foci: (1) the birth of a new type of anti-Semitism that was secular in nature and (2), the beginning of healing and reconciliation.. As secularization of Christianity continued to grow in Europe, there was a decline of Christian anti-Semitism but an increase of a secular, non-religious form of it from the pens of Voltaire and Marx. Treatment for Jews varied from freedom to coercion but mostly on coercion, It was in the nineteenth century that the concept of race came to play. German culture embraced an unfounded theory that the Germans were of the Aryan race and were superior to others while the Jews were targeted as an alien race and not good for the social order. The Dreyfus Affaire took center stage while Roman Catholic publications accused the Jews as the killer of Christ, ritual murder, traitor, and financier. The second half of Chapter Six is devoted to healing and reconciliation. Two primary movements occurred: Zionism and the Messianic Jewish Movement. Zionism led, in part, to the birth of the State of Israel in 1948 while seeds were planted of Jews coming to believe that Jesus is the Messiah but want to maintain a Jewish lifestyle. Kinzer (2015) outlined ways the Roman Catholic Church can reach rapprochement The last element of this reconciliation is the growth of a global intercessory movement called Towards Jerusalem Council II. Further to this were reconciling events such as the new teaching of the relationship between Christianity and Judaism from the Second Vatican Council and the Catholic Catechism. Wounds of anti-Semitism are being healed and there is now potential to unite the two segments of the Body of the Messiah, Jewish believers in *Yeshua* and Gentile believers in Jesus.

Chapter seven documented the era of the worst tragedy of human history, the *Shoah*. Historians theorize that it was not formed by Christianity but the anti-Semitism within the religion was a necessary but insufficient cause of it.

The last chapter, chapter eight, addressed the question of eschatology and the return of the Messiah. Five views were presented: Rabbinic Judaism, the Jerusalem church, two from Messianic Judaism, and the Catholic Church. Included in the insights from Messianic Judaism, an interpretation of the Book of Revelation was given.

GLOSSARY

Adaddon: (in Greek, Apollyon) or Destruction, corruption horrible pit, shadow of death, neither world, deep valley.

Adonai: "My Lord."

Adonai Shamah: *Adonai* is returning to the land of Israel.

Adversos Judaeos: Simply meant: "Against the Jews" . It refers to a series of homilies preached at various times and places in the Late-Classical Era. These texts, which go back to the second century, are directed against the Jews, Judaism and "Judaizing" Christians, i.e., members of the Christian communities who espoused Jewish beliefs or participated in elements of their religious practice. The contents, which were initially presented as polemics and later settled into convention formed a repertoire for anti-Jewish and later Anti-Semitic ideas.

Allegorical hermeneutic: The assumption that various levels of meaning of interpretation are present especially of the Bible or literary texts.

Aljama: A term of Arabic origin used in official document in Spain and Portugal to designate self-governing communities of Jews and Moors living under Christian Rule in the Iberian Peninsula.

Ancien Régime The political and social system of the Kingdom of France from the Late Middle (*circa* 15th century) until 1789, when hereditary monarchy and the feudal system of the French nobility were abolished by the French Revolution. The term is occasionally used to refer to the similar feudal systems of the time elsewhere in Europe.

Aniconic: The term refers to images of deities, symbols, and the like) not portrayed in a human or animal form.

Antilegomenos: speaking against.

Apokalupsis: An unveiling, uncovering, or the revealing of something previously concealed.

Axis Mundi: The axis of the world–considered among Messianic Jews and some Christians to be Jerusalem.

Axis Temporis: the axis of time. considered among Messianic Jews and some Christians to be the new era of Jerusalem and Israel.

Br'it Hadasha*h* or Books of the New Covenant.

Birkat ha minim. This became part of the Jewish Synagogue ceremony. One document discovered in 1898 reads: "For the apostates may there not be hope if they do not return to Your is a Jewish curse on heretics. It included Jewish Christians before Christianity became markedly a Gentile religion. May the *nosrim* (could read Nazarenes) and *the minim* (heretics) perish in a moment.

Caesaropapism: Indicates the subordination of priestly to secular powers. It is when a civil leader (king, prince, president) acts as a priest and has power over the sacred institutions Distal.

Chiliastic: A variant of millennialism with an accent of 1000 years were the just would enjoy all the sensual pleasures of life–abundant food, longevity, and eroticism.

Demiurge: A being responsible for the creation of the universe.

Distal factors: refer to the far past surrounding an historical event.

Collegia licita: An institution within Roman society where people of like mind, were involved in a common trade, or a kind of fellowship.

Eschatological : Anything to refer to end-times or the end of the temporal world.

Einsatzgruppen: A special mobile killing unit of the German army who followed the main army into the Soviet Union as well as other countries such as the Ukraine and Poland. Their sole purpose was to murder Jews. They would force their captives to dig mass graves in fields and forests and then shoot them all. In all, about 1.5 million Jews suffered death between 1941 and 1944.

Ecclesia et Synagoga, *R*efers to symbolic representations in Christian art of the Medieval Era (typically in the form of two women (375 CE to 1500 CE) depicting the victorious Church and the defeated Synagogue, symbolizing the triumph of Christianity.

Ecclesia ex circumsione: The Church of Jerusalem—which was Jewish in nature.

Ecclesia ex gentibus: The Church of the Gentiles. Also called the Great Church.

Final Solution: This refers to the systematic plan by the German Nazis to exterminate the eleven million Jews of Europe. It was officially endorsed at the Wannsee Conference.

Gemara: Further expansions the *Mishnah* and the *Tosepha*.

Genealogical-Israel. The Jewish people as a community that traces its descent back to biblical patriarchs and matriarchs. This term is equivalent to Paul's Israel according to the flesh or physical descent.

Germanentum: the culture, history, religion, and traditions of the Germanic peoples.

Heteropraxy heresy of moral practice.

Hierocracy: designates a political system of priests, virtuosos, or clerics have power and authority over secular authorities and non-sacred social/cultural systems.

Holocaust: Called Shoah in Hebrew, refers to the period from January 30, 1933, when Adolf Hitler became chancellor of Germany, until May 8, 1945, when Germany surrendered to the allies The brutal and systematic murder of two-thirds of Europe's Jews during the second world war. The meaning in Hebrew is catastrophe.

Idea type: The term *type* comes from the Greek word *tupos* and can be translated as a pattern or a model. The sociologist Weber uses the term ideal type as an analytical construct that serves as a measuring rod to determine similarities and differences in concrete cases. It usually does not exist in its pure form, but it is of heuristic value for discussing the real world. The use of ideal types permits comparisons between different types of relations between Christianity and Judaism.

Israel-Christology Jesus is the perfect representative and individual embodiment of the Jewish people. He is the Christ- the Messiah, the King of the Jews. He demonstrates that he is such obeying the *Torah* as God always intended it to be obeyed.

Israel-Ecclesiology. The ecclesiology of the church necessarily includes Israel as the mature olive tree that the church is grafted into. It also means that the mystery of Israel remains at the center of Christian faith and ecclesiology.

Hyper cosmic imagery. Portraying the ascent of *Yesuah* from earth to heaven through seven heavens, carried by a huge angel, and flying on a chariot.

Illuminists: Those or believed or claimed to have enlightenment not accessible to human kind in general.

Kenotic leaders: Leaders who lead with humility, gentile, compassion and love.

Marcion Heresy: The heresy of Marcion (85-166 CE) who argued for the deletion of the Old Testament because it taught that God was an angry God.

Midrash: Biblical exegesis by ancient Judaic authorities using a mode of interpretation prominent in the *Talmud.*

Mikveh: cleansing font likely a baptismal font.

Mishnah: an interpretation of the *Tanakh..*

Nazarites: In Numbers 6:1-21, *Adonai* created the Nazirites to be consecrated to Him and be holy. They were commanded not to drink wine or any intoxicating liquor, to approach a corpse, and to wear long hair. Sampson (Judges 13-16) was one of them.

New religious movement: A type of religious organization the reforms a particular religious group by changing the doctrine.

Nuremberg Laws: Established in 1935, these new laws defined a Jew who had at least one grandparent who was Jewish. These laws forbade all marriages between Jews and other Germans and if a couple were already married, the marriage was to be annulled. The Jew now would not be a citizen of the state and could not hold public office.

'Olam hazel: Of this world or of this time. from *saeculum*, 'age' or 'world', i.e. this world.

Papal nuncio: An official Vatican representative in a nation.

Pogrom: The term was used to describe an organized attack or massacre, often with government support. It was primarily directed against the Jewish population. proximate indicate the close.

Proximate factors: Indicate the close factors surrounding an historical event.

Qumranites: The name of the Essenes who live in the desert monastery in the Qumran.

Rabbinic Judaism: the normative form of Judaism that developed after the fall of the Temple of Jerusalem originating in the work of the Pharisaic rabbis, it was based on the legal and commentative literature in the *Talmud* it set up a mode of worship and a life discipline that were to be practiced by Jews worldwide down to modern times (The Editors of Encyclopedia Britannica, https://www. Britannica.com/topic/ Rabbinic Judaism).

Racism: It stands apart by a practice of which it is a part and which it rationalizes: a practice that combines strategies of architecture and gardening with that of medicine—in the service of the construction of an official social order, through cutting out the elements of the present reality that neither fit the visualized perfect reality, nor can be changed to that they do.

Renewal prophets: Leaders of movements of renewal that focus on renewing a tradition rather than breaking off the original tradition as sects do.

Replacement Theology: God has ceased to be the God of the Jews who have forsaken Him but now the God of the Christians; since the Jews have failed to recognize Jesus as Messiah they shall now recognize their own demise; they are condemned and rejected by God; God has rejected their ritual practices; they are obdurate and blind; Scripture does not belong to them but to the Christians and it is they who have the gift of understanding the text and not the Jews; and the Christian Church has inherited Israel's promises.

Ruach HaKodesh: The Holy Spirit.

Secularization: From the Latin, *saeculum*, 'age' or 'world', i.e. this world. The process whereby people, losing confidence in other-worldly or supernatural accounts of the cosmos and its destiny, abandon religious beliefs and practices, or whereby religion loses its influence on society. It then came more loosely to refer to the transition from the religious to the non-religious world.

Sanbenito: During the Spanish Inquisition, it was clothing with a mark of guilt.

Sect: A type of a religious tradition which tries to reform the church but also separated itself from the tradition. It has a strong sense of doctrine and morality, that the leaders were not likely to be professionally trained, that it stood strong against secularization tendencies and was not over accommodative to the external environment and was organizationally precarious. By not tending to be secularized and non-accommodative to the Greco-Roman culture, it tended to be in a high-tension relationship.

Secular leaders: leaders who lead with power, control, and coercion.

Secular Antisemitism: by a new, international, secular, anti-Jewish rhetoric in the name of European culture rather than in religion.

Shekinah: The divine presence.

Shtetl: A Yiddish word for town or small city. It was an eastern European town with a large cohesive Jewish community whose life revolved around Judaism and Jewish culture. Every shtetl had a market, a synagogue, and other communal buildings and homes.

Shoah: The holocaust. The brutal and systematic murder of two-thirds of Europe's Jews during the second world war.

Sh'ol: The underground, death, hell.

Siddur Is the Jewish prayer book. It presents all the prayers to be recited at the various daily and Sabbath worship services, in their proper order according to the tradition of the community that printed it." Since it was written the first time in the ninth century, it has evolved and changed a lot but still maintaining the heart of Judaism. It consists of collections of the Tanakh, material drawn from the *Talmud*, and special prayers and hymns composed by individual writers and poets over the centuries (Karesh and Hurvitz 2008: 478–479).

Social Action: Our relations with one another. According to Weber, there are four kinds of social action: value-rationality (action based on justice), affectual (action based on affection and intimacy), traditional (based on past practices) and instrumental rationality (when the end, the means, and the secondary results are all rationally taken into account).

Sukkot: The Feast of Booths, celebrating the forty years when the people of Israel in *sukkots* (booths or tents) in the desert between Egypt and Israel.

Supersessionism. An etymological meaning of the term connotes something coming later supersedes something that went before. Christian supersessionism is the belief that the Jewish people and religion have been entirely replaced by the Christian people and religion, and that divine favor rests only with those (both Jew and Gentile) who follow Jesus as God's Messiah. Jews therefore can find religious legitimacy only as members of the Christian church.

Supra-historical election: The election of Israel was above history wherein *Elohim* entered into humanity as an active God and beyond human initiative.

Tannaism: The first *midrash* of an interpretation of the *Tanakh* to form classical Judaism.

Tanakh: This is an acronym for the Hebrew Bible: **To**(rah), **N**evi'im (the Prophets) and **K**'tuvim (Writings).

Targum: ancient Jewish commentary on the Scripture.

Tisha B'Av. In Jewish tradition, this day was to be remembered as a day of mourning and lamentations.

T'zva'ot: of hosts.

Theopolitics, Concerned with to establish as certain people, in a certain historical situation under the divine sovereignty, so that his people are brought nearer to the fulfilment of its task, to become the beginning of the kingdom of God. *Torah* (Hebrew for teaching) refers to: sacred scripture, the five books of Moses (Genesis, Exodus, Leviticus, Numbers and Deuteronomy), oral law which includes the *Talmud* and all Jewish law.

Topheth led astray.

Tosefa : a commentary on the Mishnah and addition to the *Mishnah.* and the *Gemara* (further expansions of al

Volkisch movement. The term accented a link to the soil and to the forest. Germans were to find their identity in the soil, in nature. It was a spiritual movement that accented exclusivity based on a mystical relation to the land in contrast to industry and commerce. It is from this movement that the swastika became the symbol of the Nazis. The four F's indicate "fresh," "pious," "happy," and "free."

Wannsee Conference: This was a high-level Nazi leaders conference in the Wannsee Villa in southwest Berlin on January 20, 1942. The final solution to the "Jewish problem" was officially endorsed. Only the extermination of all European Jews could permanently cleanse Nazi controlled Europe.

Yud-Heh-Vau-Heh: Without the vowels, the name is YHVH. It is also the holy name of God that should not be recited. It also is the *Tetragrammaton* or "the Name". This name is not to be used as God is most holy. seems to have been regarded and the "unpronounceable name" and is said only once by the high priest in the Holy of holies of the temple.

Yeshua: The Hebrew name for the Greek name Jesus.

Zionism: A Jewish nationalist movement born in the late 19th century, a period of rising nationalistic feelings throughout the world. Its founders believed in a Jewish return to a permanent, independent homeland in Israel.

Printed in the United States
by Baker & Taylor Publisher Services